What Readers Are Saying About *Designed for Use*

An encyclopedic narrative of the life cycle of software UX design, stuffed with best practices, timely examples, and solid design methodologies. I wish I had it years ago!

▶ **Keith Lang**
COO and interaction designer, Skitch

It's hard to write about usability concepts without sounding overly academic, but that's exactly what Lukas has done. This book is a must-read if you are familiar with basic usability concepts and are ready to learn more.

▶ **Jon Bell**
Interaction designer, Windows Phone

Designed for Use distills Lukas's brilliant insight into the much neglected area of usability, UX, and UI design. An essential, authoritative, and enlightening read.

▶ **Paul Neave**
Interaction designer, Neave Interactive

This book is smooth and pleasing like Swiss chocolate and has the eloquence of a cherry blossom. It's a must-read and real gem for everybody who is eager to learn about usability.

▶ **Michael D. Trummer**
Senior engagement manager, Appway, Inc.

Make good use of this book! It will help you to improve your work.

▶ **David Naef**
Creative director, Design Management, Visionaer

Designed for Use

Usable Interfaces for Applications and the Web

Designed for Use

Usable Interfaces for Applications and the Web

Lukas Mathis

The Pragmatic Bookshelf
Raleigh, North Carolina   Dallas, Texas

Many of the designations used by manufacturers and sellers to distinguish their products are claimed as trademarks. Where those designations appear in this book, and The Pragmatic Programmers, LLC was aware of a trademark claim, the designations have been printed in initial capital letters or in all capitals. The Pragmatic Starter Kit, The Pragmatic Programmer, Pragmatic Programming, Pragmatic Bookshelf and the linking *g* device are trademarks of The Pragmatic Programmers, LLC.

Every precaution was taken in the preparation of this book. However, the publisher assumes no responsibility for errors or omissions, or for damages that may result from the use of information (including program listings) contained herein.

Our Pragmatic courses, workshops, and other products can help you and your team create better software and have more fun. For more information, as well as the latest Pragmatic titles, please visit us at http://www.pragprog.com.

The team that produced this book includes:

Editor:	Jill Steinberg
Indexing:	Potomac Indexing, LLC
Copy edit:	Kim Wimpsett
Production:	Janet Furlow
Customer support:	Ellie Callahan
International:	Juliet Benda

Printed in the United States of America.

ISBN-13: 978-1-93435-675-3

Printed on acid-free paper.

P2.0 printing, August 2011

Version: 2011-8-4

For Regula and Werner

Contents

Before We Start, a Word

This is a book for visual designers and programmers. It's not, however, about visual design or about code. Instead, it's about something much more important: the people who will be using your product.

The best product is of no consequence whatsoever if people don't use it. You can create the most beautiful, sturdiest, most elegant brush in the world, but if nobody uses it to paint a picture, your work was in vain.

This book helps you make products—applications and websites—that people will want to use.

There are two kinds of chapters in this book: "technique chapters" and "idea chapters." Each technique chapter explains a specific technique you can use during the design process to make your product more user-friendly: storyboarding, usability tests, or paper prototyping, for example. Technique chapters explain concrete things you can do—the tools for your designer's tool belt.

Idea chapters, on the other hand, talk about ideas or concepts in more general terms: how to write usable text, how realistic your designs should look, when to use animations, and so on. Idea chapters explain things to think about and consider while coming up with designs.

Technique Chapters

You can identify technique chapters by the cog on the first page.

All technique chapters follow the same basic outline. Since not all techniques work well in all situations, I start by quickly outlining the kinds of situations to which the technique applies. Then, I explain what the technique is and how to use it. I end many of the technique chapters with a specific example of the technique as applied to a fictional application we design as we proceed through the book.

Since Twitter[1] apps are our generation's "Hello World" example application, for the technique chapters we'll design a Twitter app. To make things interesting, we're not designing a generic Twitter app. Our app is aimed at people who have to update Twitter accounts for their companies. We call this fictional application BizTwit.

Think of the technique chapters as recipes. It's OK to read the book from start to finish, but it's also OK to delve into a specific topic. To that end, these chapters are typically short and to the point, and they contain references to further information both inside the book as well as in other books or on the Internet.

Idea Chapters

While technique chapters introduce specific techniques and explain how to apply them, idea chapters are less specific. They introduce concepts and are mostly meant as sources of inspiration, rather than as strict rules. Some of the idea chapters mention techniques or refer to technique chapters, but they *focus* on more general concepts: How realistic should design be? How can we use animation most effectively? What are modes? What can we learn from video games?

You can identify idea chapters by the light bulb on the first page.

The ideas in these chapters may not always apply to the projects you're working on, because to some degree, people are unpredictable. When using your products, they don't always behave as you expect them to behave. And they don't always act as your rules predict.

To illustrate how people's behavior is often different than predicted, let's look at an example outside of user interface design. Let's assume you are concerned with public health and safety. Where do you start? Given that tens of thousands of cyclists are injured in traffic accidents every year, bicycle safety is a good place to start.

Studies show that helmets help cyclists avoid injuries. So, getting people to wear helmets should decrease the number of injuries, thereby increasing people's health and safety. The predicted outcome seems

---

1. In case you don't know what Twitter is (possibly because you're reading this book in the year 2053, when brainjacking is how people communicate), Twitter (at http://twitter.com) is a popular Internet service that people use to publish short text messages—*tweets*—and subscribe to other people's messages.

Typing Web Addresses

This book contains a lot of web addresses. Some of them are pretty long. Maybe you're reading a printed version of this book. Copying these long addresses from your book to a web browser can be cumbersome. To make it a little bit easier, I've set up http://designedforuse.net. This site contains a list of all the long addresses in this book. Instead of typing a long address, type http://designedforuse.net, and click the link there.

---

obvious: people get into bike accidents, helmets prevent injuries, people who wear bike helmets can avoid injuries. Conclusion: force people to wear helmets.

Over the years, a number of bike-helmet laws have been introduced. However, these laws have not led to the predicted outcome.

In a 2009 study titled "The Health Impact of Mandatory Bicycle Helmet Laws,"[2] Piet de Jong, from the Department of Actuarial Studies at the Macquarie University in Australia, evaluated the effects of such laws. He discovered that people really don't like bike helmets, so much so that many of them simply stop using their bikes altogether if they are forced to wear helmets while riding.

This outcome prompted de Jong to conclude that bike-helmet laws actually have a *negative* effect on societal health as a whole. Yes, the laws prevent some injuries, but for people who stop using their bikes entirely (and often use their cars instead), the health consequences are overwhelmingly negative.

The bottom line is, no one bothered to *test* the laws before enacting them. The people who were affected by the laws did something completely unexpected by the people who designed the laws.

You will often observe the same effect when designing user interfaces. Design changes don't always create the result you intended and sometimes have the opposite effect of what you expected.

When you read the ideas and rules in this book, I want you to keep this in mind. You can do your best to come up with a usable solution; you can follow all the rules and make what seem like obviously

---

2. You can read the study at http://ssrn.com/abstract=1368064.

usable choices when designing your user interface. But people will still surprise you by finding creative ways of misunderstanding your application's user interface, getting lost on your website, behaving in unpredictable, seemingly illogical ways, and being unable to do the very tasks that seem most obvious to you.

Never assume you can apply a list of usability rules to a product and end up with something usable. Use common sense when designing user interfaces, but don't *rely* on it. Know the rules, but break them if it improves your product. The point is not to do exactly what I tell you to do but instead to take my words as a source of inspiration—and to always test your designs.

How the Book Is Organized

The chapters in this book are presented roughly in the order in which they are applicable during a typical design process, which I've divided into three stages: research, design, and implementation.

Research

> It's tempting to jump right in and start designing a product as early as possible (or perhaps even to start writing code if you're a programmer). In some cases, that may be OK, but it's usually better to start by doing a bit of research. Who is your product for? What problems do you want to solve?

Design

> Think about how to solve your audience's problems. Design solutions and then test them before writing any code. Fixing mistakes on paper is a lot easier than fixing them in code.

> From a design point of view, this stage is probably the most important in the development process and, consequently, represents the largest part of the book.

Implementation

> Create the product, but keep testing it. Were your earlier assumptions correct? Does your design work? How do people interact with it now that it's running? Is your implementation good enough? How does your product deal with errors and real data? Does it perform well enough?

Deciding where to put idea chapters was more of a gut call than an exact science. I've put these chapters where you're likely to find them useful, but most ideas are applicable most of the time. The organization is more pertinent for technique chapters.

I introduce each technique chapter with a timeline that looks like this:

This timeline should help you understand when a technique is most important or most commonly used. The example timeline indicates a technique that is typically used at the beginning of the "implementation" part of the product development process. However, many techniques are useful at different times of the design process. The timelines are there to help put techniques into context, not as strict rules.

Now, this representation makes it look like the typical development process is a linear affair that goes from research to design to implementation. But typically, design processes are iterative. Your development process is more likely to look a bit like this circle.

However, since we often think of our development process as a number of linear iterations on a product, the linear timeline should be easy to understand.

Just One More Thing

Before we start, I should note that this book has its own web page.[3] It offers a book forum and an errata page. Of course, now that I type this, the errata page is still empty, but by the time you read it, it probably won't be.

And with that out of the way, let's get started!

---

3. You can find it at http://www.pragprog.com/titles/lmuse.

Part I

Research

The first part of this book is about research. You'll learn why research is important and find out which kinds of research work well (and what you should avoid). You'll learn how to observe what people actually do and how to interview people. You'll see how to use personas to keep track of your research and to focus your product's design. Later, you'll see how to structure your product using card sorts.

So, let's start by figuring out why research is important.

Chapter 1

User Research

When designers talk about their design process, they usually mention that it is "human centered" or "user centered." In a very vague sense, this means they are constantly thinking about the people who are going to use their product and trying to create the best possible product for these people.

But how do we do that?

This question is more difficult to answer than it seems, but the answer generally starts with user research.

How do we find out what goals people have, and how we can solve these goals? The most obvious answer would be to simply ask them. Although this can sometimes lead to useful information, we need to be careful when evaluating such opinions.

Henry Ford is quoted as saying, "If I'd asked people what they wanted, they would have said faster horses." And why shouldn't they answer in this way? Most people are not product designers. They don't spend a lot of time thinking about where their issues are (such as that they constantly have to care for their horses) and how a new product could solve these issues. They just work around the issues (by building stables for their horses and hiring people to care for them) and then promptly become blind to them. Rather than asking for something different that actually fixes their problems, they ask for the same thing that's slightly better.

As a result, people often aren't able to tell us how we can solve their problems. Worse, people may not even be able to tell us what their problems are. And worst of all, people are pretty bad at predicting whether and how they would use a product if we proposed to build it for them.

Focus Group

The term *focus group* describes a kind of user research in which a brand, a service, a new design, a device, or a similar product is shown to a group of people and the group's subjective reaction and opinion are recorded. The goal is to use this data to predict the general public's response to the product.

Take the Atari Lynx, for example. Back in the early 1990s, the Japanese video game company Nintendo owned the handheld gaming market with its Game Boy.

Almost every kid had one, and those who didn't were adding it to their wish lists and eagerly waiting for their birthdays to arrive. Atari, a competing video game company, wanted in on the action.

After talking to focus groups, Atari decided to go with a console that was much more powerful than Nintendo's little gray device. Atari put a color screen and a faster processor into its device and called it the Lynx, clearly trumping the comparatively puny and punily named Game Boy. Atari also went with a huge case for the device, because people in the focus groups said they preferred a larger model.

The device bombed. Nobody wanted a Lynx.

When I contacted Lynx co-designer RJ Mical and asked him about this,[1] he told me the following:

> One of the most valuable lessons I learned from the Lynx: never trust focus groups. We did a lot of focus group testing with the Lynx, especially regarding the size and shape of the case. We presented a number of different models and asked, "Which one do you like? Which one feels best to you?" We showed them big ones and little ones. We showed them gigantic ones and little tiny ones! Over and over again they preferred the big ones. They all told us, "Big! Make it big! I

---

1. You can find out more about RJ Mical at http://www.mical.org.

want to feel like I'm really getting my money's worth." OK, so we made it big. And then when Lynx came out, suddenly they all said, "So big?! Why is this thing so big?" It was awful. The original Lynx was mostly air space inside! We should have followed our instincts; instead, we did what the focus groups told us to do, and that was a mistake.

It turned out that people didn't really know what they wanted from a handheld gaming device; they were not capable of correctly predicting how they would use it. Despite what people claimed, they did not want large, powerful devices. Instead, kids liked to put these devices into their school bags and carry them around. The Lynx was too large for this, and the powerful processor and the color screen ate through a set of batteries within less than four hours; in other words, a full set of fresh batteries typically didn't even last a single school day. What's more, all the hardware power of the Lynx made it expensive enough that a lot of parents were not comfortable handing one to their kids.

People thought they wanted a big device with a powerful processor and a color screen, because they imagined how awesome the games on such a device would be. In reality, they wanted a cheap, small device they could easily carry with them and play for a long time on a single set of batteries.

Atari scrambled to release a smaller version of the console, but by the time it hit the market, it was too late for the device. Atari sold a mere 500,000 Lynxes. Nintendo, on the other hand, went on to sell almost 120 million Game Boys.

At this point, we know who our audience is going to be. But we've found out that they don't know what they want, so we can't just ask them what they need. Instead, we need to figure it out on our own. Our goals are rather straightforward:

Find Problems	Find Solutions
Find out what people are currently doing.	Find a way of making what they are already doing easier and more efficient.
Find out what people have to do but really dislike doing.	Find a way of making the things they dislike obsolete, or at least more fun.
Find out what they would like to be doing.	Find a way of making what they want to be doing possible.

You'll find out how to do that in the following chapters.

Chapter 2

Job Shadowing and Contextual Interviews

Research	Design	Implementation

What Are the Techniques?

Job shadowing and contextual interviews are two techniques used to find out what people actually do, where they need help, and how your product can help them. To do that, you will be accompanying people while they do their jobs and talking to them about their jobs.

Use these techniques if your application or website is targeted at a specific audience and if you have the ability to interact with people from your audience. For example, if you're creating a product for photographers, read this chapter. If you're creating a product that will be used by employees of a company and you can talk to employees of the company, read this chapter. If, on the other hand, the audience of your product is not well-defined or you don't have access to your audience, don't feel bad about skipping this chapter.

Why Is This a Good Idea?

Your users are different from you. Getting to know them and getting to know their problems will help you understand how to create a product that is truly usable to them.

> **Users**
>
> It was astronomer and author Cliff Stoll who famously asked, "Why is it drug addicts and computer aficionados are both called users?" It's unfortunate that the term *user* is used in both contexts, but I don't have a good alternative to the word. So, it is with considerable chagrin that I admit defeat and begrudgingly continue to use the word in this book.
>
> Whenever possible, I try to use a better term, though. *Human* and *person* and *customer* are each often perfectly serviceable replacements for *user*.

Are There Any Prerequisites?

You should have an idea of who your target audience is and be able to easily access the people who make up your target audience.

2.1 Observing Your Audience

In the previous chapter, we established that most people are not product designers. They are hard-pressed to explain what kind of product they need to help them achieve their goals, and they are often unable to correctly evaluate their own feelings about a product.

As a result, we can't just ask people what they want. Instead, we need to figure it out on our own. *Job shadowing* and *contextual interviews* are two techniques we can use to do just that.

2.2 Job Shadowing

Since people don't know what they want, a good approach is to simply observe what they do. The idea of shadowing is to visit users in our target audience at the place where they will use our product. The goal is to find out how our product will help them achieve their goals. This is a bit like doing a usability test, but instead of inviting people to test and telling them what to do, we visit them and observe what they do.

With usability testing, the goal is to find issues with the user interface. When you are shadowing somebody, the goal is to figure out what kind of product to create or how to change your product on a more fundamental level.

- Are there specific tasks that this person is spending a lot of time on?

- Is the person doing the same thing repeatedly?

- Is she doing something that looks like a workaround?

- Is she doing something that seems to bore or annoy her?

- Is she forced to memorize steps or technical aspects of a task or other things that the computer could manage for her?

- Is she using other tools in conjunction with her computer, such as paper lists or a calculator?

As a general rule, you should not interfere with the person while she's working, but if you're unsure what she's doing, feel free to ask.

2.3 Contextual Interviews

What you see is more important than what people say. Still, by asking the right questions, you can often get some useful information out of people.

After shadowing somebody, spend half an hour asking that person about the things she was doing. The kinds of things you're looking for are areas where improvements seem possible. Don't ask for opinions, and avoid questions that force the person to play product designer.

We want to ask the person about tasks he is performing, so questions should include the following:

- Are there tasks you often do that I did not see today?

- What kind of problem are you solving most often?

- Why are you doing [something you've seen] in this specific way?

- What happens if you don't have all the information you need to complete a task?

- Who are the people you regularly interact with, and how do you do that?

- What do you have to do if somebody you need is not at work or if some other problem occurs?

Keep in mind, though, that people are spontaneously providing this information; therefore, it is often incomplete and may include personal idiosyncrasies or even errors. Still, contextual interviewing gives us a useful overview of the things people do and potential areas where improvements are possible. Also, by doing interviews with several people, we can figure out much of the missing or misreported information.

2.4 Remote Shadowing

If visiting people is out of the question, you can ask them to start their screen-recording software, let it run for half a day or so while they work, and then have them send you the resulting movie. At first, this sounds like it would create immensely large movie files. Fortunately, there are a few factors working to our advantage:

- You can record at a low frame rate. In almost all cases, a frame rate of one or two pictures per second is plenty to tell you what the user is doing.

- You don't need to see all the details, so you can scale the image down to about 30 percent of the screen's full resolution and use a strong compression setting.

- You probably don't need sound at all.

- Most of the time, only small parts of the screen change while people are working, so the resulting movies typically compress well. But do tell people to turn off their screensavers, especially if they are using visually complex ones.

Using these guidelines, recording a screen for four hours can compress down to a file size below 100MB while still yielding perfectly viewable results.

Alternatively, if that is not an option, send them a video camera, and have them set it up behind their workplace. That way, they can simply return the camera to you once they've finished recording.

Fast-forwarding through this movie can give you a pretty good idea of the kinds of things people do. Then, you can get back to them with specific questions.

2.5 Limitations of Contextual Interviews

Humans can do something almost no other animal can: they can imagine themselves in hypothetical situations. In his book *Stumbling on*

Happiness [Gil07], Harvard psychologist Dan Gilbert explains that "the greatest achievement of the human brain is its ability to imagine objects and episodes that do not exist in the realm of the real, and it is this ability that allows us to think about the future."

Although thinking about the future is indeed a great achievement, the unfortunate fact is that we're quite bad at it, as we saw in the Atari Lynx story in the previous chapter. Gilbert notes that "we make a systematic set of errors when we try to imagine *what it would feel like if.*"

His explanations of why this is are fascinating,[1] but for the purpose of this book, you merely need to know that these errors exist.

As a result, you can't rely on people's opinions. When doing contextual interviews, try to focus on finding out what people actually do, what tasks they need to accomplish, and what problems they encounter. Don't expect them to be able to tell you how the solution to their problems should look. Figuring this out is *your* task.

The fact that humans are bad at predicting how they will use a product is unfortunate. Even more unfortunate is that this also applies to us designers. We simply don't know what will work, and we can't be sure how a new product will be used.[2]

User research can help us make better predictions, but it can't remove all uncertainty. Don't get drawn into endless research. At some point, you have to take a leap of faith, try something, and see whether people find it useful.

The BizTwit Case

For our BizTwit example app, we spend half a day with a number of people at ACME Corp, a company that maintains a Twitter account, both as a means of publishing information about the company (this includes things such as links to articles that mention its products, links to press releases, or quotes from customers) and as a way of interacting with customers.

---

1. You should really read Dan Gilbert's book; I believe that you would enjoy it. Or, if the obviously wrong simulation of the future that your brain generated when it thought about reading the book disagrees with my statement that you would enjoy said book, you should at least watch Dan Gilbert's TED talk at http://www.ted.com/talks/dan_gilbert_asks_why_are_we_happy.html.

2. Cognitive science expert Don Norman talks about this and other problems of design research in a great presentation that you can watch at http://vimeo.com/12022651.

While at ACME Corp we meet with the three people who update the Twitter account to find out when and how they use Twitter. At the end of each half day, we take 30 minutes to ask them some specific questions.

During our visits, we notice that the CEO of the company starts his workday by browsing articles related to ACME Corp's industry. Sometimes he publishes links to articles he likes on the company's Twitter account. For the rest of the day, he occasionally checks Twitter but rarely writes or responds to messages. He writes about two or three messages a week. He currently uses a desktop Twitter app to do this, but during the interview, he explains that he sometimes posts from his cell phone when he's not at the office.

The second person who publishes to ACME's Twitter account is the company's PR representative. It's his job to get the company mentioned in trade magazines, and when a magazine covers the company, he writes about it on Twitter. He publishes a message on Twitter about once a week.

The last person to publish messages on the company's Twitter account is an engineer, who is tasked with writing messages during the company's events, when the CEO and PR rep are busy talking to guests. During such events, she'll mostly post short messages from her cell phone, describing new announcements made at the event. She rarely posts to Twitter, but when she does, she may post a half dozen messages within one or two hours.

While we are interviewing each of these three people after shadowing them for half a day, some additional ideas come up. The PR rep says:

> One of the issues I have is that our CEO tends to make typos while publishing Twitter messages from his cell phone. It would be great if I could somehow correct his messages.

The engineer explains:

> During our events, the people who normally do these things are busy, so it's up to me to publish updates on Twitter. But I'm not a trained writer, and I often worry that the things I write sound too colloquial or don't properly represent what I'm intending to say.

ACME Corp is just one company we visit to find out what kinds of problems our Twitter app BizTwit should solve; however, these three people alone have provided very valuable information that helps us understand what kinds of problems our product needs to solve.

Takeaway Points

- People don't know what they want, so you have to visit them and observe what they do.

- If you ask specific questions, you may get useful information, but do interview several people before coming to conclusions.

Further Reading

Cennydd Bowles and James Box have a chapter on this kind of user research in the book *Undercover User Experience Design* [BB10]. Robert Hoekman covers shadowing and contextual interviews in *Designing the Obvious* [Hoe06].

Chapter 3

Personas

Research	Design	Implementation

What's the Technique?

This chapter explains how to create and use *personas*. Personas are fictional people representing specific groups of your target audience.

Personas might be useful to you if you are doing user research *and* if you are part of a larger team where the results of that research need to be communicated. If you're working alone or in a smaller team, don't feel bad about skipping this chapter.

Why Is This a Good Idea?

Personas can be useful because it's easier to talk about an imaginary person than it is to talk about a "market segment." Personas also help you focus your product.

Are There Any Prerequisites?

To create personas, you first need to do user research.

What Are Personas, Again?

By now, you've probably done some user research. You know what problems your product should solve, and you know what kinds of people will benefit from using it. While designing your product, you'll often refer to this information. But how do you do that? Talking about target demographics can be hard. Which part of your target audience has this problem? What's their skill level?

Personas give you a way of synthesizing the information you've found during user research into a limited number of imaginary people.

When Alan Cooper first introduces personas as a software design technique in his book *The Inmates Are Running the Asylum* [Coo99], he describes them like this:

> Personas are not real people...they represent them throughout the design process. They are hypothetical archetypes of actual users. Although they are imaginary, they are defined with significant rigor and precision. Actually, we don't so much "make up" our personas as discover them as a byproduct of the investigation process.

Personas help you communicate. But they have some other advantages:

- They force you to focus your product. By creating a small number of personas, you are clearly defining the audience for your product. This takes away the futile idea that you have to please *everybody*.

- They make it easier to talk about your audience, and by thinking deeply about your target audience, they can help you make your design process more human-centered.

3.1 Problems with Personas

The goal of using personas is to make the design process more human-centered. But be aware that there are a number of problems with this.

Personas can be too elastic. Since personas are essentially imaginary people, they can't defend themselves. As a result, they can sometimes reinforce predetermined conclusions: if you're using imaginary people as your target audience, you can always come up with an imaginary scenario that validates whatever opinions you currently hold.

Personas give the impression of being human-centered without anyone having to interact with actual humans. They can be a fig leaf used to cover up a design process that is not human-centered at all. Personas can absolve designers from actually doing any of the hard work, such as going out there and testing design decisions on real people.

Creating personas can be time-consuming. Distilling all of your user research into specific people who represent parts of your target audience takes time. You also have to come up with back stories and communicate these to everyone involved in the process. Sometimes, the time required to do this may not be worth the advantages personas offer.

Talking about imaginary people can be uncomfortable. Pretending that "Emma" is an actual human being who wants to use your product when she's just a story somebody made up is not something everyone on your design team may want to do.

Especially on small teams, personas may not provide much benefit. It's likely that everybody involved has a pretty good grasp of who the target audience is. There's not much need to create imaginary characters to help with communication, and your product may already be tightly focused by necessity, since a small team may not be able to create a product that pleases a large audience even if it wanted to do so.

Still, if you keep these potential issues in mind, personas can be a valuable tool.

3.2 Creating Personas

Start with contextual interviews. Talk to people. You may start out thinking that there are many different people in your audience and that you need many different personas to cover them all, but as you talk to more people, you notice that a lot of them have similar goals. Based on this information, create simplified characters that cover the goals of a broad group of people in your audience. The fewer personas you create, the better. Having about three personas works well, but depending on your product, you may need more.

Each of your personas should have clearly defined goals. Why would this persona use your product? What does he want to achieve?

Next, you should add details relevant to the design. What's each persona's skill level? How old is this persona? What is the gender? What does a typical day look like for her? Is one of the personas more important than the other so that her goals should be satisfied even if it's to the disadvantage of another persona? What kinds of devices does each of your personas use? For example, if you design a website, does one of these people access it from a cell phone?

Once you've nailed down the relevant details, it's time to add some irrelevant, personal details. There are several reasons for doing this. First, adding personal details makes it easier to remember personas. Human brains like personal information. Second, details make personas less elastic. I noted earlier when talking about disadvantages that it is easy to project one's own ideas on a persona, because the persona can't defend herself. Well, the more specific details you add, the harder it becomes to do that. And finally, it's always possible that some of the details added here may suddenly become relevant during the design process. Add information about the persona's family, her job, and her interests and hobbies.

Finally, give her a picture and a name.

The picture should be distinctive and easily recognizable but not a photo of a person people know. Everything from stock photography to simple drawings tends to work well.

It can make sense to pick names that tell you who the person is (for example, the initials of the name could be the same as the first letter of her job, or the person's function could be used as a last name), but you should avoid names that have might have negative connotations (such as "Harry Hacker") or that might remind people of specific real people (like "Britney Bieber").

3.3 Working with Personas

When we talk about a product's design, we tend to think of our audience as generic "users." Will users like the ability to automatically upload a picture to a photo-sharing site? Will they be able to figure out how to use the uploading feature?

It's hard to figure out users' needs in such generic terms. With personas, this becomes easier.

Which one of our personas—if any—will want to upload a picture to a photo-sharing site? Given that persona's skills and intentions, how should we design the feature to satisfy her goals?

Instead of speaking in generic terms, talk about specific personas.

3.4 Personas Do Not Replace User Research

When using personas, it may be tempting to assume that since "Emma" knows how to use her computer and we designed the product for people like her, we don't have to involve actual users in our design anymore. That would be wrong.

Personas can help you communicate with other people involved in the design process, evaluate data from user research, and use that data when making design decisions. But they shouldn't replace actual users. You still need to test your design with real people to make sure it works.

The BizTwit Case

In the previous chapter, we visited a number of people working for different companies. The goal was to find out what kinds of problems our Twitter application for businesses could solve.

Now, we want to distill this information into a number of archetypal personas, each of which represents a specific part of our audience. Figure 3.1, on the following page shows how one of these could look.

This is a pretty succinct persona—in a real project you would probably flesh it out with additional details.

Takeaway Points

- Personas are imaginary people who represent specific groups of users in your target audience.

- Personas are not for everybody. Maintaining them takes time, and it's sometimes easy to project your own ideas onto a persona.

- Personas do not replace user research; they merely help you incorporate the results from user research into your product.

- Personas help you evaluate the information you find during user research, focus your product on a well-defined group of people, and communicate within the design team.

- Use personas to help with design decisions. Instead of talking about generic "users," talk about concrete personas. These are questions to ask: Who is this feature for? Will any of your personas want to use it? What kind of preexisting knowledge does this persona bring to the table? What kind of requirements does the persona have? Does the feature meet the persona's goals?

Mark Miller

Job	Management. Mainly involved with product development and customer acquisition, but sometimes also likes to focus on marketing.
Age	50 years
Gender	Male
Skill	30 years of experience (starting with an Atari ST) have given Mark good user-level knowledge of computers and smartphones. Knows how to install applications, but leaves operating system installs to the system admins at the company.
Goals	Would like to be able to post messages to Twitter from his PC and his phone. Messages often consist of a link to an article, with a few words of commentary. Would like to have the ability to check other people's messages before they publish them to the company's Twitter account.
Background	Has two kids who don't live at home anymore. Married to his wife Mandy, who works as a marketing executive at a stationery company. Likes to discuss marketing topics with her and tends to be quite involved in marketing at his own company.
	His personal style is somewhat understated. Drives a silver Mercedes and usually wears a dark gray suit. Uses a Lenovo ThinkPad and considers his choice to use an Android phone instead of a BlackBerry to be a fashion statement.
	Plays squash and tennis in his spare time.

Figure 3.1: A SAMPLE ARCHETYPAL PERSONA

Further Reading

Alan Cooper writes about personas in *The Inmates Are Running the Asylum* [Coo99] and in *About Face* [Coo95].

A good book that focuses solely on personas is John Pruitt's book *The Persona Lifecycle* [PA06].

Software for Use [CL99] by Larry Constantine and Lucy Lockwood is also a good place to get started on this general topic. The book advocates a different approach that the authors call *user role models*.

Chapter 4

Activity-Centered Design

So far in this book, we've assumed that human-centered design processes are always a good idea. The fact is, they are not always the *best* idea. Another approach is to make activities the center of your design process. For many products, this makes more sense.

In human-centered design, the idea is to get a deep understanding of the people who are going to use your product and design something that is tailor-made for them. In activity-centered design, products are tailor-made for activities or goals.

This isn't really a new idea; most design is activity-centered. A door handle is not designed for a specific audience; it's designed to make the activity of opening a door as easy and obvious as possible. The steering wheel of a car, the buttons in an elevator, probably most of the applications on your computer, and a majority of the websites you use on a regular basis—each is designed to make a specific activity, or a number of activities, as easy and obvious as possible.

An activity-centered design process may not be the perfect solution for all projects. Sometimes, you want to create a product that is optimized for a limited audience. Compare, for example, the two computer mice shown in Figure 4.1, on the next page.

The mouse on the left is the one that ships with Macs. It is designed with the widest possible audience in mind. The person who touches a mouse for the first time should be able to use it just as easily as somebody with twenty years of computer experience. To that end, in its default configuration, it has only a single button, and that single button can be activated by pushing down anywhere on the mouse.

Figure 4.1: TWO DIFFERENT COMPUTER MICE

The mouse on the left is *simple*. It might not be people's *perfect* mouse, but almost everybody will be able to use it.

The mouse on the right is the Cyborg R.A.T.,[1] a mouse designed specifically for people who play action games. It sports five different buttons and a three-position mode switch, which allows people to assign fifteen different commands to the buttons. It comes with interchangeable panels and palm rests that accommodate the different ways in which gamers hold their mice. The mouse sensitivity can be adjusted on the fly. It has removable weights so that people can make the mouse heavier or lighter. It's also a wired mouse. It's wired because people who play action games dislike the slight input lag that wireless connections can cause.

All of these features make this mouse perfect for its target audience, but many of these same features make the mouse *less* desirable to people who are not in its target audience. A wired mouse with fifteen programmable actions and removable weights is essentially unusable for most people.

The mouse on the right is *complex*. This means it's some people's perfect mouse, but it also means many people will not be able to use it.

Whether you want to focus on users or on activities depends on the specific nature of your product. Each design process creates different outcomes; deciding early where your focus lies is important.

---

1. Learn more at http://cyborggaming.com.

So, how do you *do* activity-centered design? Don Norman, one of its biggest proponents, says it's mainly a difference in attitude. Framing the problem in terms of activities, rather than individual users, allows you to think about it differently. Larry Constantine and Lucy Lockwood, authors of *Software for Use* [CL99], explain that "in the final analysis, understanding your users as people is far less important than understanding them as participants in activities."

Instead of designing for specific users or for personas, think of their activities and then design your product for those activities. Rather than adapting your product to individual people, design it in such a way that they can adapt to it.

Takeaway Points

- Depending on your product, it may make sense to make *activities* the focal point of your design process.

- Do user research to find out what activities you need to support, but don't design the activities themselves for specific people.

- Be critical when evaluating user feedback. Sometimes, making your product better for a specific audience makes it worse for everybody else.

- Keep in mind that people have the capacity to adapt to your product; you don't always need to adapt your product to them.

Further Reading

Don Norman writes about activity-centered design in his controversially titled essay "Human-Centered Design Considered Harmful."[2]

In *Software for Use* [CL99], Larry Constantine and Lucy Lockwood advocate "usage-centered design," rather than "user-centered design."

Robert Hoekman writes about activity-centered design in *Designing the Obvious* [Hoe06].

Of course, there are other kinds of design processes than the ones mentioned in this chapter. For example, Alan Cooper explains a design process called Goal-Directed Design in *About Face* [Coo95].

---

2. At http://www.jnd.org/dn.mss/human-centered.html.

Chapter 5

Time to Start Working on Documentation

Research　　　　　Design　　　　Implementation

What's the Technique?

In this chapter, I'll talk about manuals, blog posts, screencasts, press releases, and similar things. Broadly put, this is about stuff that will get people interested in your product and will help people learn how to use your product. Starting to work on this at the very beginning of your development process is sometimes called *working backward*.

Why Is This a Good Idea?

Creating documentation as early as possible will help you evaluate your designs. If you can't easily explain something, there's a good chance that it is not designed well.

Starting work on the manual during the design process also means you're less likely to regress into jargon and more likely to explain things from a user's point of view. The longer you work on something, the harder it gets to explain it to people who don't share your knowledge.

Are There Any Prerequisites?

Yes. You should have a general idea of who your audience is and what kinds of problems your product will solve.

5.1 The Manual

Many products come with some type of manual that explains how to use the product. Most manuals are pretty awful, which is bad, because people tend to open the manual when they can't figure out how to use a product. In other words, they're already annoyed and unhappy, and *then* they get to slog through a distressingly crappy manual.

Manuals don't have to be crappy. But creating a great manual means giving it high priority. And that means starting to think about—and work on—the manual early on.

During the design process, your brain is still free of implementation details. This helps you see the manual from the point of view of the user, who *also* doesn't have a clue about all the technical minutiae that makes your product tick.

Starting to work on the manual early has another benefit: it forces you to explain how your product works. Few things make you think about the details of your design quite as much as having to describe how to use it; if something is hard to explain, it's probably hard to use and in need of rethinking.

So, how do you go about writing a manual?

Look at the manual as part of your product. A great manual is a useful feature; maintain it the same way you maintain other features. (If you're writing code as well as the manual, check the manual into your version-control system.) Design the manual the same way you design any other feature of your product. Ask yourself these questions: How will people use the manual? How should the manual be structured? What should be included?

Your product's manual shouldn't be an afterthought. It's an important feature of your product and deserves the same attention you give to any other important feature.

5.2 Blog Posts

Manuals are important, but they are not the only way you can talk to people about your product. In fact, some products don't have manuals at all.

Blog posts are another important tool for communicating what your product can do, and like manuals, they have two advantages: they help people understand your product, and they help you find potential problems with your product.

After designing a feature, write a blog post telling your users why the feature is awesome and how they can use it to do cool stuff. You don't have to publish it (yet). Just write it. Can you easily explain why people should care about the feature? Can you easily describe how simple the feature is?

If the answer to one of these questions is "no," then maybe there's some way you can change your design to make it more compelling, more useful, or more easily explainable.

As a side note, you should probably save all of the design documents and mock-ups you create during the design process. They might make an awesome "this is how I came up with this design" blog post.

5.3 Screencasts

Screencasts are a great tool for introducing new products or new features of existing products. If you're working on a design, think about how you would present it in a screencast. What hook could you use to get people interested in a feature? Is there a specific problem that you could show how to solve in a screencast? Can you explain the new feature in a linear narrative?

If you have a prototype, go ahead and create a screencast explaining how it works. You don't have to publish it; merely creating the screencast will probably alert you to issues with your design. (If you can't come up with a problem to solve in the screencast, maybe the feature doesn't need to exist at all.) What's more, this is great practice for when your product is done and you're creating screencasts for public consumption.

5.4 Press Releases

Press releases are another thing you can write during the design process. Can you explain your product in the space of a press release, making it sound exciting?

If the press release doesn't sound useful and exciting, there's probably something wrong with your plan.

One company that starts product design by writing a press release is Amazon. Werner Vogels, Amazon's CTO, notes[1] that "writing a press release up front clarifies how the world will see the product—not just how we think about it internally."

Similarly, you can try writing an ad or even just a slogan for your product. Can you describe your product in a single sentence? If not, why not?

5.5 Talk About Tasks

Whether you're writing the manual, writing a blog post, or recording a screencast, it's always a good idea to talk about tasks, rather than features.

Documentation often simply explains how the individual features of a product work. But unless you are creating the most basic of products— say, an alarm clock—explaining individual features is not particularly helpful. People don't want to learn how to use features; they want to learn how to *do things*. People have goals, and they use your product because they think it can help them reach these goals.

For example, rather than describing in your blog post how layers work in a photo editor, explain how to frame a photograph and add cool effects to it—and include layers in that process. Rather than showing in your manual how tabs work in a word processor, explain how to design a beautiful letter—and explain tabs as part of this.

In their book *Getting Real* [FHL09], the guys at 37signals recommend that "if you do find yourself requiring words to explain a new feature or concept, write a brief story about it." Avoid technical details. Instead, just talk about it.

Think of yourself as a teacher, rather than a technical writer.

The BizTwit Case

To clearly define what BizTwit does, the design team has written a blog post that could be used to introduce the product once it is finished.

---

1. You can read more of his thoughts on the topic at http://www.allthingsdistributed.com/ 2006/11/working_backwards.html.

There are a lot of Twitter apps out there. A lot. We've tried to look at all of them, but we gave up after we ran out of disk space from downloading them. Clearly, what the world needs right now is *even more* Twitter apps! So, today we're introducing our own. Say hello to BizTwit!

Why does the world need another Twitter app?

Well, most of the Twitter apps we've looked at are for every-day Twitter users. They allow you to follow other people, respond to their tweets, and write your own tweets. The more advanced Twitter apps also support multiple accounts and neat features such as integration with Instapaper. But they're pretty much all aimed at regular people.

BizTwit is different. It's aimed at people who have to update a company's Twitter account:

- Several different people can use the same account.

- Everybody can share the same drafts.

- Different people can have different rights.

In the coming days, we're going to explain these features and more. For now, go ahead and download your copy!

Even a short, simple blog post like this one goes a long way toward defining what kind of product you want to build.

Takeaway Points

- Writing manuals and blog posts, as well as creating screencasts, forces you to explain your design to other people. This helps you find issues with your design: if something is hard to explain, it may be hard to use.

- People read manuals when they're already unhappy, so manuals should fix the problem, not make people even more unhappy.

- Press releases and blog posts help you think about your product's goals and put the focus on the problems you want to solve. Can you explain your product in a single sentence? If not, maybe you're trying to do too much or you're not solving a specific problem.

Further Reading

In his essay on writing manuals, Bruce Tognazzini offers some valuable ideas on how to improve manuals.[2]

If you're working on user manuals and need ideas on how to test them, you can find some in the paper "Towards a usability test procedure for technical documents" by Menno de Jong and Pieter van der Poort, which is on Google Books or in the book *Quality of Technical Documentation* [SJ94].

If you want to know more about *how* to write, read the next chapter, Chapter 6, *Text Usability*, on the facing page.

Apple recommends starting out with an "application definition statement," which is similar to the idea of working backward.[3]

---

2. You can find the essay at http://www.asktog.com/columns/017ManualWriting.html.
3. You can read more at http://developer.apple.com/library/safari/documentation/UserExperience/Conceptual/MobileHIG/AppDesign/AppDesign.html.

Chapter 6

Text Usability

When we discuss design and usability, we tend to focus on visual elements first—text often gets overlooked. This is unfortunate, because text is one of the main ways in which people interact with your application or website. In fact, in tests that track the movement of people's eyes as they scan a screen, text is often the first thing people look for.[1]

In his paper[2] on how to write for the Web, usability expert Jakob Nielsen says:

> When asked for feedback on a web page, users will comment on the quality and relevance of the content to a much greater extent than they will comment on navigational issues or the page elements that we consider to be "user interface" (as opposed to simple information). Similarly, when a page comes up, users focus their attention on the center of the window where they read the body text before they bother looking over headerbars or other navigational elements.

The guys at 37signals concur. In *Getting Real* [FHL09], they write that "good writing is good design." Words need to be considered as part of the interface design.

6.1 Why Words Matter

Have you ever tried buying a computer online, and instead of telling you in plain language what capabilities it has, the site lists a bunch

---

1. This article lists lessons gleaned from eye-tracking tests: http://www.virtualhosting.com/blog/2007/scientific-web-design-23-actionable-lessons-from-eye-tracking-studies/.
2. You can find the paper at http://www.useit.com/papers/webwriting/writing.html.

of marketing buzzwords? Hurm...do I want the one with "MagSafe" or the one with "OneKey Theater" or the one with "One-button ThinkVantage" or the one with "Multi-Convergence UltraTouch Enterprise Panel Extensibility"? OK, I made the last one up, but the other ones are real.[3]

Words are how people interact with your product. Design is communication; if people don't understand you, they can't use your product.

Since words are used everywhere in your product, on your website, in your manuals, in the things you say when people interact with you personally, and even in the class names and comments in your code, it's best to get them right early on.

But how do you know which words to use?

6.2 People Don't Want to Read

This might sound strange coming after a section about the importance of text, but the hard truth is this: most people avoid reading whenever possible.

Merely by reading this book, you have proven that you are quite unlike most of your users. In 1987 in "Paradox of the Active User,"[4] John M. Carroll and Mary Beth Rosson pointed out that "learners at every level of experience try to avoid reading." Not much has changed in the last two decades. In fact, it may be getting worse: a 2007 study by the National Endowment for the Arts[5] concluded that Americans are not just reading less than they used to, but they are also reading less well.

You have probably been on the receiving end of a "my printer has stopped working" call:

Friend: *I really need to print this document, but my printer just doesn't work anymore.*

Me: *OK, what exactly happened?*

Friend: *I'm trying to print, but it doesn't work.*

Me: *Did you get an error message?*

---

3. Neven Mrgan mentions another example of a site that uses words that make sense to the company but not to its customers at http://mrgan.tumblr.com/post/3241126895/what-does-the-user-see.

4. You can read that paper at http://dl.dropbox.com/u/16760174/Papers/Paradox.pdf.

5. Find out more here: http://www.nea.gov/news/news07/TRNR.html.

Friend: *Oh, yes, an error popped up.*

Me: *What did it say?*

Friend: *How should I know? I just clicked it away, of course, but that didn't fix the problem.*

A paper from the psychology department of the North Carolina State University titled "Failure to Recognize Fake Internet Popup Warning Messages"[6] analyzed how people deal with fake pop-up warnings. When discussing the results, the researchers note:

> Data from the post task questionnaire indicated that 12% of those who clicked on the OK button indicated that they did so because the text told them to, while 23% said they always click on that button when they encounter error messages. Just under half (42%) responded that they just wanted to "get rid of it."

Pop-up windows don't even consciously register with people before they click them away. They are just a nuisance that keeps people from doing their work, and making them go away usually seems to fix the problem.

But this doesn't just apply to text in pop-up messages. People skip text whenever they think they can get away with it.

6.3 Say Less

Since people don't read, it's best to avoid bothering them with text whenever possible.

For example, don't warn people when they are about to do something destructive. Instead, allow them to undo their change.

Similarly, if an error occurs and you have a way to make your product recover on its own without telling the user, do it. If the user has entered a website address that is truncated but your website receives enough information to identify the page he's looking for, simply forward him to that page. If your application tries to connect to a server but the connection times out, make the application try again before telling the user there's something wrong. Notify the user only if your product really can't fix the problem on its own.

---

6. Read it at http://media.haymarketmedia.com/Documents/1/SharekWogalterFakeWarning_publicationFinal_805.pdf.

If people don't understand some part of your user interface, don't add explanatory text. This just adds more clutter and makes the problem worse.

If it's impossible to avoid communicating, design your user interface under the assumption that people won't read what you write. For example, use verbs as button labels, and make sure that each button has a specific, mutually exclusive label. Instead of labeling two buttons "Yes" and "No," label them "Delete File" and "Cancel." That way, people don't have to read the text in the dialog box to figure out what each button does.

6.4 Make Text Scannable

Often you can't avoid text. To know how to write, first you need to know how people read.

Jakob Nielsen's research shows that people typically don't read text on the Web word by word. Instead, they "scan" the page, looking for sentence fragments that contain what they are looking for. To help people do that, Nielsen suggests[7] the following rules:

- Use words that make sense to your audience.
- Convey one idea in each paragraph.
- Introduce the paragraph's idea in the first sentence so people can quickly decide whether to read the paragraph.
- Use meaningful headings.
- Highlight keywords.
- Use bullet lists.
- Keep text short, simple, and informal.
- Start text with conclusions, and include a summary of its content.

6.5 No Fluff

People are trying to achieve a goal and are reading your text because they think it might help them with their task. Write short, clear, obvious

---

7. You can find a collection of Nielsen's essays on this topic at this address: http://www. useit.com/papers/webwriting/.

sentences. Keep individual paragraphs short. Don't waste your readers' time. Keep their goal in mind.

As Patricia Wright puts it in the book *Quality of Technical Documentation* [SJ94], "Writers often believe that they should communicate more than readers want to know."

When you're writing, ask yourself, "Does this sentence help the user?" If it doesn't, get rid of it.

6.6 Sentences Should Have One Obvious Interpretation

Avoid sentences that can be interpreted in two different ways and sentences that lure your readers into an improper understanding when they have read only part of them.[8]

Readers try to make sense of sentences before they reach the period at the end. Some sentences can mislead the reader. Consider the first few words of this headline:[9]

"Burger King fries the holy grail..."

Now why would Burger King fry the holy grail? The sentence's meaning becomes clear when you finish reading it:

"Burger King fries the holy grail for potato farmers"

Ah, the fries *are* the holy grail. It's still not entirely unambiguous, but the meaning is reasonably obvious now.

Reading such a sentence requires more work on the part of your readers, since they're forced to backtrack if they start with a wrong interpretation. To avoid confusing them, ask yourself whether a sentence is unambiguous even if you've read only part of it. A simple change makes this sentence completely clear:

"Burger King fries are the holy grail for potato farmers"

Can you spot the problem with the following sentence?

---

8. These are often called garden-path sentences, from the saying "to be led up the garden path." The intuitive understanding of such a sentence is misleading; reaching the end of the sentence forces the reader to backtrack, looking for a different interpretation. Wikipedia has more on the topic: http://en.wikipedia.org/wiki/Garden_path_sentence.
9. I found this example via the excellent Language Log blog at http://languagelog.ldc.upenn.edu/nll/?p=1762. Language Log is definitely worth reading if you're interested in writing.

"Lukas told his editor that he would write a project plan to finish the book by the end of the month."

Will I write the *plan* by the end of the month, or is the plan to *finish the book* by the end of the month?

If your text requires less thinking on the readers' behalf, they are more likely to read it and get something out of it.

Clarity is especially important for titles. Start titles with relevant words so people still get the meaning of the title, even if they view it on a device with a small screen that cuts off words at the end of the title.

BAD TITLES ON DEVICES WITH SMALL SCREENS, IT CAN BE HARD TO TELL WHAT THE CUT-OFF TITLES MEAN.

6.7 Talk Like a Human, Not Like a Company

Companies often use style guides to enforce a consistent tone throughout all of the company's content. Writers are encouraged to use the third person and a neutral tone. As a result, they are discouraged from letting their personalities show through in their writing.

Unfortunately, such guides encourage text that is boring and bland. People don't want to read that, and it can be a soul-crushing experience for the people who have to *write* the text.

If you focus on consistency, you'll bring everybody down to the level of your worst writer. It's better to focus on engaging your readers. Address them directly. Write sentences that would sound natural when used in a conversation. Be informal. Talk to the reader. Avoid marketing buzzwords. Say "you" and "we" when it works (although avoid that overly patronizing "we" you sometimes hear when adults talk to children).

> **The Passive Voice**
>
> When people give writing advice, they often claim you should "avoid the passive voice." Although there is some truth to that ("click Backup to create a copy" is better than "a copy is created by clicking Backup"), the case against the passive voice is often overstated. There is nothing wrong with writing something like "Don't worry about the Backup button—your documents will be backed up automatically," even though "your documents will be backed up automatically" uses the passive voice. In fact, changing this to active voice would simply add useless words to the sentence, making the end result worse: "the application will back up your documents automatically."
>
> I suspect that people don't really mean you should avoid the passive voice. After all, passive voice merely means that the subject of the sentence doesn't initiate the sentence's action but is its *recipient*.
>
> Instead, what people mean is that you should avoid writing in a way that makes it unclear who a sentence's active party is. People often use the passive voice to shift responsibility away from themselves ("Mistakes were made"). Avoiding that kind of writing is generally good advice.

BLEEDING-EDGE COLLABORATIVE DELIVERY CHANNELS ALLOW USERS TO ENGINEER PLUG-AND-PLAY E-SYNERGIES!

Read the text out loud. Ask yourself whether this is something you would want to read. Ask yourself whether the text contains information anyone not working in your marketing department would find useful.

6.8 Illustrate Your Points

Maintaining images and screenshots can be a lot of work. With each product update, you have to go through all of the pictures and fix the ones that are out-of-date. It's tempting to just avoid pictures altogether. But pictures can make your text more understandable and readable.

Pictures help illustrate points. A good screenshot can replace several paragraphs of text and may be easier to understand. Depending on your audience, even simple explanations can benefit from an illustration.

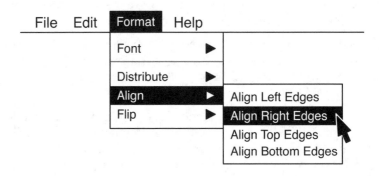

Although the preceding text is reasonably clear, an image makes it even more obvious.

Images can also give your text a more inviting look. Facing a wall of text is discouraging, but add a few images, and the text looks more enjoyable to read. In their paper "What's Psychology Worth? A Field Experiment in the Consumer Credit Market,"[10] Marianne Bertrand et al. show that that merely adding a picture of a woman to a loan offer caused a statistically significant increase in loan interest. However, Jakob Nielsen also revealed that users ignore photos if they look like generic stock photography or pure filler.[11]

6.9 Use Words People Understand

Don't let your pet peeves guide your writing. Some people don't like to use the word *podcast*. Some people don't like *blog*. Some people don't like to use *Lite* for free versions of iPhone apps. But pretty much every-

---

10. Read it at http://karlan.yale.edu/fieldexperiments/pdf/Bertrand%20et%20al_2006.pdf.
11. Read more about his results at http://www.useit.com/alertbox/photo-content.html. You can find links to other research on this topic at http://uxmyths.com/post/705397950/myth-ornamental-graphics-improves-the-users-experience.

body else uses and understands these words. People know what a podcast is, what a blog is, and what to expect if an iPhone app has the word *Lite* after its name. Just use the words people understand, even if you don't like these words. As former *Guardian* science editor Tim Radford puts it,[12] "No one will ever complain because you have made something too easy to understand."

Keep in mind that the people who read your text probably use different words than you do. If you know your audience, write for it. Your audience may have an age range, skill level, or domain knowledge that is different from the average person. Taking these things into account when writing text will make it easier for your audience to read and understand your text.

But above all, just keep it simple. In *On Writing* [Kin00], Stephen King explains that "one of the really bad things you can do to your writing is to dress up the vocabulary, looking for long words because you're maybe a little bit ashamed of your short ones." His rule of thumb: "Use the first word that comes to your mind, if it is appropriate and colorful. If you hesitate and cogitate, you will come up with another word—of course you will, there's always another word—but it probably won't be as good as your first one or as close to what you really mean."

Now, King is talking about writing novels. But then, why shouldn't your writing be just as engaging and interesting as a Stephen King novel?

6.10 Test Your Text

Since text is part of your user interface, you can test text as part of a regular usability test. But that's not all you can do. Usability expert Angela Colter encourages also testing your text using a Cloze test.[13]

In a Cloze test, you remove some of the words of your text and then ask test participants to find the missing words. A sample is shown in Figure 6.1, on the next page.

Colter suggests picking sample text from your product that is between 125 and 250 words and then removing every fifth word. Ask participants to fill in the missing words. Calculate the test score by dividing the number of correct answers by the total number of removed words.

---

12. Find Tim Radford's "manifesto for the simple scribe" at http://www.guardian.co.uk/science/blog/2011/jan/19/manifesto-simple-scribe-commandments-journalists.
13. You can read more of her suggestions for testing content at http://www.alistapart.com/articles/testing-content/.

There are a lot _____ Twitter apps out there. _____ lot.

We've tried to _____ at all of them, _____ we gave up

after _____ ran out of disk _____ from downloading

them. So _____ course, today, we're introducing _____

own Twitter app. Say _____ to BizTwit!

Figure 6.1: A SAMPLE CLOZE TEST

If the score ends up being below 0.4, your audience likely won't be able to understand your text, and you should rewrite it. If it's below 0.6, they might have a bit of difficulty, and some changes may be required. Scores above that indicate audience-appropriate text.

6.11 Display Legible Text

Making the content itself usable is important, but the way you present it also matters.

Pick a large font size. Although most people hold books quite close to their faces, computer screens tend to be further away. While sitting in front of your computer and looking at your site or application, hold up a book at typical reading distance, and compare the font sizes.[14]

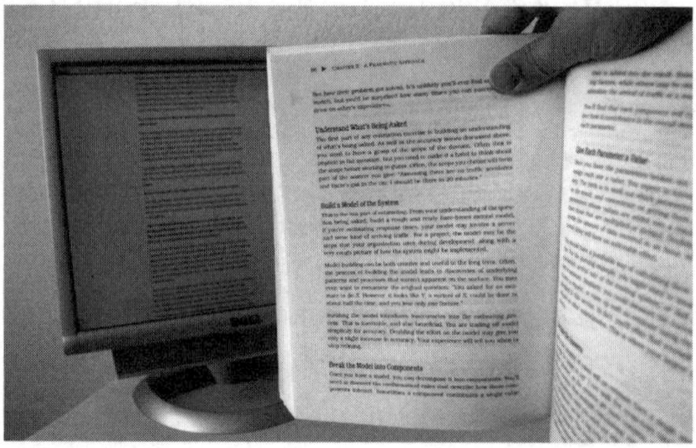

---

14. I first saw this idea mentioned in an essay by Oliver Reichenstein, which you can read here: http://informationarchitects.jp/100e2r/.

If you notice that the text on your PC looks significantly smaller than the text in the book, make the screen text larger. Keep in mind, though, that the same font size can appear to be larger or smaller on screens with lower or higher resolutions.

Of course, if you're creating content for a cell phone, the situation reverses. People typically hold their phones reasonably close to their eyes, so you can get away with smaller font sizes.

Pick a readable typeface. There is a great difference in legibility between different typefaces and even between different members of the same type family. Choosing a good typeface matters.[15]

Takeaway Points

- Avoid text if you can.

- If you can't avoid text, keep it succinct, clear, and scannable.

- Keep paragraphs short, and convey one idea per paragraph.

- Be engaging and personal, rather than boring and professional.

- Use pictures to illustrate your points and make your text look more approachable.

- Use large font sizes and readable typefaces.

---

15. Note that studies show that whether a typeface has serifs or not probably doesn't make a difference in terms of legibility. If you are interested in reading studies on this topic, you can find out more at http://www.alexpoole.info/academic/literaturereview.html.

Further Reading

Jakob Nielsen has a number of good essays on the topic of writing for the Web.[16] If you're writing a manual, Patricia Wright's *Quality of Technical Documentation* [SJ94] contains a ton of useful information. Joel Spolsky tackles reading in *User Interface Design for Programmers* [Spo11].

Science author Carl Zimmer has written an essay about good science writing.[17] Tim Radford has compiled a set of rules for good writing based on his experience as a journalist.[18] If you're interested in good writing in general, I really liked Stephen King's *On Writing* [Kin00].

You should also read Angela Colter's essay on testing content.[19]

---

16. At http://www.useit.com/papers/webwriting/.
17. At http://blogs.discovermagazine.com/loom/2011/01/12/death-to-obfuscation/.
18. Read the rules at http://www.guardian.co.uk/science/blog/2011/jan/19/manifesto-simple-scribe-commandments-journalists.
19. At http://www.alistapart.com/articles/testing-content/.

Chapter 7

Hierarchies in
User Interface Design

In thinking about how websites are organized, you'll find that they often make use of hierarchies. Sometimes, these hierarchies are even used as explicit user interface elements. Here is an example of a "breadcrumbs" navigation element as it appears on sites like Google Directory:

Software

    <u>Science</u> > <u>Biology</u> > <u>Bioinformatics</u> > Software

This navigation element tells people where in a hierarchy the current page is and allows them to "jump up the hierarchy."

The headers of many news sites also show a hierarchy of sorts but often use two or three levels of tabs instead of breadcrumbs:

U.S.	**World**	Europe	Technology	Business	Science	Opinion

Africa | Asia | Middle East | Japan

These two examples show how whole websites (or products in general) can be organized into hierarchical structures. But the individual screens themselves also use hierarchies to structure their content. Check out this screenshot from Google's Chrome browser:

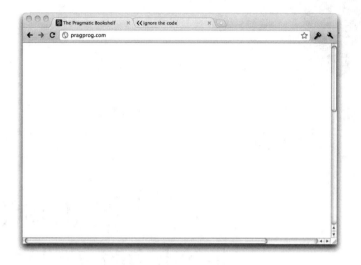

This is a very simple user interface, but even so, it implies a hierarchical structure. For example, buttons inside a tab only apply to other things inside that tab. If you hit the "back" button, anything outside of the currently active tab won't be affected. But if you hit the window's "close" button, the whole window will be closed, including both open tabs. Buttons affect only things that are on the same or on a lower hierarchical level.

7.1 Creating Hierarchical Structure Visually

If you look at any user interface, usually you can discern a hierarchy of user interface elements relatively quickly. Most Western users understand intuitively that hierarchies go from left to right, from top to bottom, and from outside to inside. Here are several examples showing representations of A hierarchically above B:

For example, take an MP3 player that shows the currently playing track of an audio book. How would you arrange the following elements: track number, chapter number inside a track (for audiobooks, or podcasts with chapter markers), and the playhead's current position in the chapter? Obviously, the relationship between these elements is as follows:

Track→Chapter of current track→Playhead position in current chapter

Here's how this is arranged in the iPod app on iPhones:

The chapter number and track number are shown in "reverse" order, with the current track's chapter number appearing *above* the track number:

This visual arrangement implies the following, wrong hierarchy:

Chapter of current track→Track→Playhead position in current chapter

This trips me up every time and makes me think that the number next to the playhead is the chapter number, rather than the track number.

The Audible app for iPhones solves this problem by not showing the track number at all and moving the chapter number next to the playhead, which fixes the misleading arrangement:

It's natural to assume that the elements shown on-screen are in a hierarchical relationship arranged from top to bottom. When designing screen layouts, keep the visual hierarchy consistent with the hierarchical relationships between the individual elements.

Let's go back to the browser example. Reduced to its main elements, Chrome's user interface looks like this:

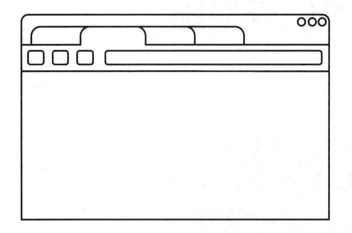

When people look at this, they intuitively assume that the hierarchy of the elements in this window looks a bit like this:

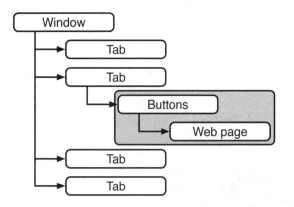

This assumed hierarchy allows people to figure out how the user interface behaves: closing a tab causes everything that is hierarchically below it to disappear. Clicking a button in the button bar influences the part of the user interface that is hierarchically on the same level or below the button bar.

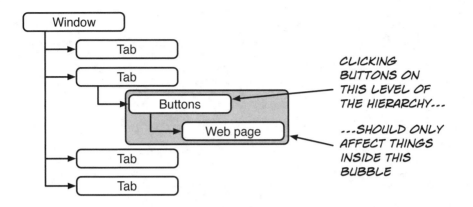

Interacting with a user interface element shouldn't affect things that are placed above it in the visual hierarchy.

Hierarchies are everywhere, and they affect how people expect your product to behave. By using hierarchies properly, you can give people hints that allow them to figure out how to use your product.

Takeaway Points

- Think about how the elements of your product can be arranged hierarchically.

- Use hierarchies to give your users hints about how your product works. Individual screens convey implicit or explicit hierarchies to the user.

Further Reading

What most people call "organizing things," designers call *information architecture*. There are a number of great books on the topic. Donna Spencer has written one called *A Practical Guide to Information Architecture* [Spe10]. The book *Information Architecture for the World Wide Web* [MR06] by Peter Morville and Louis Rosenfeld is another good place to get started.

Chapter 8

Card Sorting

Research	Design	Implementation

What's the Technique?

Card sorting allows us to gather data on where people think the individual parts of our product should be shown or what parts belong together.

Consider doing card sorts if your product is complex enough that you have to "sort things." For example, if you're designing a site and have to decide how to organize the individual pages, or you're working on an application that offers lots of different features that have to be organized in a way that makes sense to your users, this chapter is for you.

Why Is This a Good Idea?

Our view of our product is very different from that of our users. For example, if we're creating a website for a company, we have a pretty good idea of the company's internal organization, which may influence how we think the website should be organized. The people visiting the website, on the other hand, probably don't know how the company is organized. This difference in knowledge may mean that something that makes perfect sense to us is incomprehensible to our users.

Card sorting helps us find out how people really see things.

Are There Any Prerequisites?

No.

8.1 Designing Hierarchies

In the previous chapter, we saw that products are often organized using hierarchies. Here's another example.

Open any website, and it's likely to be arranged in a hierarchy. Let's say your laptop's internal camera doesn't work anymore, and you need help. You open the manufacturer's website in your browser. Where do you go to find help? If your computer is from a big electronics manufacturer, you probably start by clicking "Computers" and then "Notebooks." Here you'll see a list of laptop lines from your manufacturer. Clicking the proper line of notebooks should take you to a list of laptop models, and you should be able to find yours in that list. On the page for the specific model, you'll probably look for "Support." Ideally, this will show a support page for your model, with a number of potential laptop issues. With some luck, you'll find your problem (and a solution to it) in that list.

Here's the path you took through the site's hierarchy:

Computers → Notebooks → Notebook Line → Notebook Model → Notebook Model Support → Answer to a specific question

But that's not the only way you could have arrived there. You could also have gone straight to the Support section of the website. The question is, if you are designing this website, how do you know what path the user will take? And how do you know where people expect to find the individual pages of your site?

Card Sorting

A common way of finding answers to these questions is to use card sorting—a great way to determine where people expect to find things. Card sorting is really easy. In her book *Card Sorting: Designing Usable Categories* [Spe09], Donna Spencer explains that "at its core, card sorting is a pretty simple technique—write things on index cards and ask people to sort the cards into groups."

Of course, there are nuances, so let's look at some of the details of how to do this.

8.2 Preparing for a Card Sort

To prepare for a sort, you simply take a bunch of index cards and put the things you need to sort on them. For example, if you're structuring a website, you represent the individual pages or areas of your website as the individual cards to sort. If you're structuring an application, you use the names of features, properties, menu items, commands, windows, tasks, goals, or visible elements as your cards.

It sometimes makes sense to pick things that are roughly on the same level in your product: don't mix terms that are high up in the hierarchy with terms that are far down in the hierarchy. Instead, do multiple card sorts to get information on different levels of the hierarchy.

It's best to use terms that are obvious and easily understandable. If you absolutely can't avoid using jargon, explain the meaning before the card sort, and allow participants to substitute their own terms.

When coming up with words to use in the card sort, you need to make sure they can't be grouped on the basis of superficial similarities, such as how the words look or sound. The risk of picking words that look or sound similar is that people may group them based on that similarity, rather than on their meaning.[1]

You should end up with anywhere from twenty to eighty cards. If you have fewer than twenty, then you're probably not thinking hard enough. If you have more than eighty, then you might overwhelm your participants.

Also prepare some empty cards.

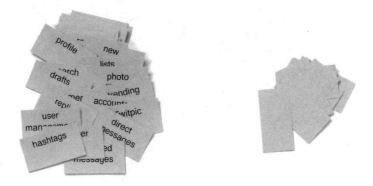

Since people might write on cards during a card sort, or otherwise alter them, and since you'll want to do more than just one card sort, making multiple card sets by hand is often too time-consuming. Instead, it's easier to print cards out and cut them up.

8.3 Participants

You can do each card sort with one person at a time or with several people at once. Both have advantages. Having more than one user in one session can be harder to schedule, and one person typically dominates the process anyway. On the other hand, having multiple participants may create conversations that offer valuable insights into how people think about these things.

If you go with multiple participants, be careful not to overdo it. More than three or four people typically won't be able to participate in a card sort at the same time.

---

1. Jakob Nielsen talks about this problem and offers solutions for it at http://www.useit.com/alertbox/word-matching.html.

How many card sorts should you do in total? Jakob Nielsen recommends fifteen card sorts with one user each.[2] Since card sorts are simple, doing many of them is easily possible. Different people may expect things to be in different places; the more card sorts you do, the clearer the picture becomes.

8.4 Running a Card Sort

After you've welcomed the participant or participants, explain what they are about to do. This introduction should go something like this:

> Hi, my name is Lukas Mathis. I'm currently working on the design for a new Twitter application. Twitter is a social networking tool, similar to Facebook.
>
> Right now, I'm working on the basic organization of the app—you know, where to put which feature, stuff like that. The exercise we're about to do will help me understand where people expect to find things in our application.
>
> In a minute, I'm going to give you a bunch of index cards that have words written on them. These words are things that exist in our application, like features or objects. What I want you to do is to group these index cards into little piles. Each pile should contain things that, to your mind, belong together. Let me explain this a little bit more clearly. We're not looking for superficial similarity, like grouping words that sound similar or start with the same letter. Instead, imagine that you are using this application. Which things would you expect or want to see on the same screen, for example? If there's a list of items on a screen, which items would you expect to see next to each other in the list?
>
> If there are cards you can't group anywhere or think don't belong in the application, feel free to put them in their own group. I have empty cards handy, and there's a marker on the table, so if the word on a card seems unclear to you, feel free to cross it out and replace it with a better word. You can also make copies of cards, if you feel that certain cards should be in more than one group.
>
> Before we start this, let's go through all the cards.

---

2. Read his essay at http://www.useit.com/alertbox/20040719.html.

Next, go through the cards with the people doing the card sort, and make sure they understand what each word means in the context of your product.

Now, ask the participants to sort these cards into categories that make sense to them, stacking cards they think belong together.

Invite them to think out loud and to ask questions. Start taking notes at this point. If participants come up with new words, you can either make additional cards as necessary or add the words to existing cards as relevant.

If the participants create many small groups of cards, encourage them to merge similar groups. If they come up with only a few large groups, encourage them to break them up.

Alternatively, depending on the situation, you can also do a "closed" card sort, where you define a number of groups beforehand and let participants sort the cards into the different groups.

It's important to let people discard those cards that they feel don't fit anywhere. These rejected cards may indicate product features or website areas that are not important enough to include or that are extraneous to the problems your users usually solve with your product.

Next, ask the participants to identify names for each stack of cards. Add a card with the name of the stack to the top of each stack (preferably in a different color).

If there are enough stacks, ask participants to arrange them so that those that belong together are located near each other. Depending on the people participating in your card sort and the words you've picked to put on the cards, you might even want to ask people to draw connecting lines between associated stacks. (If you intend to do that, do the card sort on a large sheet of paper.)

Finally, collect the data. A quick and easy way to do this is to take a picture of the whole arrangement and then secure the individual groups of cards with rubber bands.

8.5 Running a Remote Card Sort

You don't necessarily have to invite people to a physical place to do card sorts. Card sorting can easily be done remotely. In fact, there are a number of good card-sorting websites like websort.net or OptimalSort[3] that are specifically designed for doing remote card sorts.

Remote card sorts give you more exact data, since you can do card sorts with a lot more people. However, you'll miss a lot of the qualitative information you get from doing card sorts in person. What words are people confused by? What synonyms do they use? What kinds of associations do they have to the words on the cards? Remote card sorts won't tell you these things.

Of course, nothing prevents you from doing both kinds of card sorts.

8.6 Evaluating the Results

If you're working with predefined groups of cards (a closed card sort), evaluating the results is simple. Count how often each card got sorted into each group, and you'll get a pretty good idea of where most people would expect to find the thing that the card represents.

	Group 1	Group 2	Group 3	Group 4	Group 5	Group 6	Group 7
Card 1		4			3		
Card 2			2	6			
Card 3	7						
Card 4				5	1	1	
Card 5				5	4		
Card 6	1	4					3

If you're working with user-defined groups of cards, on the other hand, start by defining the groups. Sometimes different people use different words to describe the same group. In those cases, it may make sense to combine these groups. Other times, different people come up with entirely different ways of sorting the cards, creating entirely different groups. If this happens, it may be an indicator that you need to provide different ways of accessing the same things. Once you've hashed out which groups to use, you again count how many times each card was sorted into each group.

3. At http://www.optimalworkshop.com/optimalsort.htm.

Now you can develop a hierarchy based on the information you've collected and then use this hierarchy for your visual layout and for your information architecture. I would advise against formal, statistical evaluations of the data because you probably haven't collected enough information. Card sorting provides input for your design decisions, not proof that a specific solution is the "correct" one.

Simply take the information you've collected into consideration when working out things like the storyboard of your application, the hierarchy of your website's content, or the hierarchy of individual screens. What you gain from a card sort is insight into how people think about the things in your product, the criteria people use to put the concepts present in your product into different mental boxes, and people's mental model of how your product is supposed to work.

After you've decided on a hierarchy, it is generally a good idea to create a simple paper prototype and run a few short rounds of usability testing. (See Chapter 11, *Paper Prototype Testing*, on page 97 for more information on how to do this.) This way, you know whether your interpretation of the results is correct.

8.7 Guidelines for Creating Usable Hierarchies

The data from card sorts can help you design good hierarchies. Here are some additional guidelines that should help you do that.

Allow Things to Exist in Several Places

Keep in mind that hierarchies don't have to be strict: things don't have to be in exactly one place inside the hierarchy. You can give users several paths that lead to the same result. This is sometimes called a *polyhierarchical classification*. There's an example in Figure 8.1, on the next page.

I mentioned a bit earlier that some users who experience problems with their computers might start by searching the website for their exact laptop model. Others may prefer to go directly to the Support section of the website to look for their laptop model. Still others may go to the Support section and start a search based on their specific problem. If you find that different people tend to sort cards into different groups in a card sort, it makes sense to create such a nonstrict hierarchy.

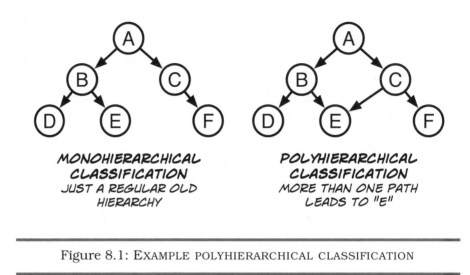

Figure 8.1: EXAMPLE POLYHIERARCHICAL CLASSIFICATION

Shallow or Deep?

A lot of the time, people evaluate user interfaces by counting clicks. How many times does the user have to click to reach the goal? It makes intuitive sense to assume that fewer clicks are better.

This focus on counting clicks might tempt you to keep hierarchies as shallow as possible, making every possible goal reachable with the fewest clicks. Although it may often make sense to make sure that people can access a small number of important, often used features with few clicks, I advise against intentionally trying to achieve shallow hierarchies, because these force users to choose from a bigger number of possible actions at each level of the hierarchy. By cutting down on the depth of a hierarchy, you are increasing the potential choices at each level of the hierarchy.

In fact, research shows that optimizing for fewer clicks doesn't necessarily yield positive results. Summarizing the research,[4] uxmyths.com writes that "the number of necessary clicks affects neither user satisfaction nor success rate. That's right; fewer clicks don't make users happier and aren't necessarily perceived as faster."

---

4. At http://uxmyths.com/post/654026581/myth-all-pages-should-be-accessible-in-3-clicks.

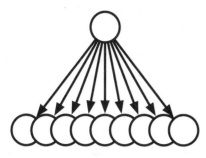 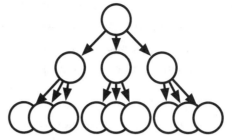

SHALLOW
THE USER CAN REACH EACH
OF THE NINE GOALS IN ONE
SINGLE CLICK, BUT HAS TO
PICK OUT OF NINE DIFFERENT
CHOICES

DEEP
THE USER HAS TO CLICK
TWICE TO REACH ONE OF THE
SAME NINE GOALS, BUT
ONLY HAS TO PICK OUT OF
THREE CHOICES EACH TIME

A rule similar to the "the fewer clicks, the better" rule is that you must constrain the number of options given to the user; do not make her choose from more than seven options. The reason given for this idea is that humans are incapable of processing more than seven possible choices. Like the "fewer clicks" rule, this rule is wrong.

The "seven rule" originates from a paper published in 1956 by Princeton University's cognitive psychologist George A. Miller.[5] In the paper the author concludes that the average human can hold only about seven different objects in working memory. Although this may be true, it doesn't apply to picking from a number of options, because you don't have to keep all the options in working memory. You merely have to look through them and pick the first one that seems like it would bring you closer to your goal. This behavior is called *satisficing*, a term coined by psychologist Herbert Simon in 1956. Instead of comparing all available options in order to find the perfect choice, most people will simply pick the first option that seems sufficiently satisfying.

In *The Paradox of Choice* [Sch05], however, Barry Schwartz notes that some people are "maximizers"—those who try to find the *best* possible solution, rather than the first suitable one. What's more, although most people can cope with a large number of choices, many don't like doing so. Schwartz writes that "a large array of options may discourage consumers because it forces an increase in the effort that goes into making a decision."

---

5. Wikipedia has a great article about this paper at http://en.wikipedia.org/wiki/The_Magical_Number_Seven,_Plus_or_Minus_Two.

In other words, even though most people are perfectly capable of picking from many choices, they may not like it.

A great user interface is not one where each goal can be reached with the smallest number of clicks possible, or where the user has to pick from only a small number of choices at each step, but one where each individual click is as obvious as possible. If your users have a clear goal in mind, each level of the hierarchy should have one option that clearly satisfies their goal—or at least gets them closer to that goal. As long as users feel that they are getting closer to their goal with each step, they don't mind drilling down into a deep hierarchy.

Grouping Things

Humans may be capable of picking from dozens of choices, but that doesn't mean you should throw ungrouped lists of choices at them. Being confronted by a wall of seemingly equally valid choices is discouraging.

It helps users when you group or order choices in a meaningful way. Better grouping allows users to more easily scan the available options. The maximum number of choices that can appear on a single screen is mainly constrained by the design of the page that shows the choices to the user. If many different choices appear at the current level of the hierarchy, grouping them—in a way, adding a local, visual hierarchy to the choices—helps users find the option they are looking for among a large number of choices.

○○○	
Option 1	Option 9
Option 2	Option 10
Option 3	Option 11
Option 4	Option 12
Option 5	Option 13
Option 6	Option 14
Option 7	Option 15
Option 8	Option 16

○○○		
Group A		**Group C**
Option 1	Option 5	Option 11
Option 2	Option 6	Option 12
Option 3	Option 7	Option 13
Option 4	Option 8	Option 14
		Option 15
Group B		Option 16
Option 9	Option 10	

SHOWING MANY OPTIONS AT THE SAME TIME CAN BE OVERWHELMING

STRUCTURING THE OPTIONS INTO A LOCAL VISUAL HIERARCHY HELPS THE USER SORT THROUGH THEM

Using proximity isn't the only way you can create this kind of local structure. In his book *Vision Science: Photons to Phenomenology* [Pal99], Stephen E. Palmer describes a number of different ways of grouping elements. These eight dots are ungrouped. Individual dots don't seem to belong together in any way.

Even by merely shifting them a bit, we can make it look as if there were four pairs of dots, rather than eight individual dots. This is called *proximity*, as mentioned earlier.

Here's another way of grouping the dots into pairs: changing the *colors* of four of the dots again turns the dots into four pairs of similarly colored dots.

We can also change the *size* of the dots to achieve the same effect.

Or we can change the *orientation*.

These three examples show groupings based on color, size, and orientation. But these aren't the only similarities you can use to group things. Different font styles, for example, might be another way of achieving this.

A more obvious way of grouping elements is to put them into common regions.

Or you can connect them directly.

There are many ways of creating structure and grouping things. Use these methods when you need to show a large number of individual items on a single screen.

Takeaway Points

- Don't use internal structures as blueprints for hierarchies that users see in your product or website.

- Use card sorts to find out where people think individual things should go.

- Don't optimize whole hierarchies for low click counts.

- Use grouping to organize individual screens.

Further Reading

There's really only one book you need to read to find out pretty much everything there is to know about card sorting: Donna Spencer's *Card Sorting: Designing Usable Categories* [Spe09].

If you're interested in the larger field of information architecture, *Information Architecture for the World Wide Web* [MR06] by Peter Morville and Louis Rosenfeld and *A Practical Guide to Information Architecture* [Spe10] by Donna Spencer are both good ways to get started. Spencer also writes a great card sorting blog[6] and a blog about information architecture.[7]

If you're interested in how humans perceive things, *Vision Science: Photons to Phenomenology* [Pal99] is a fascinating read.

---

6. At http://rosenfeldmedia.com/books/cardsorting/.
7. At http://practical-ia.com.

Chapter 9

The Mental Model

The people who use your products are not neutral or unbiased. They have ideas about how your product should work before they've ever used it. And yet, most products don't work the way people expect them to; people have to *learn* how to use things.

Instead of forcing people to learn how to use your product, wouldn't it be better if you created products that work the way people already expect them to work? Joel Spolsky notes in *User Interface Design for Programmers* [Spo11], "A user interface is well designed when the program behaves exactly how the user thought it would."

Of course, different people have different ideas about how things work. But even so, you can make an effort to minimize the gap between what people expect from a product and how the product actually works.

9.1 What People Think

The concept a user forms about how something works is called a *mental model*. Mental models are usually much simpler than reality. In *About Face* [Coo95], Alan Cooper refers to mental models as "a cognitive shorthand (...), one that is powerful enough to cover [the user's] interactions with [the product], but which doesn't necessarily reflect its actual inner mechanics."

Jakob Nielsen says, "A mental model is *what the user believes* about the system at hand."[1]

---

1. At http://www.useit.com/alertbox/mental-models.html.

Here's an example. Somebody driving a car might think there is a direct mechanical connection between the gas pedal and the engine, assuming that pushing down on the gas pedal opens some sort of valve that causes more fuel to enter the engine, thus making the car run faster.

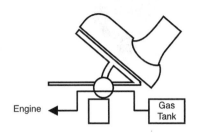

This mental model of how cars work is not actually correct. Instead, the gas pedal is connected to a computer. The input from the gas pedal is just one of many data points the computer takes into account, and the fuel system is just one of many systems the computer controls.

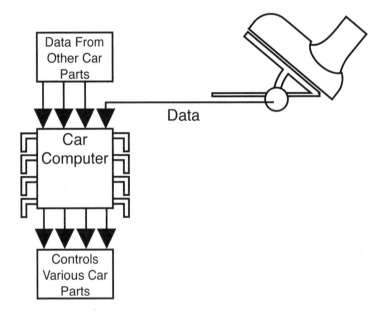

Based on all of this data, the computer then tries to figure out what the driver is doing. Is he trying to accelerate quickly because he has just gotten on the highway? Is he starting from a complete stop because the red light has just turned green? Is he suddenly letting go of the gas pedal because he's trying to stop the car as quickly as possible?

If the computer works correctly, the driver doesn't notice any of this. Stepping on the gas pedal makes the car go faster, just as you'd expect it to do.

There's an important point here: the user's mental model of how the car works is technically wrong. However, it still helps him understand how to control the car, because the interaction logic of the mental model—push the gas pedal to make the car go faster—matches the car's behavior (most of the time).

In other words, the user's mental model doesn't have to be correct. It just has to be consistent with the product's behavior.

9.2 Three Different Models

Our product actually reflects three different models:

- How the user thinks the product works. This is the user's mental model of the product.

- How the product is presented to the user in the user interface. I call this the UI model.[2]

- How the product is implemented. I call this the implementation model.[3]

In an ideal product, these three models are consistent with each other. The user interface perfectly represents the implementation, and the user perfectly understands what he sees.

9.3 Hiding Implementation Details

In reality, the three models are never entirely consistent. For example, the implementation model may be complex and archaic, so you have to simplify what the user sees. This is at odds with the goal of making the implementation model consistent with the UI model.

---

2. The model espoused by the visual representation of the product (its user interface) is sometimes also called the *design model*, *manifest model*, or *designer's model*.
3. The model espoused by the implementation is sometimes also called the *system model* or the *programmer's model*.

Anthropomorphism

People tend to attribute human characteristics to applications, websites, and other products.* This is a kind of mental model; people assume that machines work similarly to humans. So when a coin-counting machine finishes too quickly, we think that it hasn't put the proper effort into its task. We get angry at our computers as if they ate our documents on purpose. We suspect that our car's navigation system has led us astray deliberately. We give our devices names.

Car manufacturers are especially good at making use of our tendency to anthropomorphize their products. They intentionally design their cars to look as if they have human characteristics, making them look friendly or aggressive.

As designers, we should keep an eye on what kinds of human characteristics people will attribute to our products. Do our products behave like nice people or like unfriendly ones? Do they seem cold and unconcerned, or do they have a bit of personality? Are they tardy or so efficient that people might become suspicious?

---

*. Clifford Nass writes about research on this topic in *The Man Who Lied to His Laptop* (NY10).

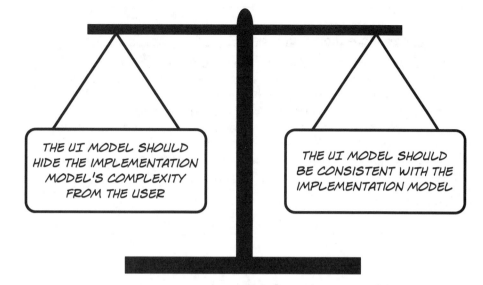

It's a trade-off. You are simplifying the user interface so that most users will have a better experience. But this means your UI model may not be entirely consistent with the implementation model.

Let's say you're creating an online platform for purchasing download-able movies. Your potential customers probably know how buying a movie works:

1. Go to a store.
2. Browse through a number of movies until they find one they like.
3. Exchange money for the chosen DVD.

This is the user's mental model of how buying a movie works.

But this isn't how buying a movie works on the Internet. Your customers don't give you physical money; instead, software running on your server asks a credit card company to change some numbers in a database. Then, your software updates some stuff in your database, signaling that the customer is now allowed to download a file. When the customer starts the download, the file is typically watermarked and possibly encrypted. Once the file is downloaded, software on the customer's computer decrypts the file, decodes the stored movie, and shows it on the customer's screen.

How do we represent this complex string of actions in the user interface?

You Know More Than Your Users

If you're creating a user interface for a product, you probably know how the product is implemented. If you're creating a website representing a company, you probably know that company's internal structure. Your users (most likely) don't know these things. So, right from the beginning, your mental model of how things work is different from your users' mental models, because yours is informed by things your users don't know.

Just because something makes sense to you doesn't mean it will make sense to your users.

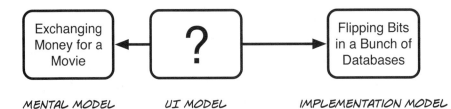

MENTAL MODEL   UI MODEL   IMPLEMENTATION MODEL

The user interface sits between the customer's mental model of how movie-buying works and the implementation model. Those two things are very different, so it's the user interface's job to translate between the two worlds, to present all of those strange things that happen outside of the user's view in a way that the user can understand and relate to. To help the user understand what is going on, the UI model has to be closer to the user's mental model than to the implementation model, hiding some of the implementation's complexity.

9.4 Leaky Abstractions

Hiding implementation details from the user makes your UI model easier to understand. But it creates a different problem: whenever some of the hidden implementation details leak to the user, it will not match his mental model of how your product behaves.

Going back to the earlier example of somebody buying a movie, let's say that same person now wants to buy a movie for her sister. Her mental model of buying a movie as a gift is simple:

1. Go to a store.

2. Browse through a number of movies until she finds one her sister likes.

3. Exchange money for a DVD.

4. Wrap the DVD in nice wrapping paper.

5. Deliver the wrapped DVD to her sister.

When it comes to buying a movie for her sister *online*, this user's mental model breaks down. The UI model hides a crucial aspect of the implementation model: the movie she bought is encrypted and needs to be decoded in order to be viewed. It can be decoded and shown *only on her own computer*. It would be reasonable for her to assume that she could put the downloaded movie on a memory stick and give that to her sister, because that matches her mental model of how movies work. But in fact, her sister would not be able to watch that movie.

How can you prevent these kinds of problems?

9.5 Designing for Mental Models

First, you need to find out how people think something works—by having a conversation with them to figure out what their preexisting mental model is (see Chapter 2, *Job Shadowing and Contextual Interviews*, on page 9). Then you do a card sort to find out how people think things fit together (see Chapter 8, *Card Sorting*, on page 53). Next up is usability testing with paper prototypes (see Chapter 11, *Paper Prototype Testing*, on page 97) to come up with designs that match people's mental models. You show them your design, describe an interaction, and ask them what they expect to happen. ("If I type some text and then close this document, what do you think will happen?")

Using the information you've gathered from conversations and usability testing, you can design a UI model that is consistent with your users' mental models. If you're creating your product from scratch, make sure that the implementation model matches that UI model.

This isn't always possible. Sometimes, you have to deal with an existing product that simply doesn't work the way people expect it to, and you can't change how it works. If that happens, make sure that the things your users have to learn are few and simple so that people can easily change their mental model of your product to fit how it actually works.

If you discover that people always form false mental models of your product when they use it (say, during usability tests), try changing how it looks, for example, by avoiding metaphors that don't fit your product's behavior (for more on metaphors, check out Chapter 12, *Realism*, on page 113). You can also try making your product appear unique so that people will immediately understand that it behaves differently from what they already know.

In their paper "Mental Models and Usability,"[4] Mary Jo Davidson, Laura Dove, and Julie Weltz describe seven user interface design principles that help users form valid mental models:

Principle 1: Simplicity

Mental models are simplified versions of reality. If your product follows a small number of simple rules, your users' mental models are more likely to be consistent with how the system actually works, and people will be able to learn these rules more easily.

The Flip video camera,[5] for example, has a huge red button on the back. Even if people have never used one, they have to take only one look at it to form a correct mental model of how the camera works. Push the button to start recording. Push again to stop.

(Photo courtesy of Cisco)

---

4. You can read the paper at http://www.lauradove.info/reports/mental%20models.htm.
5. For more about the Flip, go to http://www.theflip.com.

Principle 2: Familiarity

Users bring a lot of prior knowledge to your product. You need to be consistent across similar products and with how things work in the real world, and people will be more likely to form correct mental models.

An example of this is the way people delete files in most modern operating systems: they throw them into a bin and then empty the bin. You don't need to explain to people how to tell an empty bin from one with files in it; their prior knowledge of how bins work suffices.

EMPTY WINDOWS 7 BIN   BIN WITH FILES INSIDE

Of course, this prior knowledge of how trash bins work can cause problems. On Mac OS X, dragging a DVD onto the Trash icon (which then turns into an eject symbol) ejects the DVD. Predictably, a lot of people are confused by this; after all, they don't want to risk accidentally destroying the DVD by throwing it into the trash.

A lot of the music apps on Apple's iPad also make use of familiarity. Figure 9.1, on the following page shows an app called djay.[6]

This looks exactly like a real, physical dual-turntable DJ system. As a result, people familiar with such systems can start using this app without having to learn anything. They already have the mental model that allows them to make perfect sense of what they see.

Principle 3: Recognition

Instead of making people recall how to do something, show them the cues or obvious choices that allow them to understand the options currently available to them.

For example, the menu bar in Windows 7 displays actions related to the files the user is currently looking at. If she's looking at pictures, it offers commands related to sharing or viewing pictures, shown in Figure 9.2, on the next page

People don't have to remember how to show pictures in a slide show. The option is right there when they are likely to need it.

---

6. Find out more at http://www.algoriddim.com.

Figure 9.1: THE DJAY APPLICATION INTERFACE

Figure 9.2: WINDOWS MENUS ARE CONTEXT SENSITIVE

Principle 4: Flexibility

Let users perform actions in any order, using different techniques if possible.

In modern word processors, users can switch to the different styles they want to use for different parts of a document while they're typing. Or they can type all of their text first and then go through the document and apply different styles.

Principle 5: Feedback

Always give immediate, useful feedback to user interactions. If the user clicks something, it should highlight immediately. If she drags something, it should move in line with her mouse or finger, without any lag. If she initiates an action that takes a bit of time, show an activity indicator such as a progress bar to inform her that the computer has received her command and is working on it (there's more about this in Chapter 23, *Speed*, on page 193).

Getting immediate feedback helps people correct flaws in their mental model and builds trust in their own actions when their mental model is correct.

Figure 9.3, on the next page shows two pictures of different buttons used in trams in Zürich. You push them when you want the tram to stop. The one on the right lights up once pushed; the one on the left doesn't. While riding trams in Zürich, you will often notice people repeatedly pushing the button in the style shown on the left, just to make sure that their push was really registered; there's no obvious feedback that it was. You rarely see that with the one on the right.

Of course, it's possible to overdo things. Buttons in some trains use a scheme with different colors, one to indicate that the button can be pushed (which activates only shortly before the train stops) and one

LACK OF FEEDBACK MAKES IT
HARD TO LEARN HOW
EXACTLY THE BUTTON
WORKS AND TO TRUST THAT
IT WORKS AT ALL

THE BUTTON LIGHTS UP ONCE
PRESSED. THIS IMMEDIATE
FEEDBACK MAKES IT EASY FOR
THE USER TO LEARN HOW IT
WORKS

Figure 9.3: PUSH THESE TO STOP A TRAM

to indicate that it has already been pushed. Since people can never remember which color is which, they tend to push the button several times, just to make sure it has switched to the correct state. Adding some feedback helps people form correct mental models. Adding too much or unclear feedback can cause even more confusion.

Principle 6: Safety

User actions should not be harmful, unless the user intends them to be. Closing a document with unsaved changes should not destroy those changes without giving the user the opportunity to get them back. Always allow users to undo their actions (see Chapter 19, *Instead of Interrupting, Offer Undo*, on page 165). Give them the freedom to explore without fear of permanent harm, and they'll be more open to learning and to adapting their mental model to how your product works.

For example, if someone closes a window containing several tabs in Google Chrome and then decides that she really needs to get some of those tabs back, she can simply restore the closed window using the History menu.

Assuming Causality

People tend to assume causality when things happen at the same time or close to each other. If B happens right after the user does A, he will often conclude that A caused B. Although you can use this causality element as a way to help people form correct mental models, keep in mind that this can easily create *incorrect* mental models.

This issue often appears in troubleshooting behavior; if something doesn't work and the user does something in an attempt to fix it and then it works, it's natural for the user to assume that what he did fixed the problem. After all, the user doesn't know whether it would have worked if he hadn't done anything.

In Switzerland, you often see people scratching coin-operated machines with coins the machine didn't accept on their first attempt:

Since the coin is usually accepted after scratching the machine, it's natural to assume that scratching the machine was what fixed the problem, even though the coin would have worked on the second attempt independent of the scratching.

Similarly, if Chrome crashes, she can restore all of the windows that were open at the time of the crash.

Principle 7: Affordances

Your user interface elements should be created in a way that suggests to your users how they can interact with them. Design details that communicate possible interactions are called *affordances*.

In *The Design of Everyday Things* [Nor88], Don Norman writes:

> A good designer makes sure that appropriate actions are perceptible and inappropriate ones invisible.

Nintendo's old NES controller (below, pictured on the left) doesn't make it obvious how you're supposed to hold it. In fact, the two red buttons are placed so far down the right side that it's more comfortable to hold the controller upside down. Compare this to Nintendo's newer GameCube controller. Although the newer controller is a lot more complex, it's immediately obvious how you're supposed to hold it, thanks to the nubs on each side of the controller that invite you to wrap your hands around them.

User interfaces often use bevels and highlights to indicate elements you can interact with.

Highlighting user interface elements when you move the cursor over them further indicates that they are clickable.

Of course, if this "hover effect" doesn't work correctly, the affordance is misleading, suggesting to the user that he can interact with a user interface element when he really can't. For example, Mac OS X highlights the buttons in its windows' title bars even before the user moves the cursor over a clickable area; this can cause users to click too early, missing their target.

Similarly misleading affordances can often be found in audio software like Propellerhead Software's ReBirth. These apps often use knobs that look like real knobs, indicating that the user can interact with them by turning them.

IMPLIED
INTERACTION

ACTUAL
INTERACTION

Instead, you change their values by dragging vertically.

I'll talk a bit more about how affordances apply to user interface design in Chapter 12, *Realism*, on page 113.

Takeaway Points

- Humans have ideas about how things work. The closer your product matches these ideas, the less people have to learn in order to use your product.

- To match your users' mental models, you often have to hide implementation details from them. Watch out for leaky abstractions.

- To design for mental models, make your product simple, familiar, flexible, and safe. Provide feedback, and make it obvious to people what options they have at any given moment.

Further Reading

Alan Cooper has a good chapter on mental models in his book *About Face* [Coo95]. Robert Hoekman also covers mental models in *Designing the Obvious* [Hoe06]. Joel Spolsky's *User Interface Design for Programmers* [Spo11] covers mental models from the perspective of a developer.

Jakob Nielsen has written about mental models.[7]

---

7. At http://www.useit.com/alertbox/mental-models.html.

Part II

Design

By now, you have a pretty good idea of who your audience is and what kinds of problems you want to solve. You probably even have a basic idea of how the solution might work. But be careful: you don't want to settle on any particular solution yet. The human mind is pretty good at rationalizing information that goes against its current opinion. So, don't form opinions too quickly. Try not to focus on a specific design or solution; doing so might make you blind to *better* approaches.

Instead of immediately going for fully formed ideas, start slowly. In this part of the book, you'll start by doing flow diagrams of your product. These are very simple, high-level ideas that will help you figure out how your product might work. Slowly, you'll add details, moving from flow diagrams to storyboards to simple sketches and eventually to fully formed mock-ups and even to interactive prototypes.

Always remain open to the possibility that you're wrong. The longer you hold on to a design that doesn't work, the harder it will be to change it. Failing early is a good thing.

To make sure you're on the right track and to allow you to fail early, you'll test your design ideas with actual users. Pretty quickly, you'll find out what works and what doesn't.

This part of the book is about iteration. Avoid strong opinions. Instead, design, test, accept if something doesn't work, and iterate.

Chapter 10

Sketching and Prototyping

Research	Design	Implementation

What's the Technique?

By now, you probably have a pretty good idea of what you want to create. It's time to flesh out the design, first by sketching the structure of your product and then by progressively zooming in on the details by designing the individual screens.

Why Is This a Good Idea?

Changes you make once you've started implementing your product can be expensive. A small user interface change can have vast implications.

Changing a sketch, on the other hand, is cheap and quick. All you need is an eraser, a pencil, and a few seconds.

Basically, you are creating simple prototypes of your product. If you're designing a remote control, you don't create the molds and start producing them. Instead, you start with simple wood or clay models of the remote to get a feel for how it should be proportioned. Then, you add more and more detail until you end up with the final design.

Sketching is the clay model prototype of your product. The more details you nail down before committing to code, the better.

Are There Any Prerequisites?

You should have a pretty good idea of what your product is going to be.

10.1 Designing the Structure

In *Rework* [FH10], Jason Fried and David Heinemeier Hansson write that "architects don't worry about which tiles go in the shower or which brand of dishwasher to install in the kitchen until *after* the floor plan is finalized."

This is what flow diagrams and storyboards are: your product's floor plan. We're at the very beginning of the "design" part of our design process. Flow diagrams and storyboards are not about details. They are about the big picture: the structure.

10.2 Flow Diagrams

Flow diagrams answer the following questions: What does the user have to do to get what he wants? What steps does she have to follow to reach her goal?

Pick the most important user goals, and think about the required steps.

For our Twitter app example, a simple flow diagram for replying to a message would look a bit like this:

REPLY TO A MESSAGE

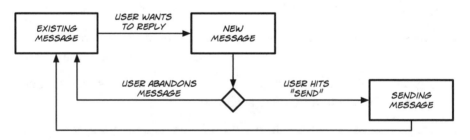

It's OK to add branching to flow diagrams, but don't make them too complex. In theory, you could have one enormous flow diagram that describes your whole product. In reality, it makes more sense to create several flow diagrams for the most important user goals. That way, you can keep the individual flow diagrams concise and clearly arranged.

The goal of this exercise is to think about what's involved in each goal. What kinds of screens do you need to show to the user? What kinds of decisions does he have to make at what point?

10.3 Storyboards

Storyboarding is a technique originally developed to plan animations for movies. Storyboards break animations down into their important frames; they turn a moving picture into a comic book. In user interface design, we use storyboards for a similar purpose. They break down the user's path into a series of snapshots.

Storyboards mostly ignore branching and focus instead on interaction details. What exactly is the user seeing on each screen? What do you want the user to do? Where should you use animations or graphics to help the user understand what he should do?

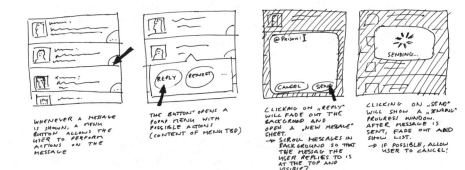

You can indicate where and how interactions happen by drawing arrows or hands (if it's a touch-screen user interface).

Making storyboards can take a lot of time, so you want to use them only for those parts of the application where the design is not obvious. Everybody who is familiar with comic books can follow a storyboard—it's a great tool for communicating design. If you need to explain to a programmer how to implement something, storyboards can be a huge help.

10.4 Sketching

After architects design the floor plan, they design the individual rooms. After you design the structure of your product, you want to design the individual screens. By making flow diagrams and storyboards, you should have a pretty good idea of what screens your product requires and what functionality each screen should provide.

You've already done simple sketches of some of the screens while doing storyboards. In the storyboard example, some of the screens already contained things that were unrelated to the task performed in the storyboard. For example, the pop-over menu didn't just have a "reply" button; it also had a "retweet" button. Now, we want to nail down the contents of the individual screens.

Usability consultant Bruce Tognazzini notes:[1]

> Jumping into complex, finely-tuned prototypes is perhaps the worst mistake a team can make. (...) Users (and clients) [feel more free] to express contrary views if models look less than perfected. But there's another side, too: designers and developers are more willing to listen to dissent if they haven't lavished ultimate care on what should have been a storyboard or quick-and-dirty prototype.

Experiment with using simple sketches to figure out how individual screens should look at a very basic level. Everybody can sketch, so you're free to involve other people in the process. Show them your ideas, and see whether they come up with their own.

Once you're happy with the basic design of your screens, move on to wireframes.

---

1. Read more at http://www.asktog.com/columns/005roughsketches.html.

Lorem Ipsum

People often use filler text like Lorem Ipsum in wireframes. If you really don't have anything better, using filler text is OK. If you can, however, include text that users might actually see. That gives you a better idea of how well the user interface will work and how big the text is going to be (if it's something that has specific lengths, like Twitter messages).

10.5 Wireframes

Wireframes represent the exact structure of a screen but without the decoration—no colors, shadows, or pictures. Wireframes are about the content. What do you want to show on each screen, and where do you want to put it? How big should things be? How close to each other should they be? Figure 10.1, on the following page shows a sample wireframe (on the left).

This is also the time when you start working on the copy. You don't need to get this exactly right yet, but you should think about text you want to include and where to put it.

The goal of wireframes is to identify exactly what you need to show on each screen and where you want to put things. Once you've done this, you can move on to decoration.

10.6 Mock-ups

Wireframes tell you about the layout of a screen. Mock-ups add the decoration, or visual details: shadows, textures, images, transparency. This is how you want the screen to look based on your current knowledge. Compare the mock-up in Figure 10.1, on the next page (on the right) with the wireframe (on the left).

Adding visual details is not just about making your product look pretty. Of course, the goal is for the end product to look good, but visual design can also give the user hints about the functionality of your product. User interface designers often call these *affordances*. If you've missed it, I've talked about this back in Section 9.5, *Principle 7: Affordances*, on page 80. For now, here are some examples of affordances: textures to let the user know that he can touch and drag something, shadows and

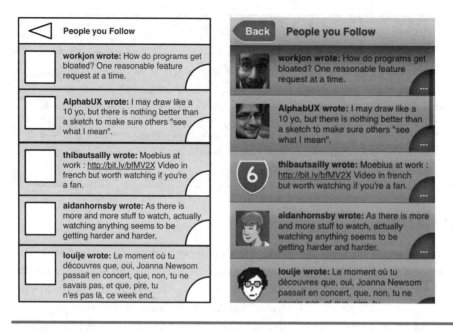

Figure 10.1: A SAMPLE WIREFRAME (LEFT) AND MOCK-UP (RIGHT)

bevels to show that he can push something or to emphasize hierarchies, and colors to convey importance and draw the user's attention.

These are the kind of things you need to keep in mind when you do a detailed mock-up of how your screen should look.

You don't necessarily have to create mock-ups using a graphics application. If you prefer, you can do mock-ups in code. Simply use the medium that will be easiest for you when you have to make sweeping changes. But keep in mind that you are creating prototypes, not early versions of the final product. In *The Pragmatic Programmer* [HT00], Andrew Hunt and David Thomas write:

> With a prototype, you're aiming to explore specific aspects of the final system. With a true prototype, you will throw away whatever you lashed together when trying out the concept, and recode it properly using the lessons you've learned.

Even if you do mock-ups in code, the goal is still to explore ideas in a way that makes it easy to throw things away if they don't work out.

Terminology

In this book, I use the following terms:

Sketch	Any representation of a user interface as a drawing.
Wireframe	A static representation of a user interface where the individual elements are at least roughly where they are supposed to go, at their supposed sizes.
Mock-up	A (usually static) representation of a user interface where decorations like shadows and colors are introduced.
Prototype	Any representation of a product that is not the final product.

Not everybody uses these terms in that way. Sometimes, the term *prototype* denotes only interactive, high-fidelity representations. Sometimes, the term *mock-up* is used for any type of sketch of the final user interface. When you read about these things on the Internet or in other books, be aware that the author may use these words differently.

10.7 Tools

Sketching and prototyping are popular activities in the software development community—enough to have given rise to a whole ecosystem of products. The sole *raison d'être* for these applications and services is to help you sketch or prototype your product.

There are many good reasons for using such products. One of the main ones is that they make it easy to collaborate on designs even when designers live far away from each other.

Balsamiq[2] and Mockingbird[3] are online tools that allow you to create and share sketches of your user interface.

Google Docs has a drawing component called Google Drawings, which allows several people to collaborate on a design. Morten Just has a set of Google Drawings templates with user interface elements.[4]

---

2. At http://balsamiq.com.
3. At https://gomockingbird.com.
4. At http://mortenjust.com/2010/04/19/a-wireframe-kit-for-google-drawings/.

On the Mac, OmniGraffle[5] fills many of your user interface sketching needs. People have created user interface stencils specifically for OmniGraffle.[6] If you're an iPhone developer, check out Briefs[7] and Review.[8]

Some people also use tools like PowerPoint[9] or Keynote[10] to create mock-ups and prototypes. These tools even allow you to add simple animations and interactions. Sites like Keynotopia[11] and Keynote Kungfu[12] provide user interface templates for these applications. Templates can help you create pixel-perfect mock-ups that use a platform's standard user interface elements.

All of these tools can make your life a lot easier. On the other hand, there are good reasons for going with paper. It's faster, it's more natural, and as long as everybody is in the same room, it's easy to collaborate with other people; the only thing people need in order to contribute ideas is their own pencil. And since everybody has some kind of gadget with a built-in camera nowadays, sending the sketched user interface to somebody else is as easy as taking a picture and emailing it.

Just use what's easiest for you. If sketching on paper works best, sketch on paper. If you prefer to use an application specifically created for user interface designers, use that. If you want to use a graphics application instead, that's fine too. Or simply use all of these tools, depending on your current task.

Takeaway Points

- Start with a bird's-eye view and work your way down to the details, from flow diagrams to storyboards to simple sketches to wireframes and eventually to detailed mock-ups.

- Fix problems early. The earlier you notice a problem with your design, the cheaper it is to fix it.

- Flow diagrams help you make it as simple as possible for your users to reach their goals.

---

5. At http://www.omnigroup.com.
6. For example, at http://graffletopia.com/categories/user-interface.
7. At http://giveabrief.com.
8. At http://www.getreviewapp.com.
9. At http://office.microsoft.com.
10. At http://www.apple.com/iwork.
11. At http://keynotopia.com.
12. At http://keynotekungfu.com.

- Storyboards help you flesh out and communicate the interaction design of your product.

- Simple sketches help you figure out *what* to put on individual screens.

- Wireframes help you decide *where* to put things on individual screens.

- Mock-ups help you iterate quickly on the visual design.

Further Reading

Flow diagrams, storyboards, wireframes, and mock-ups are the four techniques I use most often. They allow me to start with a bird's-eye view and progressively move down to the details. Other designers, however, prefer a different combination of techniques. *Undercover User Experience Design* [BB10] by Cennydd Bowles and James Box teach you these and other techniques.

Bill Buxton's *Sketching User Experiences* [Bux07] is another great book on this topic, and Robert Hoekman also covers some of these techniques in *Designing the Obvious* [Hoe06].

Tyler Tate writes about different sketching and prototyping methods.[13]

---

13. At http://www.uxbooth.com/blog/concerning-fidelity-and-design/.

Chapter 11

Paper Prototype Testing

Research	Design	Implementation

What's the Technique?

In the previous chapter, I explained how to sketch your product. I said that you should sketch before you commit to code because sketches are easier to change. But I kind of skirted around the issue of how you know what changes to make.

In some cases, issues with a design—such as features that are available at the wrong time or overcrowded screens—become obvious once you see it sketched out before you.

But in other cases, it's not obvious. When is a design good? If you have more than one idea of how to do something, which idea will work best? Where are the issues with your current idea? This chapter will help you find answers to these questions.

Your sketches are basically primitive forms—prototypes, if you like— of your product. As such, you can run usability tests with them and see whether your designs work the way you expect them to work. The easiest way to do that is to show them to people and see whether they understand them.

If you're working alone or in a small team, feel free to skip the part of this chapter that explains how to run full usability tests with paper prototypes.

Why Is This a Good Idea?

The earlier you find issues with your design, the easier it is to fix them. Every problem you fix with a pencil on paper is a problem you don't have to fix in code.

Are There Any Prerequisites?

You should have started doing sketches.

11.1 Guerilla Paper Prototype Testing

At this point in the process, you have static representations of your product. Whether it's simple, crude sketches, wireframes, or detailed mock-ups, your product exists in the form of a series of pictures.

At its most basic, paper prototype testing simply means you get a real person to "interact" with those pictures in order to gauge whether your planned user interface is understandable to your users. This could be as simple as showing somebody a drawing of a user interface and asking them something like "If you wanted to change the font size of the text document on this screen, where would you click?"

You need a reasonably detailed sketch, wireframe, or mock-up of one of your product's screens to do paper prototype tests. Then, find somebody willing to spend five minutes with you. Show them the screen, and ask a generic question: *"What do you see on this screen? What do you suppose this product could be used for?"*

Alternatively, you can ask a simple task-based question: *"If you had to use this application to add a picture to a document, what would you do?"*

Paper?

This chapter is about "paper prototypes," but the "paper" part isn't meant too literally. You don't necessarily need to do sketches on paper to do these kinds of tests. You can also do mock-ups on a computer and print them out. Or, instead of printing them, put them on a tablet computer, and show that to people. You could even create a simple interactive prototype of your product by putting sketches into an application like PowerPoint or Keynote.

I guess this chapter should really be called "how to do usability tests with (mostly but sometimes not entirely) static sketches or mock-ups of your final product," but that didn't fit into the book's layout.

This kind of test will give you a general idea of whether people understand your design and what parts people don't get. That way, you know where you have to make changes and where you're on the right track.

Simply showing people a mock-up of one screen of your product helps you understand whether people understand that screen. This is useful, but we can go a step further and test interactions. To do this, prepare more than one screen in advance. If you need pop-up elements or other elements that have to be added or removed from the screen, also prepare them in advance; draw them on Post-it notes so you can easily add them to the prototype.

Prepared in this way, you can run actual task-based usability tests. Of course, you can't let people veer too far off track, but if they do, you already know that there's a problem with your design, because people don't follow the path you expected them to take.

You can do this type of simple test with pretty much anyone. It takes only a few minutes, and it's quite easy to explain:

> I'm working on a new Twitter app. You know what Twitter is? OK, great. I'm currently working on the design of my app, and I'm trying to figure out whether people understand what I've done. You know, when you work on something for weeks, you lose any objectivity, and it's hard for me to tell whether what I'm doing makes sense to anyone else. I was wondering

whether I could show you some of these designs and ask you a few questions about them to see whether people can figure them out? It won't take more than five minutes.

You can start doing this with friends and family members to get used to running these tests. Then, ask random people. A good place to start is a café. People usually have a few minutes to spare.

Once you see how people interpret your designs, it will be easy to figure out where your designs work and where potential problems lie.

11.2 Running Full Usability Tests with Paper Prototypes

The simple tests I've described so far will allow you to do some early usability testing on your designs. There is, of course, a much more elaborate way of doing prototype testing. I don't recommend this process for most smaller teams, but if you have the time and the people required to do such tests, they can give great feedback even before a single line of code is written.

A prototype typically represents only a subset of your finished product. Not every screen of your final product will be part of your prototype. Not every feature will be represented. For this reason, prototype usability tests are almost always based on specific tasks: you will give a person a specific task and ask that person to execute that task on your prototype. That way, you have a pretty good idea of what screens and UI elements you will need to prepare.

So, the first thing you want to do is define tasks you want to test.

Defining Tasks

Now that you've created a storyboard and mock-ups, you probably have a pretty good idea of where potential user interaction problems might be found. If it was hard to come up with a user interface for a feature, this is probably something you want to test early. If it is a critical, central feature of your product, it's definitely something you want to test early. Pick the features that are important to your product, that you think might be hard to use, or that you think might cause problems.

Next, come up with tasks that use these areas of your product. You can draw upon the user research you did in the first part of the book, if you need.

Remember that you're not looking for opinions. Usability tests are not focus groups. The goal of a usability test is to observe people as they interact with your design so that you can find flaws in the interaction design. Pick tasks that cause people to actually use the product.

It's important that the task not be too prescriptive; tell the user what goal he has to achieve, rather than what steps he has to follow. The task should *not* look like this:

Task 1: Posting a Picture

1. Use the "New Message" button to create a new message

2. Click on the camera icon to attach a picture

3. Select a picture from the browser, and click "Add Picture"

4. Add some text to your message

5. Click on "Publish Message"

A task like this tells you only whether people are capable of following instructions. It doesn't tell you whether your product is usable. Instead, the task description should state the goals and leave the individual steps up to the user. It should look something like this:

> You are at one of your company's customer events. You want to take a picture of the room and publish it on your company's Twitter account.

This is a scenario one of your users might find himself in. It will show you how somebody in this situation might interact with your product.

Perhaps counterintuitively, tasks are one area where you should avoid using your official terminology. If you use words in the task description that people can find in the user interface, you are essentially giving them a hint about how to perform the task.

It's a good idea to prepare at least five or six tasks; more is better. Each task should take between two and ten minutes. It's likely that you won't make it through all of the tasks, but it's hard to tell before doing the actual test, so it's better to be prepared if people blow through your tasks quickly.

Creating the Paper Prototype

Based on the tasks you've come up with, it's pretty easy to tell which screens you will need to show to people (but be liberal when deciding which screens to include in your prototype; people may not always take the most obvious steps toward the goals you've set).

You can use existing sketches for paper prototypes, if they're not *too* crude and simple. Using very simple sketches can cause problems if they are not easily readable by people who are not already familiar with your product.

To turn a sketch or mock-up into something suitable for a usability test, you need to add the user interface elements surrounding your own user interface. For example, if you're testing a website, add relevant parts of the browser user interface to the prototype (forward and back buttons, the address bar, the title bar, and so on). Similarly, if you're testing an application, you should add the menu bar and maybe even parts of the desktop if it is an application running on a desktop operating system.

After you've created the screens, you should think about state changes on individual screens.

What happens if somebody clicks a drop-down menu? You should prepare any pop-up windows in advance. Some people like to use Post-it notes for them, which makes it easy to stick them to the paper prototype once the user activates them.

What happens if the user has to type data into a field? There are several ways of handling this. If you are not going to reuse the paper prototype, you can simply give people a pencil and an eraser and let them change the data on the screen using these tools. If you are going to reuse the prototype (say, you're doing more than one test), you could use transparencies. Put them over your prototype, and let people draw on the transparency.

Finally, you should print each task on its own piece of paper. Since you don't know how many tasks a user will get through, using individual pieces of paper for each task allows you to hand out tasks as you go along or switch the order of the tasks on the fly if you need to do so.

At this point, you should run through each task. Make sure that the individual goals are feasible and that you've included every screen and pop-up element you're likely to need.

Paper Prototype Creation Checklist

- ☐ Prepare all the screens people are likely to progress through while doing your tasks. Don't make them too crude.
- ☐ Add the surrounding user interface elements (such as browser windows around sketches of a website) where necessary.
- ☐ Create the pop-up elements you might need.
- ☐ Prepare some way for people to draw on top of your prototype.
- ☐ Print out the tasks on individual pieces of paper.
- ☐ Do a test run of each task, and make sure you've prepared all of the screens and pop-up elements you're likely to need.

Preparing for the Test

To run a usability test with your paper prototype, you need at least one additional person: the person who is going to do the tasks. This person is sometimes called the test subject, but since you're not testing this person, I usually call her the tester. She's the one who is testing your design, after all.

I won't go into great depth on how to recruit testers in this book. There are many good resources on the topic,[1] but generally, pretty much anyone outside of your company will do. It's best to avoid recruiting testers from within your company. They are too familiar with your product and your company's jargon; this familiarity may mask usability problems with your product. It sometimes makes sense to recruit testers from your product's target audience, but generally, it doesn't matter too much. Almost anybody will do, including friends and family.

How many tests should you run with any version of the paper prototype? Paper prototypes take a bit of time to create, so it makes sense to test each prototype with more than just one person. Additionally,

---

1. This Nielsen Norman report does a great job: http://www.nngroup.com/reports/tips/recruiting/.

The Original Computers

It seems funny to us that we would call a human *the computer*. Historically, though, computers actually *were* humans. The term was first used around 1600 and referred to people who carried out calculations.

It was only during World War II that machines started to take over this task, when people like Konrad Zuse and Alan Turing created the first computing machines. As these machines became more prevalent, the term *computer* eventually changed its meaning.

with a paper prototype, it's easily possible to make small adjustments between tests. A good solution is to invite three or four testers and schedule them two or three hours apart. That way, you have enough time between tests to quickly go through the issues you've found and, if possible, make changes to the paper prototype accordingly.

While you can run a paper prototype usability test on your own, it's helpful to have at least one additional person there to assist you. Since you have created the paper prototype and since you know how the storyboard of your application looks, you are the perfect person to "play the computer" during the test. This means you will have to switch screens, show pop-ups, and simulate the user interface. This leaves you with little time to interact with the tester. Although you can do both if you have to, it makes sense to find a second person who can help you with this. This person is called the *facilitator*. Figure 11.1, on page 107 shows a typical setup for paper prototyping.

The facilitator is the person who guides the usability test by introducing the tester to how the test works by giving out tasks and by answering any questions the tester might have.

Computer	Controls the paper prototype, reacts to user input
Facilitator	Introduces the tester to the process, gives tasks, answers questions
Tester	Interacts with the paper prototype according to the given tasks

The facilitator should take notes during the test and (if you record the session) add the recording's timecode to the note so that each note can be matched to a video of what occurred. Taking good notes during the test can keep you from having to sift through hours of recorded usability tests.

Recording the session can be a good idea. It allows you to go through the session after it's over. Viewing a session after the fact allows you to focus specifically on what the tester is doing and will provide a ton of insight into the kinds of problems she encountered; often these are small things you might not have noticed during the test. Additionally, if you're not the one making the relevant decisions, a movie that shows people repeatedly failing at the same task can often quickly persuade people who otherwise don't believe that there even *is* a problem with the user interface.

I tend not to go into legal issues in this book. But remember that in addition to having testers sign a consent form,[2] the facilitator should also explicitly get permission from the tester to record the session if a recording will be made.

Test Preparation Checklist

- ☐ Recruit three to five testers, and schedule them about two hours apart.
- ☐ Find and train somebody to act as the facilitator.
- ☐ If you want to, prepare a way to record the test.
- ☐ Prepare a consent form for the tester.

Preparing the Tester

Have the tester sit across from the person playing the computer so that the computer can change the prototype in front of the tester. The facilitator should sit next to the tester, preferably slightly behind her so as not to be in the way.

Once everybody is ready, the first thing the facilitator has to do is to explain to the tester that it is not she who is being tested, but the user interface. This is basically the standard introduction you give at

---

2. If you don't already have a consent form for usability tests, I suggest you write one with the help of a lawyer familiar with the legal requirements in your location. Just make sure that your testers will be able to understand any legal provisions in the consent form.

Observers

The three roles I've mentioned so far are *computer* (the person who controls the paper prototype), *tester* (the person who interacts with the paper prototype), and *facilitator* (the person who leads the test). For most smaller companies, these are often all the people you will have in a usability test for a paper prototype. However, in larger companies, it makes sense to have more people participate and observe the tests. In my experience, programmers and people from the management team can profit tremendously from seeing how users interact with their products.

We call the people who observe tests *observers*.

For a usability test of a paper prototype, observers can either sit in the same room as the other three people, observe from a different room, or watch the video after the fact. If they sit in the same room, they need to know that they should not interfere or influence the tester in any way. Generally, I think it is a bad idea to have observers in the same room as the tester, but since tests of paper prototypes already require a computer and a facilitator, adding two or three observers might not make much of a difference.

Tell your observers to take notes during the test. Afterward, you should spend an hour or so going through the issues found during the test. The more people who observe the test, the more issues they will find. You can use affinity diagrams to prioritize issues coming from several observers. This is explained in Carolyn Snider's excellent book *Paper Prototyping: The Fast and Easy Way to Define and Refine User Interfaces* (Sni03).

Figure 11.1: THE ROLES IN PAPER PROTOTYPING

every usability test; you can read more about it in Chapter 28, *Usability Testing*, on page 241. A short version of the introduction might go:

> Hi, I'm Michael. I work here as a software designer. This is my friend Sandra. She also works in the design department, and she will help me with this test.

> First of all, I want to thank you again for taking the time to help us with this.

> Today, we are testing a new design for our product to see whether it works the way we intended. I want to make it very clear that we are testing the design, not you. This new design has never been used outside of our design team, so we are hoping to find problems in the design by observing people interact with it. So, don't worry if you get stuck or if something doesn't work as you expect it to; this is exactly the kind of feedback we are looking for!

> As you can see, we haven't implemented the design yet; it's still on paper. We want to iron out any problems before we start writing code. So today, my friend Sandra will play the part of the computer—she'll do all the things the computer would do. Since she's playing the computer, she won't say much today, but she will change what you see according to your input, like a real computer. While you interact with our design, please feel free to tell me whatever is on your mind and ask questions. Since we are trying to see how people interact with this product when we are not around, I may not always be able to answer your questions immediately, but they will still help us understand what is going through your mind.

> With your permission, I will record this session. This is just so we can go back and figure out how to improve our design. We will never publish this recording in any way.

> Do you have any questions about how this will work?

Then, have the tester sign the consent form.

It's a good idea to make some notes or keep a checklist about what to say beforehand, just to make sure that the facilitator mentions every relevant point. There's a lot of ground to cover, and it's easy to forget something.

Next, the facilitator should quickly introduce the tester to the paper prototype. Explain what she is looking at: "This is the home page of our new website." Next, explain how to interact with it:

> You can use this just like you would use a regular computer. To click something, point with your finger. You can also drag things as you would with a mouse. To type something, use a pencil to write directly onto the prototype—don't worry, we have extra copies. To delete something, use the eraser. If something you do changes the screen, our human computer will take care of this and replace the screen or add pop-ups or menus to this screen. Again, feel free to talk out loud. The computer will only react to clicking and typing, though.

You can use an example sketch to demonstrate things such as pointing, dragging, writing, and erasing while you explain this.

The facilitator should point out that the tester should talk only to him or her, not to the computer. If the tester starts talking to the computer during the test, make sure that the facilitator is always the one who responds. And again, take care to point out that it's the design that's being tested, not the tester.

Running the Test

Finally, introduce the first task:

> OK, now that we have that out of the way, let's start testing the design. I have written a task on this piece of paper. Take your time to read it. Once you're ready, you can start interacting with the design.

There are a few things the facilitator should keep in mind during the test. First of all, it's important to avoid influencing the tester. This is especially relevant when the tester gets stuck and starts asking questions. Once it becomes obvious that the tester won't be able to solve the problem by herself, it's OK to give a hint (or move on to the next task), but generally, the facilitator must take care not to lead the tester.

At most, the facilitator can ask questions but, again, should make sure not to accidentally influence the tester by offering hints on how to use the design. Avoid terminology seen in the design. The facilitator's questions should be as generic as possible, along the lines of "What are you thinking right now?" or, if the tester is stuck, "Tell me what you see on that screen." For more common mistakes made during usability tests, see Chapter 31, *How Not to Test: Common Mistakes*, on page 271.

Generally, as long as the tester seems occupied by the interface, it's best to remain silent. After all, people using your product at home don't have one of your employees looking over their shoulder, constantly asking them how they feel about your product.

The facilitator should avoid doing anything that may make the tester feel uncomfortable. Having people observe your errors can already be stressful; don't add to the stress. If the facilitator notices that the tester is getting frustrated, it's OK to intervene and offer a bit of help, encouragement, or even a quick break. Indicators that intervention is necessary are the tester asking for help, the tester starting to blame herself for problems, or the tester getting stuck. Make sure to avoid sounding condescending when you offer encouragement or a break.

The computer's job is to update the prototype based on the tester's input. If everything goes as planned, with paper prototype testing this mainly consists of replacing the current screen with a different screen or adding and removing Post-it notes of interface elements as needed. In some cases (for example, when the tester uses the search function), the computer can also erase things from screens or write text onto screens. For data-heavy applications, especially if they include a prominent search feature, it may make sense to prepare some screens that you've already filled in with data for the path you expect the tester to take.

Sometimes, the tester takes a route nobody expected. In those cases, the computer can create a quick mock-up of the screen, or, if the tester goes too far off track, the facilitator can intervene and either stop the test or bring the tester back on track.

After the tester has finished the first task, both the facilitator and the computer can take a minute to ask any questions they might have and didn't want to (or could not) ask during the test—for example, "You hesitated before clicking the Buy button; do you remember what went through your head at that point?" Personally, I prefer it if the facilitator doesn't ask too many questions during the test and instead waits until the task is finished. This makes it less likely that the facilitator influences the tester's behavior. The disadvantage is that the testers often don't clearly remember exactly what they did during the test or why they did something.

Once this is done, give the tester the next task, and have her continue with the test.

When the last task is over or you're about to run out of time, you can finish up by asking the tester for some opinions, if you want. Opinions are generally not what we're looking for, but people sometimes come up with interesting thoughts after a test. For example, you could ask what the tester *didn't* like about the design, whether she would use your product, and what she would use it for.

It's a good idea to ask what the tester thought of the whole experience. As a sort of meta-test, the things people point out after such a test can often be useful input for improving future tests.

Finally, thank the tester again for her time, and make sure she understands that the results of the test were helpful to you.

Analyzing the Results

Avoid any kind of statistical or formal evaluation. Usability tests provide qualitative data, not quantitative data. It would be misguided to do formal analyses of the results of such a test. It would also be unnecessary. In fact, even from merely looking at a video of a usability test, it is usually quite obvious where the big problems are.

Instead of investing a lot of time into analyzing the results, identify the problems, prioritize them, let each team member pick the ones they want to solve, let them come up with possible solutions, make the changes to the design, and test again as soon as possible (with another set of testers).

Knowing When to Stop Testing

So, how do you know when your design is good enough and you can stop doing usability tests?

Basically, you don't stop testing. Testing is a constant part of the development process. During this process, as you iron out the problems with your paper prototypes and move toward writing real code, you will also gradually move from testing paper prototypes toward testing running code. However, paper prototyping will remain a valuable tool every time you work on a major design change. It's always easier to test such changes on paper first and implement them in code only once you've settled on a workable, tested design.

Takeaway Points

- To know how to improve sketches and mock-ups, test them with real people.

- Tests don't have to be complex. Show sketches to people, and ask them simple questions.

- For more extensive tests, define tasks that touch critical areas of your product. Prepare at least five or six tasks. Each should take between two and ten minutes. Tasks should not be prescriptive.

- Print out the tasks on individual pieces of paper.

- Recruit three to five testers, and schedule them about two hours apart.

- You can run the whole test on your own, but it's best if you focus on simulating the computer and have another person act as the facilitator.

- Prepare all the screens people are likely to progress through while doing your tasks. Screens should not be too crude. People unfamiliar with your product should be capable of reading them.

- Add the surrounding user interface elements (such as browser windows around sketches of a website) where necessary. Create the pop-up elements you might need.

- Do a test run of each task to make sure you've prepared all of the screens and pop-up elements you're likely to need.

- When the test starts, explain to the tester what is going on. Make sure to emphasize that you are testing the design, not the tester.

- Make a checklist of everything you want to say, and check off the points as you make them during the introduction. Don't forget to have the tester sign the consent form.

- Explain how the tester should interact with the "computer." Allow him or her to draw on top of your prototype.

- During the test, avoid influencing the tester. Don't make the tester feel uncomfortable. Intervene when you feel that the tester is getting frustrated.

- After the test, do a short debriefing, and thank the tester for her help.

Further Reading

Carolyn Snider has written the definitive book on paper prototyping. It's called *Paper Prototyping: The Fast and Easy Way to Define and Refine User Interfaces* [Sni03]. If you're serious about paper prototyping, you need to read it.

Userfocus has a neat article about paper prototyping with links to more resources.[3]

---

3. At http://www.userfocus.co.uk/articles/paperprototyping.html.

Chapter 12

Realism

Pick up any reasonably modern device—say, a tablet or a smartphone—and you'll quickly notice that a lot of work has gone into making the user interface appear realistic.

You see shadows, gradients, 3D effects, and textures. On-screen elements and whole applications are based on real objects. Even the user interactions themselves are patterned after the real world: you can touch and move sliders, you can toggle switches, and if you give a scrollable area a push, it keeps scrolling for a bit, steadily slowing down as if there were actual friction. The book application on your tablet device resembles an actual book, and the calendar application's user interface looks like an actual paper calendar.

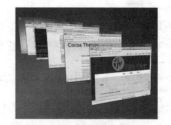

THE PALM PRE USES SHADOWS, TEXTURES, AND TRANSPARENCY	APPLE USES A PHYSICAL CALENDAR AS A MODEL FOR ITS CALENDAR APP ON THE IPAD, INCLUDING PARTIALLY RIPPED OFF PAPER	MICROSOFT USES SHADOWS, TEXTURES, AND TRANSPARENCY IN WINDOWS 7. THEY EVEN USE 3D ANIMATIONS FOR CERTAIN FEATURES OF THE OS

Unlike objects in the real world, applications and websites are not bound by the laws of nature; they can do anything. After all, they are just a bunch of glowing dots on a screen. If someone picks up a rock and lets it drop, she knows what's going to happen. But if she touches a pixel on a touch screen, there is no telling what kind of behavior the programmer imbued it with. For this reason, making an application or a website look and behave like a real-world object can be a good idea. That congruity helps people understand how things work—it tells them that the same laws that govern the real world also apply to products. It helps people understand what possibilities a user interface element offers.

Realistic details can help communicate possible actions (also called *affordances*, as discussed in Section 9.5, *Principle 7: Affordances*, on page 80). The closer the product is to reality, the easier it is for the user to figure out how it is supposed to work and to form a correct mental model for using the product.

However, if you're not careful about how you use realism, you can also create confusion.

12.1 Symbols

Many of the visual elements in a modern user interface are meant to stand for actions or ideas. The little pencil isn't meant as a literal representation of a physical pencil; it represents the idea "edit." The stop sign isn't there as a signal to stop a car; it's meant to alert you to a potential problem.

 What do you suppose this button is trying to convey?

Without any context, users can't be sure, but a likely explanation would be that they need to activate the button to take a picture.

What about this button?

Clearly, trying to make the button's camera look more like the actual object doesn't make it easier to figure out what the button means. In fact, when it comes to determining what the button does, the extra detail might just increase the user's confusion.

In his book *Understanding Comics* [McC94], cartoonist Scott McCloud points out that adding details to an image makes it less universal. The button with the realistic camera doesn't "mean" anything; it depicts a

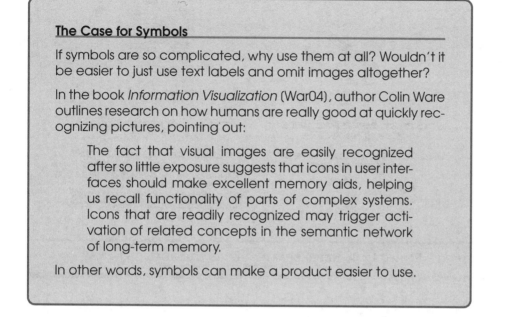

The Case for Symbols

If symbols are so complicated, why use them at all? Wouldn't it be easier to just use text labels and omit images altogether?

In the book *Information Visualization* (War04), author Colin Ware outlines research on how humans are really good at quickly recognizing pictures, pointing out:

> The fact that visual images are easily recognized after so little exposure suggests that icons in user interfaces should make excellent memory aids, helping us recall functionality of parts of complex systems. Icons that are readily recognized may trigger activation of related concepts in the semantic network of long-term memory.

In other words, symbols can make a product easier to use.

specific camera. The button without the details, on the other hand, is archetypal. It doesn't display a specific camera. Instead, it conveys the concept "camera."

At the same time, having too few details makes it more difficult for users to identify exactly what you're trying to convey.

As usual, you can find the sweet spot between the two extremes. You want to be somewhere in the middle of this entirely unscientific graph:

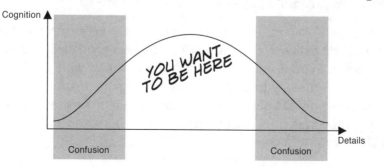

Usability testing can help you identify the sweet spot for your particular images.

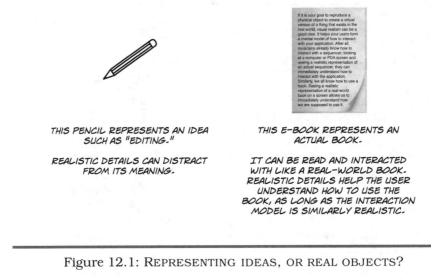

THIS PENCIL REPRESENTS AN IDEA
SUCH AS "EDITING."

REALISTIC DETAILS CAN DISTRACT
FROM ITS MEANING.

THIS E-BOOK REPRESENTS AN
ACTUAL BOOK.

IT CAN BE READ AND INTERACTED
WITH LIKE A REAL-WORLD BOOK.
REALISTIC DETAILS HELP THE USER
UNDERSTAND HOW TO USE THE
BOOK, AS LONG AS THE INTERACTION
MODEL IS SIMILARLY REALISTIC.

Figure 12.1: REPRESENTING IDEAS, OR REAL OBJECTS?

12.2 Virtual Versions of Real-World Objects

Although many of the visual elements in a modern user interface stand for actions, tasks, or ideas, some act as representations of their real-world versions. Unlike the pencil icon that is actually an edit button, the knob in a music application doesn't represent the *idea* of a knob; instead, it represents a workable knob element that behaves like a real-world knob and is used for the same tasks as a real-world knob. Similarly, some e-book applications use a realistic depiction of an open book as their user interface. The book in this application doesn't represent the idea of, say, reading; instead, it is meant to fulfill the exact same functions as an actual physical book. (See Figure 12.1)

Visual realism—reproducing a physical object to create a virtual version of a thing that exists in the real world—can be a good idea. It helps your users form a mental model of how to interact with your product. After all, musicians already know how to interact with a synthesizer; looking at a computer or PDA screen and seeing a realistic representation of an actual synthesizer, they can immediately understand how to interact with the user interface.[1]

---

1. The synthesizer shown previous in the picture is Korg's iELECTRIBE. Find out more at http://www.korg.com/ielectribe.

Skeuomorphs

When designers talk about realistic user interfaces, they sometimes call them *skeuomorphs*—new versions of objects that retain purely ornamental design details from earlier versions of the same kind of object. Example skeuomorphs: shoes with parts that are glued together but have nonfunctional, purely decorative stitching as well, or postage stamps as user interface decoration in email applications (the screenshot on the right shows an image-sharing app for the Mac called Courier).*

Both the stitching and the stamps serve no actual use.

---

*. Find out more at http://www.realmacsoftware.com/courier.

However, enabling users to immediately form a strong mental model is not necessarily always a good thing. It means that your users have very specific expectations of how your product works before they even use it. In other words, if you go with a realistic visual design, you're obligated to ensure that the interaction design is similarly realistic.

You can't create a book-reader application that uses a realistic depiction of a book as its user interface, only to then add "next" and "back" buttons to let users move from page to page. If people see a realistic book on a screen, they expect to be able to leaf through the book by "flipping" the pages with their fingers. They also expect to be able to see how far along they are in a book by looking at the layer of pages stacked up on each side of the book, because that's how real books work.

FIRST PAGE   MIDDLE OF BOOK   LAST PAGE

Conversely, offering realistic interactions in a nonrealistic user interface is typically not harmful, but chances are people simply won't discover these interactions unless you introduce some realism—textures, for example—that provide hints. Such user interfaces don't provide enough affordances.

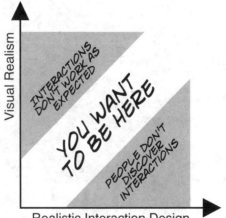

If you are creating an application or website that represents a real-world object, going with a realistic visual design and a realistic interaction design sounds like a winner. However, there are potential problems with this approach.

12.3   Replicating Physical Constraints in Digital Products

Although realistic user interface elements allow people to quickly form accurate mental models, these elements also restrict what you can do. In his essay "Overdoing the interface metaphor," Instapaper developer Marco Arment pinpoints the issue:[2]

> It's important to find the balance between real-world reproduction and usability progress. Physical objects often do things in certain ways for good reasons, and we should try to preserve them. But much of the time, they're done in those ways because of physical, technical, economic, or practical limitations that don't need to apply anymore.

Usability consultant Bruce Tognazzini agrees, noting that "in the hands of an amateur, slavish fidelity to the way a real-world artifact would act is often carried way too far."[3]

Korg's Synthesizer shown earlier looks like a real synthesizer. Here's a screenshot of Beatwave,[4] a different synthesizer for the iPad:

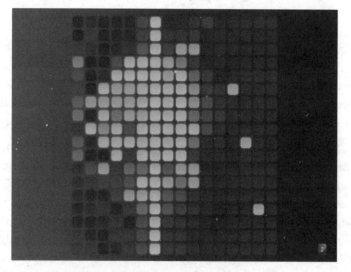

It doesn't look like a real synthesizer at all and makes use of an interaction model that wouldn't be possible in the real world.

Here's another example. A physical calendar exists on a limited number of two-dimensional sheets of paper. Since the calendar manufacturer

---

2. Read the essay at http://www.marco.org/441168915.
3. Read his essay here: http://www.asktog.com/readerMail/1999-06ReaderMail.html.
4. Learn more about Beatwave at http://collect3.com.au/beatwave.

does not know how a particular person uses his time, each day has to be the same size and include more hours than he probably needs, or the hours need to be left out entirely, so he can enter his own numbers. It's hard to keep more than one view consistent if a user has to keep track of every change in multiple places, so physical calendars typically don't have many different views of the same data.

A calendar on an electronic device is not bound by these restrictions; you can make it look however you want. For example, you can show a number of different views of the same data—including views that mix several different zoom levels so you can see a detailed itinerary for today, while still seeing how busy you are for the rest of the week.

Instead of trying to imitate real-world objects—and their limitations— on a computer screen, in many cases you'd do better to find a user interface that takes advantage of what computers can do. The Windows Phone design team did a great job of this when it came up with the Metro design language for Windows Phone 7. The team's goal was to create something "authentically digital." Windows Phone design team member Mike Kruzeniski writes that "a user interface is created of pixels, so in Metro we try to avoid using the skeumorphic shading and glossiness used in some UIs that try to mimic real world materials and objects."[5]

Of course, in some ways, this is a bit of a false dichotomy. Often, it makes sense to use design cues from the real world *and* take advan-

---

5. Read more about it at http://windowsteamblog.com/windows_phone/b/wpdev/archive/2011/ 02/16/from-transportation-to-pixels.aspx.

tage of the freedom digital devices offer. Take the Palm Pre's calendar application. Its layout somewhat resembles a real calendar, but it also does things a real calendar could not. For example, it contracts free time so a person sees only the parts of the day when she's busy.

Takeaway Points

- Adding realistic details communicates possible actions, or affordances, to users.

- Symbols shouldn't be too realistic or they will lose their meaning.

- Replicating real objects can help users quickly form correct mental models.

- Realistic graphics and an interaction design based on real objects should go hand in hand.

- Sometimes, replicating the constraints of real objects can be limiting in needless ways, since objects on screens are not bound by physical laws.

- It's possible to combine realistic elements that help people figure out how to use your product with advanced features that would not be possible in real life, but you need to make it obvious where your product's realism stops so that people can form a correct mental model.

Further Reading

Scott McCloud's *Understanding Comics* [McC94] offers insight into how people "read" images. If you want to learn more about designing icons, I also recommend Adrian Frutiger's *Signs and Symbols: Their Design and Meaning* [Fru98].

Max Steenbergen talks about the trade-off between attractiveness and functionalism in his essay "Eye Candy vs. Bare-Bones in UI Design."[6]

---

6.   At http://facevalue.virb.com/blog/text/12959219.

Chapter 13

Natural User Interfaces

Natural user interfaces (NUIs) are interfaces that ignore the traditional conventions of GUIs in favor of an interaction design based on the natural world. Instead of windows and buttons and menus, natural user interfaces are based on realistic objects and gestures. Instead of a mouse and keyboard, natural user interfaces rely on multitouch screens, cameras, microphones, pens, and other devices that allow people to interact with the interface directly with their hands and fingers, with their voice, or by moving their whole body.

CLI Command Line Interface	**GUI** Graphical User Interface	**NUI** Natural User Interface
Interaction based on a predefined set of textual commands.	Interaction based on metaphors, with icons representing data and commands.	Interaction based on direct, natural manipulation of realistic objects.

The command-line interface makes you remember its strict syntax. Graphical user interfaces improve upon this by showing you what you can do at any given time, but you still have to remember what each thing on the screen actually means. Natural user interfaces are based on things you already know. In the best case, there's nothing to remember—not how to do things (you do them as you would in real life) and not what things mean (they mean the same thing as in the real world).

Trying to reproduce the real world is an admirable goal, since it makes learning and using a product easier. But, it also has its problems; I've already pointed out some of them in the chapter on the mental model (Chapter 9, *The Mental Model*, on page 67) and in the chapter on realism (Chapter 12, *Realism*, on page 113). In this chapter, I want to touch on some ideas related to natural user interfaces that I haven't touched on before.

13.1 Avoid Gesture Magic

If you choose gestures, make sure they directly and immediately affect things on the screen in a familiar way that users understand from the real world. Gestures work best when the system gives constant feedback while the user is interacting with it. In *Designing Gestural Interfaces* [Saf08], Dan Saffer points out:

> We're used to instant reaction to physical manipulation of objects. (...) When engaged with a gestural interface, users want to know that the system has heard and understood any commands given to it. This is where *feedback* comes in. Every action by a human directed toward a gestural interface, no matter how slight, should be accompanied by some acknowledgment of the action—whenever possible and as rapidly as possible.

This kind of interaction—where the user directly manipulates objects, rather than giving commands and then watching the results—is called *direct manipulation*, a term first used in this context by Ben Shneiderman, a professor of computer science at the Human-Computer Interaction Laboratory at the University of Maryland.[1]

Shneiderman notes that allowing people to manipulate objects directly makes the user interface easier to learn and allows the user to focus on her actual task, rather than the user interface itself.

Scrolling through text by touching the text and moving the finger, for example, is an action that yields immediate feedback; as soon as the user starts moving her finger, the text starts scrolling. If the user does something wrong, it is immediately obvious that the gesture isn't working, and she can try a different approach.[2]

On the other hand, telling people to draw an S in order to save a document is bad. Like Harry Potter invoking a magic spell with his wand, the user has to finish making the gesture before the action executes. She receives no useful feedback while she is making the gesture, and if the gesture fails, it is not obvious why the system did not recognize it.

---

1. For more, read Ben Shneiderman's paper "Direct Manipulation for Comprehensible, Predictable and Controllable User Interfaces."
2. Though this interaction is not always easily discoverable, it can be made so by making sure that the last visible element of a list is only partially visible, showing the user that there is more content further down.

Furthermore, such "magic" gestures force users to remember which gestures correspond to which commands and how to execute a gesture. In that sense, it is no better than a command-line interface, except that the user is entering commands by moving his fingers on a screen, rather than by typing on a keyboard.

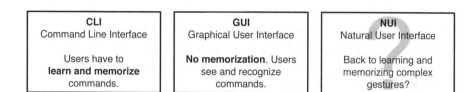

Along similar lines, natural user interfaces often avoid "traditional," established user interface elements such as visible menus or buttons. Features are sometimes hidden and accessed in a way that is not easily discoverable by the user—for example by touching and holding user interface elements until a menu pops up.

The point is, for natural user interfaces more than for any other type of user interface, direct manipulation, visibility, and simplicity are important. People need to be able to figure out how to interact with the things on their screen without having to consult a manual.

13.2 Recognizing Gestures

When you observe people using a device with a touch screen, sooner or later you will see them repeatedly fail at one of the simplest gestures: swiping. Swiping is used in many applications—most prominently in book readers to move from one page of the book to the next. If it is so simple and used consistently across applications, why do people often fail at executing the gesture properly?

One reason is that different applications implement the gesture slightly differently; the exact same swipe gesture may be recognized in one application but not in another. As a result, people may get used to swiping in one application but then get confused when the same gesture doesn't work in another.

A more important reason is that there is often no useful feedback telling the user the exact moment the device "accepts" the gesture. The user doesn't know when he can stop the gesture, because he doesn't know at which point lifting the finger will cancel the gesture and at which point it will cause the application to jump to the next screen. These issues aren't limited to swipes, of course. They affect all gestures. Don Norman explains the problem like this:[3]

> Gestures lack critical clues deemed essential for successful human-computer interaction. Because gestures are ephemeral, they do not leave behind any record of their path, which means that if one makes a gesture and either gets no response or the wrong response, there is little information available to help understand why.

The solution is not always obvious, but it often boils down to making it clear to users when the computer has recognized a gesture.

Something as simple as a toggle switch can benefit from this. On a computer with a mouse, toggling a switch is easy; the user simply has to click it. There is little room for error.

GUIS ARE DIGITAL   NUIS ARE OFTEN ANALOG

SIMPLY CLICK TO TOGGLE   HOW FAR SHOULD THE USER
THE SWITCH.   DRAG TO TOGGLE THE SWITCH?

In a natural user interface, interactions feel gradual and nuanced. Gestures don't have a clear start and end, so it's not always apparent when the user can stop sliding the switch. Giving feedback on when the gesture was successful tells the user when she is "done" and teaches her how to use the system more efficiently.

Here's an example from the official Twitter app. It tells people when they can stop making the gesture:

---

3. Read his essay on NUIs at http://jnd.org/dn.mss/natural_user_interfaces_are_not_natural.html.

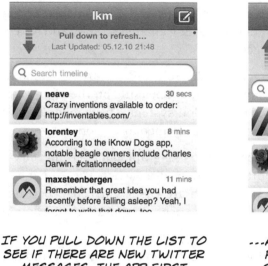

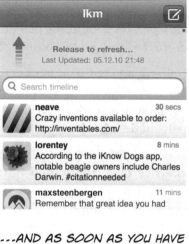

IF YOU PULL DOWN THE LIST TO SEE IF THERE ARE NEW TWITTER MESSAGES, THE APP FIRST TELLS YOU TO PULL FURTHER TO REFRESH THE MESSAGES...

...AND AS SOON AS YOU HAVE PULLED FAR ENOUGH TO START THE REFRESH, THE MESSAGE CHANGES AND TELLS YOU TO RELEASE

Creating a simple gestural user interface is not easy, but some guidelines may help. Give immediate feedback telling users when a gesture has been recognized or, if it hasn't been recognized, why not. Simple, error-tolerant gestures work best. Straight lines work best. Short gestures work better than long ones. If people need to make gestures that start or end in specific areas, make these areas large. And in case the computer recognizes a gesture incorrectly, there should be a simple way for the user to undo its effects.

13.3 Accidental Input

Some time ago, I switched from a simple pen-and-paper list to an application on my cell phone for grocery checklists. Pretty quickly, I noticed that I forgot to buy two or three items every time I went shopping. Further investigation showed that I didn't really forget these items as much as accidentally remove them from my grocery checklist. While holding my phone with one hand and putting an item into my shopping cart with the other, I would often inadvertently touch the phone's screen, thereby accidentally marking an item as "done."

Similarly, when friends and I played Kinect[4] for the first time, the game would constantly pause for no apparent reason. We finally figured out that a person behind the players was leaning against a table, and Kinect interpreted this as its "pause gesture."

Brushing against a touch screen can delete things. Leaning against a table can trigger an action in a video game. Speaking on the phone can activate a nearby device's voice recognition system. These mistakes are easily made, but the results are often not immediately noticeable.

Of course, people make mistakes when using graphical user interfaces, too. They click the wrong button, or they drag when they meant to click. But in most cases, such mistakes are easily corrected, because the problem is immediately obvious to the user. Just undoing the action fixes it.

But when users don't notice that there is a problem, they can't undo it. If the source of the problem isn't obvious, users can't easily prevent it from happening again.

When designing a natural user interface, it's important to spend some time thinking about how to prevent accidental input, how to teach people what went wrong when something does go wrong, and how to let users reverse unwanted actions even if they didn't notice the problem immediately.

13.4 Conventions

Let's say you want to give people the security they need to freely explore your application. To achieve that, you want to implement a simple way for them to undo their actions.

Designing a user interface for "undo" is easy if you're working on a desktop platform like Windows or Mac OS X. There are conventions and guidelines that explain how to do it. Figure 13.1, on the facing page is a screenshot of BusyCal (at http://www.busymac.com).

If your product has a natural user interface, on the other hand, it's a lot harder. There aren't many conventions or rules that help with this.[5]

---

4. Microsoft's Kinect is a peripheral for the Xbox 360 video game console that enables users to control games by moving their bodies and arms.

5. If people have expectations about how natural user interfaces should work, they often come from science-fiction movies, as Chris Noessel and Nathan Shedroff explain in their presentation *Learning From SciFi Interfaces*. Watch it at http://vimeo.com/15233780.

| File | **Edit** | Font | Calendar | View | Window | Help |

Undo Date Change	⌘Z
Redo	⇧⌘Z
Cut	⌘X
Copy	⌘C
Paste Text	⌘V
Paste and Match Style	⌥⇧⌘V
Delete	
Select All	⌘A

Figure 13.1: UNDOING IN BUSYCAL

You have to come up with your own design, preferably something that feels "natural." But in real life, you can't turn back time and revert to the way things were a few seconds ago. So, how do you present that concept in a natural user interface?

Unfortunately, there is no simple, obvious solution to the problem of designing "natural" user interfaces, but there are some ideas you can follow:

- If possible, copy real-world behavior. Have the computer respond immediately and behave in a way that the user will recognize and understand. That way, people can apply real-world knowledge to virtual systems.

- Copy what popular applications are doing. Chances are that your users have already seen these other applications and are familiar with their approach.

- Implement interactive prototypes of different ideas, and do usability tests to see how people react to them.

Until NUIs become more popular, we will have to live with a lack of commonly accepted user interface conventions. This makes our job harder, but fortunately, it also makes it more interesting.

Takeaway Points

- Allow direct manipulation whenever possible.

- Give immediate, live feedback to any user action.

- Use gestures that don't manipulate objects but instead invoke commands only as shortcuts rather than as primary interactions.

- Make sure people don't have to learn complex gestures.

- Make sure people don't have to make precise gestures; be liberal in accepting user input, but allow them to undo false input.

- Hardware that runs natural user interfaces is especially prone to interpreting unintended user actions as input. Whenever possible, prevent accidental input, and provide fallback solutions for when it does happen.

- Follow what nature does.

- Follow what popular applications do.

- Regularly test interactive prototypes of your user interface with actual people.

Further Reading

Dan Saffer's *Designing Gestural Interfaces* [Saf08] covers some of the things mentioned in this chapter and many additional topics. Josh Clark talks about gestures (among many other things) in his excellent book *Tapworthy* [Cla10].

Fred Beecher lists a number of useful guidelines for designing natural user interfaces.[6]

---

6. At http://userexperience.evantageconsulting.com/2010/11/ui-guidelines-for-skeuomorphic-multi-touch-interfaces/.

Chapter 14

Fitts's Law

Usability has very few universally accepted laws. Fitts's law is one of these few. It basically states that people can hit a target more quickly if the target is bigger or closer to the user's mouse cursor (on a desktop system). The target could be a screen icon users are trying to click with a mouse cursor or a button they are trying to tap on a touch screen.

CLICKING "OK" TAKES A
LONGER TIME HERE...

---THAN CLICKING "OK" IN
THIS SITUATION

The direction of the motion matters. The target object's size should correspond to the direction of the motion:

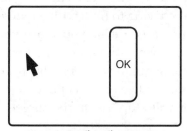

CLICKING "OK" TAKES A
LONGER TIME HERE...

---THAN CLICKING "OK" IN
THIS SITUATION

Who's Fitts?

Fitts's law is named after its discoverer, Paul Fitts, a psychologist at Ohio State University and later at the University of Michigan.

The law's name is sometimes written as Fitts' law, dropping the possessive s, but "Fitts's law" seems to be the form most commonly used by reputable sources, so I'm going with that version in my book. Please don't send me mail complaining about it. But here's my pledge to you: if you manage to change the Wikipedia article and make the change stick, I'll change it in the book, too.

This idea seems pretty straightforward, and indeed, a number of studies have shown that it is correct.[1] The relevant part of the formula used to calculate the time it takes a user to achieve a task is the index of difficulty (ID), which basically measures how difficult it is to hit a target. This part of the formula reads as follows:

$$ID = \log_2\left(\frac{\text{Distance to target}}{\text{Width of target in direction of motion}} + 1\right)$$

Since the formula for the ID is logarithmic, even small changes in size can result in comparatively big changes in difficulty if the target is small to begin with. For larger targets, small changes have little effect.

Although the law itself seems obvious enough, some of its effects may not be. Let's look at a few.

14.1 Screen Edges Have Infinite Size

If you think about it, an interface element at the very edge of your screen is essentially infinite in size if you're trying to hit it with a mouse. No matter how far in the direction of the screen edge you move your mouse, it will never leave the screen and always remain on the target. Thus, it makes sense to put important elements at the very edge of the screen. Hitting such elements is much easier because people can just slam the mouse toward the edge, and it will stop inside the target on its own.

---

1. You can find references to some of the research on this topic here: http://www.yorku.ca/mack/RN-Fitts_bib.htm.

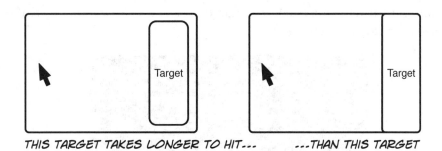

THIS TARGET TAKES LONGER TO HIT...   *...THAN THIS TARGET*

Corners are especially valuable, because they have two infinite edges.

In most cases, this same effect does not apply to touch screens, unfortunately. Touching elements closer to the touch screen's edge is not easier than touching elements elsewhere. The areas the user can most easily reach depend on how she holds the device instead.

IF YOU HOLD YOUR IPAD LIKE THIS...   *...ONLY PARTS OF YOUR SCREEN CAN EASILY BE REACHED.*

Of course, when the user is *dragging* things, the touch screen's edge becomes an easier target again, because it's not possible to drag things outside of the screen.

14.2 Radial Context Menus Decrease Average Distance

As mentioned, corners are especially easy to hit, because they have two infinite edges. There is, however, one point on the screen that is even easier to hit: the point below the cursor. You don't have to move the mouse at all to hit it. Context menus make use of this.

If a menu pops up below the mouse cursor, it makes sense to arrange the individual menu entries around the mouse cursor to decrease the average distance to each entry. One way to achieve this is by using a radial context menu.

Many games use radial context menus. Here's an example from the LucasArts title Full Throttle:

The Firefox extension easyGestures also uses a radial context menu:

So if they work so well, why aren't radial context menus used more often? One reason may be that it's hard to fit a lot of menu entries into a small circle. Maya gets around this by using regular menu labels but arranging them in a circle around the mouse:

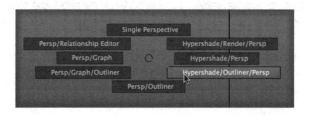

A solution retaining the familiar look of traditional context menus yet still offering some of the advantages of radial context menus would be a regular context menu with more than one horizontal level. We could just break up traditional context menus into several smaller groups of commands and then use the horizontal space to arrange them around the cursor.[2]

---

2. This is the type of context menu I use in Appway, a business process management system. You can find it at http://www.appway.com.

Perceiving Circles and Lines

One of the reasons why radial context menus may not be more popular can be found in *Vision Science* (Pal99) by Stephen E. Palmer. When explaining one model of how humans perceive visual information, he notes that "cells in the first area of the visual cortex have elongated receptive fields that respond most vigorously if stimulated by an edge or line at a particular orientation and position." In other words, it seems that humans have special mechanisms for seeing lines. What's more, we may be better at seeing horizontal and vertical lines than lines going in other directions. In *Sensation and Perception* (Cor99), Stanley Coren speculates that since humans spend most of their time in rectilinear environments and are constantly exposed to vertical and horizontal lines, our brains are biased toward lines in those orientations.

Indeed, a paper called "Perception of contour orientation in the central fovea part I: Short lines" by D.P. Andrews notes that in many experiments, "acuity for orientation was best near the horizontal and vertical directions." Other research agrees. For example, in a paper titled "Human orientation discrimination tested with long stimuli," Guy A. Orban comes to the conclusion that "orientation sensitivity is better for a narrow range of orientations around the principal meridians."

To make a really long story short, research seems to suggest that people perceive horizontal and vertical lines more quickly and correctly than oblique lines or circles.

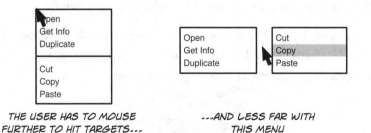

THE USER HAS TO MOUSE
FURTHER TO HIT TARGETS...

...AND LESS FAR WITH
THIS MENU

Another benefit of this kind of menu is that better usage of horizontal space allows you to show more menu items at the same time. As a result, you don't have to hide any menu items inside hard-to-use submenus.

Finally, putting the horizontal menu elements to the left and right of the cursor doesn't just decrease distance, it makes the elements easier to hit, since the cursor is moved toward the left or right, and thus the direction of the cursor motion is in line with the target area's longer dimension.

14.3 Small Targets Need Margins

Since smaller targets are harder to hit, it's very important that you put margins between small targets. Otherwise, a user may miss the correct target and accidentally trigger a wrong action.

*IT'S EASY TO HIT "DELETE"
INSTEAD OF "SEND"...*

*...ADDING SOME SPACE
MAKES THIS LESS LIKELY*

In a way, this also applies to keyboard shortcuts. Assigning destructive and nondestructive keyboard shortcuts to letters that are right next to each other on the keyboard makes it more likely that people will initiate a destructive command by accident.

14.4 Sometimes, Smaller Is Better

Since making screen elements larger makes them easier to hit, it some-times makes sense to make destructive elements smaller to decrease the probability that a user will hit them unintentionally.

For example, in the Windows 7 Start menu, the "Shut down" button is smaller than the clickable areas that start applications.

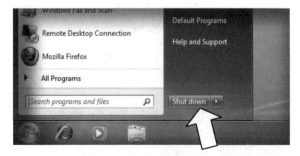

Takeaway Points

- If you want to make things easier to hit, make them bigger. If you want them harder to hit, make them smaller.

- Things that touch the screen edge are easier to hit. Corners are easiest.

- The motion of the cursor should be in line with the form of the target—that is, if the user is moving the mouse horizontally to hit a target, making the target's form horizontal makes it easier to hit.

- Things that are closer to the cursor can be reached by the user more quickly.

- Leave some room between different clickable things.

Further Reading

For a beautiful illustration of Fitts's Law, check out Kevin Hale's essay "Visualizing Fitts's Law."[3]

---

3. At http://particletree.com/features/visualizing-fittss-law/.

Chapter 15

Animations

Working with a modern computer is an immensely visual experience. Almost everything we do results in visible, graphical changes on our screens. When we write a letter, images and characters appear. When we look for something on the Web, the content of our browser window changes to represent the web page we're currently visiting. When we read email, messages open and close.

Modern user interfaces make use of both very small visual changes (a single dot next to a message disappearing or reappearing because we read a message or chose to mark it as unread) and very large visual changes (everything on our screen changing because we opened a different website). It's often easy either to miss changes or to be confused by the magnitude of a change.

Animations, when used properly, can help users understand what is happening on their computers. Animations can help explain the causal relationships between two different visual states of a screen, and they can draw attention to changes that might otherwise go unnoticed. Animations can even help people form a correct mental model of how a product works.

15.1 Explaining State Changes

Visual state changes can easily disorient people. If you're running a usability test or just teaching somebody how to use a product, often it doesn't take long until you hear someone ask, "What just happened?"

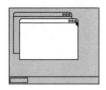
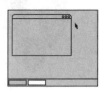

I'M JUST CLICKING ON THAT LITTLE BUTTON HERE...
HUH, WHERE DID THE WINDOW DISAPPEAR TO?

If you hear somebody say "What did I just do?" or "Where did this go?" or "How do I get back?" it's possible that you've found a problem that could be solved with an animation.

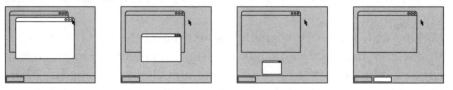

ADDING A SIMPLE ANIMATION MAKES IT OBVIOUS
WHERE THE WINDOW WENT.

Animating the change between the two states makes the state change and the relationship between the two states obvious.

15.2 Directing User Attention

When people get confused by large state changes, they usually react by asking themselves what just happened. When they miss small state changes, their reaction is typically along the lines of "Did I just do something, or not? Did it take?"

Here's something you've probably experienced. You click a link to download a file, and nothing happens. So, you click again. Still nothing. It isn't until you've clicked a few more times that you notice that you've downloaded the same file half a dozen times; the computer just didn't tell you about it.

WHEN I CLICKED ON THAT DOWNLOAD LINK,
DID ANYTHING ACTUALLY HAPPEN?

You can solve problems of this type by animating the state change, with the goal being to exaggerate the change. When somebody initiates a download, it's a good idea to show an exaggerated animation that guides the user's eyes from the link to the download window.

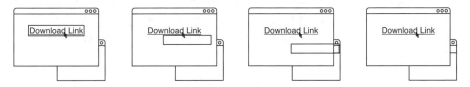

ADDING A SIMPLE ANIMATION MAKES IT OBVIOUS THAT CLICKING ON THE LINK HAS STARTED A DOWNLOAD.

Make it impossible for the user to miss what's going on. Google Chrome, for example, shows a big animated blue arrow when the user clicks a download link to indicate that a new download has started and where to look for it.

In the book *Information Visualization* [War04], Colin Ware points out that it may not be motion itself that attracts attention but the appearance of new objects. He writes:

> When early man was outside a cave, intently chipping a lump of flint into a hand axe, or when early woman was gathering roots out on the grassland, awareness of emerging objects in the periphery of vision would have had clear survival value. Such a movement might have signaled an imminent attack. Of course, the evolutionary advantage goes back much further than this. Monitoring the periphery of vision for moving predators or prey would provide a survival advantage for most animals. Thus, the most effective reminder might be an object that moves into view, disappears, and then reappears every so often.

This behavior is so deeply ingrained in our evolutionary history, it's impossible to turn off.

15.3 Avoid Unimportant Animations

As we've just seen, movement at the periphery of our vision simply can't be ignored. Our attention is naturally drawn to it. If there's a tiger sneaking through the bushes, you really, really don't want to be the last person to start running away. Unfortunately, the part of your brain responsible for this behavior doesn't know the difference between a tiger and an animated ad.

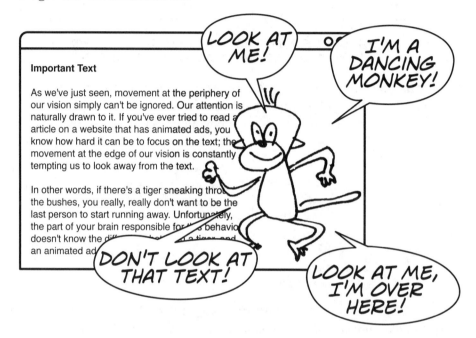

This kind of animation can drive people mad and make it impossible for them to focus on the actual content.

Use animation only if you truly want to interrupt your users and force them to look at something and if the animation is used to convey relevant information. Otherwise, avoid it.

15.4 Help Users Form Suitable Mental Models

Animations can be used to influence the user's mental model of your product. The information that animations convey should be consistent with the rest of the user interface. For example, if an animation replaces the screen content by sliding a new screen in from the right, then the back button should have an icon of a left-pointing arrow. Otherwise, the icon is at odds with the animation; the two imply conflicting models.

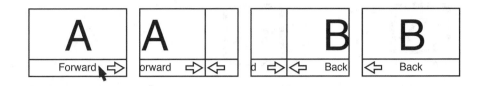

Here's an example from the iPhone app Kinetic:[1]

The icons are consistent with the animation. Arrows that point to the right move the user to the right, and vice versa.

My Android phone's home button is one example where the animation and the actual behavior are inconsistent. If I'm in an application and hit the home button, the animation implies that I'm moving to the right, even though the home button's icon—a house—doesn't imply any spatial relationship.

Indeed, if I then hit the back button, whose arrow icon implies that it should move me back to the left, nothing happens.

---

1. It's an app that helps you keep track of your running. You can learn more at http://wearemothership.com/kinetic.

HOME BUTTON
MOVES TO THE
RIGHT...

...BUT LEFT ARROW
DOESN'T MOVE TO
THE LEFT

In newer versions of the OS, Google has replaced the home button's animation. This simple fix makes it less likely that people will think that the back button works for jumping back into an application after leaving it via the home button.

Think about the user's mental model. Use animations wisely to reinforce correct mental models and dissuade incorrect ones.

15.5 Learning from Cartoons

Cartoons have a hundred years of development behind them. Cartoon animators have come up with a complex visual language that even small children can easily understand. We can follow cartoons even if they display a large number of objects or characters at the same time, each exhibiting intricate behaviors. In their paper "Animation: From Cartoons to the User Interface,"[2] Bay-Wei Chang and David Ungar point out a number of lessons we can learn from cartoons:

Solidity

In the real world, objects are solid: they have mass, inertia, weight, and balance. These are attributes that people understand intuitively. By replicating these attributes in your animations, it's easier for users to figure out what's going on.

Let users interact with objects instead of showing outlines or other placeholders during animations. For example, when people drag and drop emails in some applications, these apps show only a single icon below the mouse cursor (instead of the dragged messages). This breaks the impression that emails are solid "things" similar to a paper letter.

---

2. You can read the paper at http://research.sun.com/techrep/1995/smli_tr-95-33.pdf.

IF YOU DRAG FILES IN WINDOWS 7, YOU CAN SEE THE ACTUAL FILES YOU'RE DRAGGING

MAIL ON THE MAC, ON THE OTHER HAND, ONLY SHOWS AN ABSTRACT REPRESENTATION OF DRAGGED MESSAGES

To make objects appear to be solid, there should be no perceptible lag in your animations, and movements should seem smooth. In his paper "Principles of traditional animation applied to 3D computer animation," Pixar's chief creative officer John Lasseter notes:

> As the speed of the action increases, so does the distance between positions. When the distance becomes far enough that the object does not overlap from frame to frame, the eye then begins to perceive separate images.

As a rule of thumb, if an object moves more than half its size between frames, stretching the object in the direction of motion or adding motion blur to the animation allows users to see the object as solid, even though it actually jumps from place to place.[3]

TO HELP PEOPLE PERCEIVE A MOVING OBJECT AS SOLID...

...EITHER STRETCH IT IN THE DIRECTION OF THE MOTION...

...OR BLUR IT IN THE SAME DIRECTION.

In the real world, solid objects never just pop into existence out of nowhere. Chang and Ungar recommend that to maintain the illusion of solidity, objects should fly in from offscreen, grow from a point, or fade in (and exit the screen the same way).

---

3. As Keith Lang, COO and co-designer of Skitch points out, motion blur can also make animations more aesthetically pleasing: http://www.uiandus.com/blog/2009/7/2/blur-the-new-black.html.

Exaggeration

You can take liberty with what's possible in reality to make what's happening on the screen more obvious. Exaggerating the important parts of an animation can sometimes make the animation feel more realistic.

Similar to taking a step back before taking a leap, it can be a good idea to start an animation with a small movement that is contrary to the main movement of the animation. This is a specific form of exaggeration called *anticipatory movement*.

John Lasseter notes "without anticipation many actions are abrupt, stiff and unnatural."

Acceleration and Deceleration

Real objects don't start out at a specific speed; they have to accelerate to that speed. So, it makes sense to start animations slowly, speed them up, and then slow them down again toward the end (sometimes called *ease-in* and *ease-out*). This logic also applies to growing and shrinking animations.

Similarly, real-world objects rarely travel in straight lines. When you throw a ball, it flies in an arc. For some kinds of animations, it makes sense to mimic that behavior. For example, when you buy a Mac application in Apple's App Store, it flies into the Dock in an arc.

Finally, real-world objects such as springs sometimes overshoot their target and bounce back. Replicating this kind of behavior can also reinforce the physicality of an object.

After introducing the first iPhone at the Macworld Conference & Expo 2007 keynote and showing the device's smooth, bouncy scrolling, Steve Jobs told the following little anecdote:[4]

> I was giving a demo to somebody a little while ago, who had never seen this before, inside Apple. I finished the demo, and he told me this. He said, you had me at scrolling.

Paying attention to these kinds of details turns a merely acceptable, workable device into a delightful experience.

---

4. You can watch it here: http://www.apple.com/quicktime/qtv/mwsf07/.

User Interfaces Are Not Cartoons

It's important to remember that the goal is not to turn the user interface into a cartoon but to make it easier for people to understand how it works by using the same kinds of tools that cartoons use.

Don't use these tools, and animations in general, just because they look cute or flashy. Android, for example, provides animated home-screen wallpapers. Although it would be possible to use this feature in meaningful ways, in practice most of these wallpapers just serve as a distraction and do not show any useful information or provide any useful functionality.

It's sometimes OK to use animations to make a product more fun to use, even though the animations provide no tangible benefit. However, keep in mind that animations are distracting. Attempting to make a product more fun at the expense of its usability typically doesn't work (see Section 26.4, *Fun vs. Usability*, on page 228 for more thoughts on that).

Takeaway Points

- Use animations to draw attention to small or otherwise unnoticeable changes.

- Use animations to make large state changes understandable.

- Animations, especially at the edge of vision, are attention magnets. Don't abuse them; it'll drive people crazy.

- You can use animations to reinforce the user's mental model of your product.

- Cartoons have a visual language for animation that we can use: objects should be solid and accelerate and decelerate realistically, and movement should sometimes be exaggerated.

Further Reading

Information Visualization [War04] by Colin Ware has some information on animations. Bay-Wei Chang and David Ungar's paper "Animation: From Cartoons to the User Interface"[5] is also a great resource.

---

5. It can be found at http://research.sun.com/techrep/1995/smli_tr-95-33.pdf.

Markus Weber talks about using animation in user interface design in his blog.[6] Keith Lang has written about using animation in user interfaces.[7] Max Steenbergen also tackles this topic in his blog.[8]

And finally, John Lasseter's paper "Principles of traditional animation applied to 3D computer animation" contains invaluable information on how to use animation.[9]

---

6. At http://www.centigrade.de/en/blog/article/animations-in-user-interface-design-essential-nutrient-instead-of-eye-candy/.
7. At http://www.uiandus.com/blog/2009/2/1/interfaces-and-animation.html. He also points out that people may be blind to certain kinds of changes in his essay "The Art of Expectations" at http://www.uiandus.com/blog/2008/8/25/the-art-of-expectations.html.
8. At http://facevalue.virb.com/blog/text/12641234.
9. You can find it at http://portal.acm.org/citation.cfm?id=37407.

Chapter 16

Consistency

Consistency is a pretty popular word in the area of user interface criticism; when we dislike user interfaces, we often attribute our dislike to a "lack of consistency."

But what *is* consistency?

Merriam-Webster says that consistency is the "agreement or harmony of parts or features to one another or a whole." Simply put, when we say that a user interface isn't consistent, we mean that it isn't in agreement with its host system or with popular applications on its host system or that different features in a product don't agree with each other. We mean that it is *different* from other products we already know or that different parts of a product work differently.

16.1 Identifying Archetypes

But what kinds of differences are we talking about?

Quite often, we are talking about *appearance*. Things don't *look* quite right. Buttons in an application don't look quite like the host system's default buttons. Windows look a bit different from each other. Scroll bars look slightly strange.

Visual inconsistencies are very obvious, so people notice them easily. However, this focus on how things look is misguided. Often, when it comes to usability, appearance doesn't matter all that much. Humans are not stupid. You don't need to make elements look exactly the same in order for them to be immediately identifiable. For example, even though they look quite different, all of these buttons are clearly identifiable as buttons:

(I've written more about how much detail a user interface element needs to be easily identifiable in Chapter 12, *Realism*, on page 113.)

Elements of the same type don't need to look exactly the same. They just need to be immediately recognizable for what they are.

You can easily evaluate whether visual consistency is an issue with a simple usability test: just show people pictures of your user interface elements (preferably in the context of your whole user interface) and ask them what they are. If users have no problem identifying items for what they are, you don't have to worry about visual consistency.

Or, as Ralph Waldo Emerson put it:

> A foolish consistency is the hobgoblin of little minds, adored by little statesmen and philosophers and divines. With consistency a great soul has simply nothing to do.

So, let's ditch the foolish consistencies and move on to the areas where consistency actually matters.

16.2 Behavioral Consistency

Being good at recognizing user interface elements for what they are can cause a bit of a problem for people: they tend to apply their existing mental models liberally. The more a user interface element looks like something users already know, the more they will expect it to *work* like the thing they already know.

ALL OF THESE LOOK LIKE SCROLL BARS, BUT...

THE MOUSE WHEEL DOESN'T WORK AS EXPECTED

CLICKING ON AN ARROW WORKS DIFFERENTLY THAN EXPECTED

DRAGGING THE THUMB DOES UNEXPECTED THINGS

This problem often arises with custom versions of common user interface elements, which you may sometimes need to create. Because people will apply their existing mental models to your custom elements, you need to ensure that these elements behave *exactly* like the commonly used elements. If you violate their expectations, you will make them confused, frustrated, and maybe even angry.[1]

For example, the windows in Adobe Photoshop running on a Mac look almost exactly like *real* Mac windows, but they are not.

Adobe implemented its own custom windows. Unfortunately, in doing so, Adobe got some behavior wrong. For example, when a user clicks the little close button on a regular Mac window, the button gets a little bit darker to indicate to the user that he has hit the button. This doesn't happen with Adobe's buttons. It's just a small difference, a little detail Adobe didn't get right, but it causes a tiny bit of confusion every time the user notices it and wonders for a fraction of a second just what exactly has gone wrong.

If you *don't* want your custom versions to behave like a regular user interface element, they need to look *very* different from the regular one—so different, in fact, that your users won't identify your element as a member of the regular type of element and thus won't apply their mental model of the element to your custom, inconsistent version of it. This is pretty hard to achieve. Scroll bars, windows, buttons, and menus, for example, always kind of look like scroll bars, windows, buttons, and menus. It's almost impossible to make your custom scroll bar

---

1. If you *do* decide to reimplement existing user interface elements, don't forget to also take care of their accessibility features. These may not always be obvious to you, but forgetting them means that people with certain disabilities may not be able to use your custom user interface element.

so different from the commonly used one that people won't try to apply their expectations of how scroll bars work to your version.

It's best to stick with common user interface elements and not change their standard behavior.

Takeaway Points

- People are good at recognizing user interface elements, so user interface elements don't all need to look exactly the same.

- Things that *do* look similar need to do *exactly* the same thing, in *exactly* the same way, since people will try to apply their existing mental models to it.

- If you must create a version of a commonly used interface element that behaves differently, make sure that it looks *different enough* so that people won't form false expectations. You don't want to frustrate your users by creating a user interface element that doesn't fit the behavioral model of a common, similar-looking element.

Further Reading

In *Getting Real* [FHL09] from 37signals, the authors succinctly note that "it's OK to be inconsistent if your design makes more sense that way."

Joel Spolsky touches upon consistency in *User Interface Design for Programmers* [Spo11].

Chapter 17

Discoverability

Designers use *Discoverability* to mean whether users will be able to find and use a feature. Discoverability is important—from the user's point of view, there's no difference between a feature she can't find or can't use and one that doesn't exist.

17.1 What to Make Discoverable

Discoverability often involves a trade-off. Make one thing more discoverable, and it may detract from other things. So, you want to start by deciding which features to make more discoverable and (conversely) which parts of your product you can make less discoverable. Sometimes it's even OK to hide a feature if you know that the people who require that feature will be able to find out how to use it.

For example, a lot of browsers ship with features used only by web developers. These features are turned off by default, but the target audience is assumed to be capable of finding out that the features exist and knowing how to activate them. As Figure 17.1, on the next page shows, in Safari this involves opening the settings window, switching to the Advanced tab, and checking the "Show Develop menu in menu bar" checkbox.

Once you've decided which features must be easily discoverable and which ones can be relegated to the background, you need to assign weights to the important features. You can't make every feature equally obvious.

Figure 17.1: ENABLING DEVELOPER TOOLS IN SAFARI

Let's look at some examples. Here's the basic structure of three popular websites:

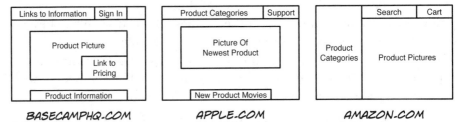

37signals' Basecamp home page puts the greatest emphasis on acquiring new customers; plans, pricing, and features take center stage. Less weight is given to things like support and the "Sign in" link.

Apple puts its most recent product in the spotlight. Some room is given to a navigation bar that allows people to reach other products; very little room is given to other elements.

Amazon puts a lot more weight on navigation, providing a lot of room for product categories and a search feature. Since Amazon sells so many different items, making navigation and search easily discoverable is the primary goal of the home page.

You should start by looking for important features and make it a priority to make them discoverable. You should also think about a feature's target audience. If the target audience is experienced with the subject matter, it may be OK to make the feature a bit less discoverable and trust the user's ability to find it.

In 37signals' and Apple's case, the designers probably assumed that the features aimed at existing customers can be a bit less obvious, since these people already know where to find them. Potential new customers have less experience with the site, so features aimed at them are given more weight.

Then, there are cases where you can make features less discoverable because they're not strictly essential and because people are likely to find out about them in some other way. For example, "pinching" an image on an iPhone to zoom in or out is not easily discoverable, but you don't need to know about this feature to use an iPhone. Plus, the feature is so compelling that people who know about it tell people who don't, creating an avenue for discovering the feature that is external to the application itself. The "pinch-to-zoom" feature is so simple that people easily remember it once they've seen it, and it works consistently in many different apps. So, once people have learned to use it, they're unlikely to forget that it exists.

To recap, you can make a commonly used feature less discoverable if

- People can get along just fine without knowing that the feature exists.

- They're likely to find out about the feature even if it's not directly discoverable.

- The feature is compelling, simple, and used consistently so people will remember it once they've learned it exists.

17.2 When to Make Things Discoverable

Not every feature of your product is relevant at all times. So after you've decided which features should be discoverable, you should decide *when* they need to be discoverable.

One way to do this is to use contextual or modal user interfaces. Let's see how this could work for a vector graphics editor. Your users probably want to be able to rotate objects, so you need to add a "Rotation" property to your toolbar or inspector window:

Rotation: 0°

But now you need a toolbar or an inspector window. And you need to make sure that the "Rotation" property is disabled when the user hasn't selected anything. In other words, you're adding user interface elements that are cluttering the user interface, regardless of whether the user has even selected something.

Another approach would be to assume that the "Rotation" property needs to be discoverable only once the user has selected the object. One approach would be to include a set of transient properties stored in a small pop-up element that appears only when the user selects an object that supports these properties.

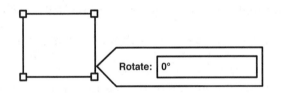

(Of course, to determine whether they work, we need to test these kinds of ideas with users.)

17.3 How to Make Things Discoverable

So far, we've considered the importance of the things in your product, and we've thought about *when* they are important. Now, let's take a look at what you can do to make these things discoverable.

Spatial Properties

You can use properties such as size, position, form, and color to make individual elements of your application more (or less) discoverable. The bigger something is, the more easily discoverable it is. By putting things at the top or down the left side of a screen or window, you make

---

Color

Recently, there's been a bit of a trend toward using less color in user interfaces. Apple's iTunes, for example, has replaced its colored icons with monochrome ones.

From a usability perspective, using color is beneficial. Colors make things easier to perceive. Our brains are really good at doing tasks such as "find the *green* icon on this screen." In *Information Visualization* (War04), Colin Ware notes that color is "preattentively processed," meaning that we identify color before we give it conscious attention. In other words, when we look at a user interface, we can find and identify user interface elements with a specific color really quickly and easily.

Do use color (for example, to make it easier to differentiate between icons), but don't rely *solely* on color. Not everybody can see color perfectly.

---

them more discoverable.[1] Certain colors (most notably red) make things appear more important. Conversely, you can use these properties to de-emphasize things you consider to be less important but still need to put somewhere visible.[2]

User Expectations

Once people have used your product for a while, they will get a feel for where the important parts are. Be consistent. Use the same kind of arrangement for every screen. Don't put the important things on the left of the screen in one layout and on the right in the next.

Similarly, if the user has an established mental model of how your product works, she probably has pretty strong opinions on where things should be. Often you can use this expectation to make things more (or less) discoverable. (For more on this topic, read Chapter 9, *The Mental Model*, on page 67.)

---

1. Jakob Nielsen calls this the "F-Pattern" because in eye-tracking studies, the heat maps created by measuring what people actually focus on when reading websites looks like a giant *F* superimposed over the user's screen. You can see examples at http://www.useit.com/eyetracking.

2. Neutral colors are also used for user interfaces in content creation applications. We don't want a colorful user interface to influence how people perceive their pictures in, say, a photo-editing tool.

Search

When people can't discover things immediately, they may turn to your product's search feature, provided they can find it. To help your users with search, you need to do these three things:

- Provide a search feature.

- Make the search feature itself discoverable.

- Make sure the search feature returns useful results.

The last point is often the hardest. Fortunately, you may be able to draw from the card sorts you did way back in Chapter 7, *Hierarchies in User Interface Design*, on page 47. This help comes in the form of feedback on terminology. What kinds of words did people use back then? If people put these words into your search engine, will they get the results they expect?

Another way of improving search results is to pay attention to how people use search once it's available to them. Especially pay attention to search terms that return zero or few results or to situations where the user searches for something, the site returns results, but the user doesn't click any of them.

Animations

Animations are your most powerful tool for drawing a user's attention. Use them wisely and sparingly; never use animation for things that are visible over longer periods of time. You can read more about animations in Chapter 15, *Animations*, on page 139.

Takeaway Points

- Decide which things need to be easily discoverable and which ones can be tucked away somewhere. Then, assign weights to the things that you decide to make discoverable, and design accordingly.

- Keep in mind that not every feature has to be available at all times. Different things can be discoverable at different times.

- Use your visual layout, a good search function, and (in rare cases) animations to make things discoverable.

Chapter 18

Don't Interrupt

In his book *Flow: The Psychology of Optimal Experience* [Csi02], psychology professor Mihály Csíkszentmihályi explained that when people are completely absorbed by an activity they are doing, they reach a state of total focus that he calls *flow*. When people talk about "being in the zone," they are often talking about that state of complete, single-minded immersion in a task.

It usually takes us a bit of time to "get into the groove," and it's often easy to pull us out again. Maybe I'm completely immersed in writing this chapter, but suddenly—*bing*—goes the computer. I think, "New email!" and then spend the next five minutes reading the new message. Just like that, I'm out of the zone.

Interruptions are expensive. They don't just cost the time it takes somebody to deal with them. They also cost the time it takes to get back into whatever they were doing when you interrupted them—if they can do that at all. A recent Microsoft study showed that after being interrupted by an incoming email or instant message, it took Microsoft workers an average of 15 minutes to return to their previous tasks. People were easily distracted, and it generally took them a long time to recover from each distraction.[1]

So, interruptions cost time. They are also annoying and sometimes even a bit rude. After all, an interruption is nothing but an outside influence that stops people from doing what they're currently doing.

Whenever possible, you should not interrupt your users. Here's how to do that.

---

1. Steve Lohr summarizes some of the research in a *New York Times* article at http://www.nytimes.com/2007/03/25/business/25multi.html.

18.1 Make Decisions for Your User

If there is a decision you can make for your users, make it. Don't check with them just to be sure.

For example, every time I plug a card reader into my Windows computer, I get this message:

How likely is it that I want to use the 4GB memory card in my card reader as a backup? How many people click the "Import pictures and videos using Windows" button in this window? Why not just default to opening the card's window, instead of interrupting people with a set of choices that most people probably will never even read?

The following happens a lot when I use my iPhone: I'm in an app, and I'm making a specific choice, such as hitting Play in a video player or tapping a link in a Twitter client. But instead of simply doing what I said, the app throws up a screen offering me additional choices. Figure 18.1, on the next page shows two examples.

Air Video[2] asks people where they want the movie to start after they hit Play. Twitter client Osfoora[3] asks people whether they want to view the web page or add it to Instapaper after they tap a link.

Both of these interruptions are not strictly necessary. Instead, just make the decision for people. Go with the most likely option, and offer them a way of changing their decision.

---

2. Air Video is a brilliant app for streaming video to iOS devices. You can find out more at http://www.inmethod.com/air-video.
3. Osfoora is a really neat, beautiful Twitter client you can find at http://www.osfoora.com.

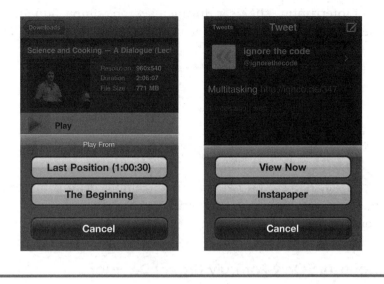

Figure 18.1: DON'T MAKE ME CHOOSE

For example, after a user selects to play a movie, simply start from the last play position. It's probably what he wanted, and if it isn't, he will easily be able to jump back to the beginning of the movie. Similarly, if he taps a link, simply open the link. It's probably what he wanted. Then, offer a way of adding open web pages to Instapaper.

18.2 Front Load Decisions

In some cases you have to ask the user to make a decision. For those instances, it's a good idea to front load decisions as much as possible so the user can make them all at once and then be left alone. For example, it's best to allow users to enter software-licensing information at the beginning of the installation process and not stop the installation in the middle to ask them for their licensing data.

Here's another example of an unnecessary interruption, this time from OpenOffice.org:

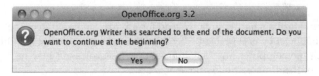

Instead of interrupting the user during a search, simply add an option to the search dialog, the way BBEdit[4] does.

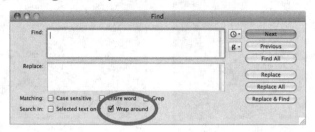

Or, best of all, don't even ask the user. Simply default to wrapping around, but show a short animation when the search wraps so that people can stop their search when they *don't* want to wrap around.

18.3 Interrupt Users Only For Truly Urgent Decisions

You should never interrupt a user just to inform her that something has happened.[5]

4. Find it at http://barebones.com.
5. Aza Raskin, Mozilla's former creative lead for Firefox, says that decisionless interruptions have "an efficiency of 0 percent," because the user can do only one thing; the user is never giving the computer any new information, regardless of how he reacts to such an interruption. Read more at http://barebones.com.

What people are actually seeing in those cases is something like this:

I'm Forcing You to Stop What You're Doing! Now Read This!
You've received a new text message.
(I receive dozens of new text messages every day. Stop interrupting me!)

If the information is not particularly important, don't show it. If it *is* important but no immediate action is required, show the information in a way that does not interrupt your users. For example, you could use a nonmodal,[6] nonintrusive way of alerting them. Here's how HP's webOS shows new messages to the user:

When a new message arrives, the small black strip with a little message icon slides up from the bottom of the screen. Touching the strip shows some more information about the message. Touch the message itself, and it opens inside its app.

---

6. If it's nonmodal, it doesn't prevent the user from doing something else. For more about modes, see Chapter 20, *Modes*, on page 169.

Interruptions Are Rude

Unless you really have no other choice than to ask your users for their input and unless you really require that information *right now*, don't interrupt them. It's just rude.

Takeaway Points

- Don't interrupt people. It makes them less happy and less productive, and it's not polite.

- Make decisions for your users, rather than asking them questions.

- If you can't make decisions for your users, ask everything you need to know once, rather than interrupting them every time you come up with a new question you need to ask.

- If there is something you really need to tell people, at least make sure it's as nonintrusive as possible so that they can deal with it in their own time frame.

Further Reading

Flow: The Psychology of Optimal Experience [Csi02] by Mihály Csíkszentmihályi explains how important it is for people to be able to focus on a task without being interrupted.

Chapter 19

Instead of Interrupting, Offer Undo

Have you ever accidentally done something stupid while using a computer and the computer warned you about it, but you just clicked the warning away, because you were thinking, "I know what I'm doing. Get out of my way, computer!"?

> **Are you sure you want to close this window?**
>
> 5 tabs are open in this window. Do you want to close the window anyway?
>
> ☐ Do not warn when closing multiple pages
>
> (Cancel)   (Close)

It happens to me all the time. We get so used to these warning dialogs that we often don't even consciously notice them anymore. *"Are you sure you want to...?"* Yeah, yeah, I wouldn't have clicked the button if I wasn't sure, would I? *" Do you really want to delete these...?"* Yes. Yes, I really wanted to. *"You will not be able to recover..."* Yes! Yes! Yes! No, wait, what did I just do?

Eventually, we reflexively click warning dialogs away. Psychologists call this *habituation*; most of the time, dialog boxes are an annoying distraction, just background noise, so we get in the habit of ignoring them. The one time we actually do something wrong, by the time we notice our mistake, we've already clicked OK.

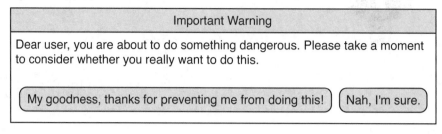

WHAT YOU INTENDED:

Important Warning
Dear user, you are about to do something dangerous. Please take a moment to consider whether you really want to do this.
[My goodness, thanks for preventing me from doing this!]   [Nah, I'm sure.]

WHAT PEOPLE ACTUALLY SEE:

Annoying Interruption
Even though you are working on something important, I'm going to interrupt you now because blah blah blah blah blah blah blah blah blah blah blah blah.
[Whatever, leave me alone, I'm working here!]

Warnings are good for shifting the blame to the users—after all, they should have read the warning, right? They are not good, however, for preventing problems.

Fortunately, in most situations, we can provide a better solution than a warning dialog.

19.1 Let Users Undo Their Actions

Instead of forcing people to deal with constant warnings, undo offers a simple, transparent solution. Unless users accidentally do something unintended, undo is invisible. Once an accident happens, it's easy to go back.

One crucial note here is that people need to trust your implementation of undo. That means you have to cover as many actions as possible and offer multilevel, "deep" undo, which allows the user to undo more than just the most recent action. If undo doesn't work reliably or doesn't go back far enough, people will lose trust in your application. They will hesitate to explore new features, they will be afraid to use features they know, and eventually they will become unhappy with your application altogether.

> ## Trust
>
> Allowing people to trust your application is one of your most important tasks. A reliable undo function is just one aspect of this. You also need to make your application predictable and stable.
>
> I once worked on a product that shipped with a very destructive bug. A specific feature of the application would destroy user data. Even though we fixed the problem very quickly, usability testing showed that people who were affected by the problem would avoid using that specific feature years after the problem had originally occurred.

Cutting down on warning dialogs in favor of undo has the added advantage that people will be less likely to automatically click away actual warning dialogs, because they won't be quite as used to them.

19.2 Temporary Undo

There are some situations where implementing undo is impossible for technical reasons. You can't let the user undo sending an email; once it's sent, it's out of your control. Similarly, while you can delete a tweet once it's sent and unpublish a blog post once it's published, that's not quite the same as preventing the action altogether.

One solution to this is to delay the action and allow the user to undo it temporarily. Instead of sending the mail right away, show an undo button for a few seconds. If the user undoes the action, don't send the mail. Otherwise, remove the undo button and send the mail. Gmail implements this in its web interface:

Graphic and interaction designer Clayton Miller calls this "delayed passive confirmation," because the user passively confirms the action by not stopping it. Here is his mock-up of how this might look in a desktop application:[1]

Takeaway Points

- Warning people before they do something potentially dangerous doesn't work, because people ignore these warnings.

- Instead, allow people to undo their actions so that they can revert accidents.

- If it is not technically possible for you to offer undo, at least delay the potentially dangerous action so that people can prevent it from happening even after issuing the command.

---

1.   You can read more about his ideas at http://iuface.net/7u8.

Chapter 20

Modes

In 1985, when writing Apple's Mac developer documentation called *Inside Macintosh* [Ros86], author Caroline Rose deemed modes to be important enough to mention them at the very start of the very first volume. She writes that "a *mode* is a part of an application that the user has to formally enter and leave, and that restricts the operations that can be performed while the mode is in effect."

Basically, a mode is a state that an application or an individual window is in that changes how the application or window reacts to user input. Modes can be a source of usability problems. Rose writes that "since people don't usually operate modally in real life, having to deal with modes in computer software reinforces the idea that computers are unnatural and unfriendly." There's another issue with modes: if people don't understand what mode an application or window is in, their input produces results that they did not expect.

Perhaps the most popular example of a mode is the Caps Lock key. Whether the Caps Lock key is active or not is a state that changes the user interface reaction to user input.

Password:    Password:

QUIZ: ONE OF THESE TWO PASSWORD FIELDS WAS FILLED IN WITH AN ACTIVE CAPS LOCK KEY! WHICH ONE IS IT?

In one mode, logging in works. In the other mode, using the exact same input, logging in fails.

20.1 Nonobvious Modes

In *The Humane Interface* [Ras00], Jef Raskin explains that "modes are a significant source of errors, confusion, unnecessary restrictions, and complexity in interfaces."

Modes are confusing when people do not realize what mode they are in—in other words, when they are nonobvious. The Caps Lock key, for example, indicates that it is active with a small light that is easily overlooked.

Another example of a nonobvious mode is the currently active tool in an image editor:

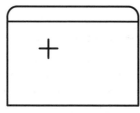 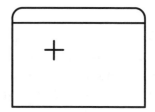

QUIZ: IN ONE OF THESE TWO CASES, CLICKING AND DRAGGING WILL CREATE A RECTANGLE. IN THE OTHER, IT WILL CREATE A CIRCLE. WHICH IS WHICH?

Since people may not realize what mode the user interface is in, their actions may create unexpected results. Logging in doesn't work properly, or the image editor creates a circle when the user wants to create a rectangle.

Modes should be obvious even if the user doesn't remember having activated them. For example, if you select the Open File menu command in Mac OS X, a modal dialog box opens. This mode is obvious to the user immediately after he has selected Open File, but if he then goes to get a cup of coffee and comes back to his computer five minutes later, he may not immediately realize that the computer is still in the Open File mode.

Now, clicking the text window merely makes the computer beep, and it may not be immediately apparent why this occurs. Of course, in this particular case, the mode isn't necessary at all. There is no reason why the Open File dialog box needs to block the whole application. However, in other cases, simply getting rid of the mode doesn't work. For example, an application installer may ask for the user's password:

If we got rid of the "asking for the user's password" mode, the user could activate the installer window with the password window still open but then couldn't continue with the installation. This is even more confusing than not being able to activate the installer window at all. You can't always get rid of modes; you just have to make it clear to the user what exactly is going on.

One way of making modes obvious is to provide visual feedback indicating that a mode is active. In a paper called "The Prevention of Mode Errors Through Sensory Feedback,"[1] user interface designer Bill Buxton describes the results of experiments, noting, "there were significantly fewer mode errors in conditions with visual feedback than those without for both novices and experts." When testing visual and kinesthetic feedback (the latter being based on perception of the motion of one's own body—for example, the vibration you feel when your phone's silent alert goes off), he further observes:

> The benefits of visual and kinesthetic feedback were found regardless of whether or not subjects were experienced users. (...) Thus, even though many of the expert subjects commented that they were used to keeping track of the mode "in their head," feedback of both kinds significantly reduced their mode errors nonetheless.

If static visual feedback doesn't work, an animation might just do the trick; animations are much harder to ignore than static visuals, as discussed in Chapter 15, *Animations*, on page 139.

However, visual feedback is not the best possible solution. Buxton's research shows that kinesthetic feedback works even better. You're probably wondering how to give kinesthetic feedback without adding special hardware to your users' computers. You could use keys on users' keyboards as mode activators; for example, dragging a file in the Mac OS X Finder moves the file, but by holding down the Alt key, Mac OS X switches to a "copy" mode. Since the user has to touch and press the Alt key to stay in this mode, this is a kind of kinesthetic, tactile feedback constantly telling the user that he's still in the copy mode. Such temporary, constantly activated modes are called *quasimodes*. I'll get back to them at the end of this chapter.

In his essay "Visual Feedback and How Modes Kill,"[2] Aza Raskin points out another option:

> Visual indication is one method for trying to bring your attention to the system state, but as Buxton showed it has a decent chance of failure. Using sound-based feedback is more likely to succeed, because while you can avoid looking

---

1. Read it at http://www.billbuxton.com/ModeErrors.html.
2. Read it at http://www.azarask.in/blog/post/is_visual_feedback_enough_why_modes_kill/.

at a visual indication, you cannot avoid listening to an audio indication (as every player who has been forced to listen to Baby Mario's cry in Yoshi's Island 2 knows).

It's probably a good idea to try various ways of dealing with this problem and do usability tests on them to find out which ones work.

But even if designers realize that they need to make modes obvious and find a workable way of doing so, people may still be confused by the result, because the way the mode is exposed is unclear. Here's an example from Apple's iPhone. The included camera application has an HDR mode.[3] Whether or not the mode is currently active is indicated on the label of the button that changes the mode:

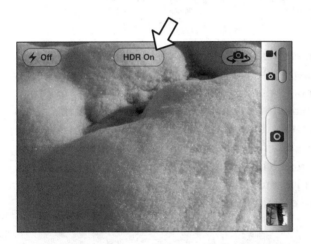

But what does "HDR On" actually mean? Does it mean that I can turn on HDR by touching the button, or does it mean that it is currently on and I can turn it off by touching it? In *The Humane Interface* [Ras00], Jef Raskin recommends using checkboxes or radio buttons to indicate active modes.

 HDR

This is unambiguous.

---

3. High Dynamic Range images combine pictures with different exposures to create an image that shows greater dynamic range than the camera would normally be able to produce.

20.2   Unexpected Modes

Dialog boxes are a specific type of mode. Unlike nonobvious modes, dialog boxes are usually reasonably obvious, at least when they first pop up. They are, however, often unexpected, therefore causing the same problems as nonobvious modes: the user interface doesn't do what the user wants because it is not in the mode the user expects.

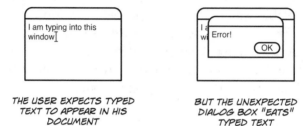

THE USER EXPECTS TYPED
TEXT TO APPEAR IN HIS
DOCUMENT

BUT THE UNEXPECTED
DIALOG BOX "EATS"
TYPED TEXT

Not only do dialog boxes change the mode of the user interface unexpectedly, but it's also possible that the user's input is mistakenly interpreted as input for the modal dialog box, rather than for the previously active window. (This is called *stealing focus*, since it moves the computer's focus from where the user wants it to be to somewhere else.) This means that the user may accidentally discard a modal window or approve something she intended to reject. Instead of moving the cursor to a new line, the Return key may unmount a network disk or delete a file, because that was the default button's action in the modal window.

20.3   Sticky Modes

This is my alarm clock. To change the time the when the alarm goes off, I have to push the topmost button. This puts the clock into its "change alarm time" mode. In that mode, the topmost button now changes the hour of the alarm. So, if I can't push this button again to exit the mode, how *do* I exit the mode?

It is often not obvious to the user how to resolve an active mode, and this causes usability problems. Another example of this is the Insert key on PC keyboards. Once the user has activated the overtype mode by hitting the Insert key (perhaps by accident), it is entirely unclear and nonobvious how to go back to the "normal" mode.

If you use modes, always make it clear how the user can exit the mode.

To solve the alarm clock riddle, you can't actively leave the "change alarm time" mode. You can push buttons all you want. In fact, pushing buttons merely ensures that you will remain stuck in that mode, since the clock will exit the "change alarm time" mode on its own a few seconds after the user stops frantically and randomly pushing buttons, trying to get out of the mode.

20.4 Modes Are Not Always Bad

Because of the problems they can cause, it's no surprise that modes have a pretty bad reputation. In reality, that reputation is largely undeserved. Trying to make a user interface entirely nonmodal increases its complexity. Modes can be used to show functionality only when it is wanted; nonmodal interfaces are forced to offer a much wider array of possible user actions at any given time.

Modes are bad only when they are nonobvious, unexpected, or hard to leave. If the user intentionally changes a user interface's mode, that mode is entirely obvious to her as long as it remains active, and she always knows how to leave that mode, then there is nothing wrong with using modes.

Keep these basic rules in mind, and your modes will improve your user interface, rather than making it more confusing.

20.5 Quasimodes

Quasimodes, as Jef Raskin calls them, are modes that are temporary and exist only as long as the user explicitly keeps them active. In *Inside Macintosh* [Ros86], Rose calls them *spring-loaded* modes. The quasimodal counterpart to the Caps Lock key is the Shift key. Instead of putting the computer into a permanent mode, the Shift key introduces a transient mode that is active only as long as the user holds the key down. Since the user has to keep the quasimode alive explicitly, there is no chance that the mode will be nonobvious, unexpected, or hard to leave.

Another quasimode that Rose mentions in her book is pressing down on the mouse key; it's active only as long as the user keeps pressing. Computers behave differently when the mouse key is held down, but people are never confused about whether they are currently pushing the mouse key.

If you need to use modes, consider whether quasimodes might solve your particular user interface need.

Takeaway Points

- Modes can be a source of confusion if they're not designed properly.

- Modes can be useful since they help you avoid overcrowding your product with user interface elements.

- To work well, modes should be obvious, expected, and easy to leave.

- Use quasimodes instead of full modes whenever possible.

Further Reading

Modes are mentioned in many books on user interface design. *About Face* [Coo95], for example, mentions modes in several different contexts. Jef Raskin's *The Humane Interface* [Ras00] has a chapter on modes. Aza Raskin has written a great essay on modes.[4]

Inside Macintosh [Ros86] only covers modes superficially, but it's worth reading in general.

---

4. At http://www.azarask.in/blog/post/is_visual_feedback_enough_why_modes_kill/.

Chapter 21

Have Opinions Instead of Preferences

If you're are not sure about a specific design choice, it's always easiest to leave it up to the user. When Mac users minimize windows into the Dock, some probably want it to elegantly flow into the Dock. Others may prefer their windows to just zoom away, linearly scaling down. So, why not give them both?

Every unnecessary checkbox in your Settings window is a design decision that you're leaving to a person who is less qualified at making that decision than you are. You are in the best position to come up with the correct solution. Don't let somebody who knows less about your product make that decision for you. Chances are, their decisions will be worse than yours.

Designer and developer Mike Rundle puts it like this:[1]

> If there's a choice between setting a value to A or B and you always choose A, why not just make A the main, unsettable, unchangeable choice? If you think A is the best decision, why even let people choose B? (...)

> [Steve Jobs] builds what he wants because he knows he's building great stuff. That's what you should do, too.

You are trained to make these decisions, and you have the necessary information to do so correctly. Your users probably don't.

What I'm Not Talking About

Not everything you see in a settings window is bad. I'm specifically talking about preferences—things that could work either way but that some people *prefer* to work in a certain way. Let's define how I use these terms in this chapter:

Settings	A global change the user can make to your product's function or behavior.
Configuration	Settings that are necessary for your product to work correctly, such as the screen resolution or network settings. If you're creating a Twitter client, for example, you need to allow the user to configure it to show his personal Twitter messages.
Preferences	Settings that change your product's behavior and are not strictly necessary but that some people may prefer to be set differently—for example, the number of recent items in the Apple menu or Windows Start menu, or the place where the scroll arrows appear in Mac OS X's scroll bars.
Personalization	Settings that have purely visual effects and do not change the actual behavior of your product—for example, the desktop wallpaper.

---

1. Read his essay at http://flyosity.com/iphone/kill-the-settings-build-opinionated-software.php.

When I say that you should avoid preferences, I'm explicitly not talking about configurations (after all, these are necessary for your product to work properly).

I'm also not talking about personalization. Although personalization isn't required for a product to work properly, it can increase the user's enjoyment tremendously. Being able to change the lock screen on your phone to a picture of your dog will make the phone much more delightful to you.

It's not always completely clear whether a setting should be considered a configuration, preference, or personalization. But thinking about settings in terms of these three categories will help you make better decisions about what to keep and what to throw out.

21.1 Why Preferences Are Bad

Preferences make your product unnecessarily complex in various ways.

First, since people will look in your product's settings area for things that they need to be able to change, every needless choice you offer makes it harder for them to find what they're looking for. Every preference they have to look through makes the one they actually need a little bit harder to find, and the search a little bit more frustrating.

Second, preferences make your product inconsistent by introducing modes; each preference is a mode (see Chapter 20, *Modes*, on page 169). If you ever sit down at the computer of a user who likes to play around with the operating system's preferences, you'll quickly discover that you're constantly annoyed by things that don't quite behave the way you want, because features are in different modes than you expect. For example, on some computers, inserting a CD causes a CD icon to pop up on the desktop; on others, this feature is turned off. On some computers, clicking the trough of a scroll bar scrolls by one screen; on others, it scrolls to the position you clicked. It's easy to get used to these things. If you use a computer with preferences that are set differently, you will experience a bit of frustration every time the computer is in a different mode than you expect. By avoiding preferences altogether, you avoid putting your users in that position.

Third, preferences make your product harder to use for the people who pick the wrong choice. Perhaps some people like to have the list of unread RSS items to the left of the view of the currently open item, and others prefer to have the list at the top of the view.

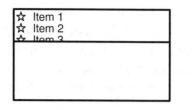

SOME PEOPLE LIKE IT
LIKE THIS...

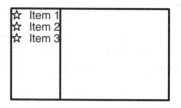

---AND SOME PEOPLE
LIKE IT LIKE THAT.

In reality, there is one solution that works best for most people. It's your job to find that solution. You can do usability tests with different configurations of your product and see which one *really* works best. Your users can't.

Fourth, leaving the choice up to the user also means you'll have to support several different ways of using your product for the rest of its lifetime. If you pick one of the options instead of leaving it up to your users, you won't have to spend time working on the other options; you'll have more time to make the one option you chose as good as it can possibly be. And when problems do occur, preferences make it harder to track them down. Every pointless preference increases the possible code paths in your product. The more ways your users can change how your product behaves, the harder it becomes to replicate problems and to provide timely help if something goes wrong.

21.2 How to Avoid Preferences

Say no to your users (and have a look at Chapter 24, *Avoiding Features*, on page 201). Some people might really like a smaller font size. Perhaps they'll even send you email, asking you to let them change the font sizes. But that doesn't mean that adding a preference for font sizes is really the best course of action. You may make some of your customers happy, but you'll inconvenience everybody else, and you'll be forced to support windows with different font sizes.

Say no to yourself. Maybe a preference sounds really good. Often, it's the easiest way out. By simply making something a preference, you don't have to make that choice yourself. But you're doing your users a disservice. Remember way back in the beginning of the book (in Chapter 3, *Personas*, on page 17), when we talked about your users? For every preference, ask yourself: How does this help my users? What goal can this preference help my users reach that they couldn't reach before? If you can't come up with an obvious answer, dump the preference.

Be consistent. If you can't decide between two choices and your users might have used similar products, be consistent with those products. Your users can then apply their existing knowledge to your product.

Run a usability test. If there are two solutions to a problem and you're not sure which way to go, create paper prototypes and test them (see Chapter 11, *Paper Prototype Testing*, on page 97). Or implement both, and run an A/B test (see Chapter 33, *A/B Testing*, on page 283). The feedback and data you get from such tests may even help you come up with a new idea that is better than the options you came up with originally.

Have opinions. If there are two equally valid ways you could go with, go with the one you like better. Which one would *you* prefer to use? It's OK to have opinions. If you try to please everybody, you will excite nobody.

Have implicit preferences. Rather than letting users set behavior explicitly, remember what they did the last time. Don't let users set the default window size; simply use the window size from the last time they resized a window as the default window size. Don't let users set their preferred protocol in a file-sharing application; simply default to the protocol they used the last time, and let them change it if necessary. Don't let users set whether they want to see a "new document" or an "open document" dialog when they open an application; simply reopen the files from the last time they used the application.

21.3 If You Can't Avoid Preferences

If you truly can't avoid preferences, make sure that the default choice for each preference works well for a majority of your users. Most people stick with the default values and never change them. Usability expert Jakob Nielsen points out:[2]

> Many previous studies, including my own, have shown that the top few entries in search listings get the preponderance

---

2. See the full article at http://www.useit.com/alertbox/defaults.html.

of clicks and that the number one hit gets vastly more clicks than anything else. (...) Users rely on defaults in many other areas of user interface design. For example, they rarely utilize fancy customization features, making it important to optimize the default user experience, since that's what most users stick to.

Give each preference a reasonable label with consistent terminology. Avoid trademarks or jargon that may be unfamiliar to your users.

BAD: ☒ Swipe down for Exposé

BETTER: ☒ Swipe down to reveal all windows

Avoid negative labels. Checkboxes should enable things, not disable them.

BAD: ☒ Disable automatic login

BETTER: ☐ Log in automatically

In the manual, explain what each individual preference does, and provide additional explanations using tooltips. If a preference is disabled for some reason, use the tooltip to explain why.[3]

Takeaway Points

- Your product's settings can be grouped into configurations (settings that are necessary for your product to work properly), personalizations (purely visual changes that are not strictly necessary but allow people to make your product "theirs"), and preferences (functional changes that are not necessary for your product to work properly).

- Preferences should be avoided, because they introduce unnecessary modes.

- Instead of offering preferences, go with the best default behaviors.

Further Reading

Designer and developer Mike Rundle has written about this topic.[4]

---

3. Some operating systems may not support tooltips on disabled user interface elements, but I'm sure you'll find another reasonably obvious way to explain to your users why a specific preference is not enabled.

4. At http://flyosity.com/iphone/kill-the-settings-build-opinionated-software.php.

Chapter 22

Hierarchies, Space, Time, and How We Think About the World

When computers allow people to organize their data, they often allow people to organize that data into hierarchies. The file system on your PC is the most obvious example of this.

```
▲ 📁 Libraries
   ▷ 📄 Documents
   ▷ 🎵 Music
   ▲ 🖼 Pictures
      ▲ 📁 Pictures
         ▷ 📁 iPhoto Library
            📁 iPhoto Library Recovered Photos
            📁 iPod Photo Cache
            📁 Photo Booth
            📁 Skitch
      ▷ 📁 Public Pictures
   ▷ 🎬 Videos
```

Hierarchies work well for a lot of things. People are used to hierarchies, since they encounter hierarchies all the time. Families are hierarchies of people (the "family tree"). We look at animals and see that individual species are related to each other in an evolutionary hierarchy. Stores arrange their products using hierarchical logic. (For example, if you're looking for strawberry jam, you'll go to the food section of the store. In the area where you'll also find peanut butter and honey, you'll look at the shelf with the jams, and you'll find different kinds of strawberry jam.) Arranging music in a hierarchic fashion (Genre → Band → Album → Song) makes sense, and the arrangement is (usually) obvious and easily understood.

When there is an obvious, generally understood way of arranging things into a hierarchy, people typically don't have a problem with understanding and using such hierarchies. The problem occurs when we ask people to create and maintain hierarchies of arbitrary items.

22.1 Hierarchies

Humans are not good at organizing arbitrary things into a hierarchy and then later remembering where exactly they sorted a specific thing. For example, Mark Shuttleworth[1] points to the hierarchical file system as a main source of usability issues in Ubuntu, saying, "People save an attachment they receive in email, and an hour later have no idea where to find it."[2] Similarly, in a paper called "Improving the Usability of the Hierarchical File System,"[3] author Gary Marsden writes:

> Anyone who has studied how application users store files realizes that the file system is quite a large barrier to all but the most advanced users.

In their paper "Hierarchical File Systems are Dead," Margo Seltzer and Nicholas Murphy write:[4]

> Users no longer know where their files are stored. Moreover, they tend to access their data in a more search-based fashion. We encourage the skeptical reader to ask nontechnical friends where their email is physically located. Can even you, the technically savvy user, produce a path name to your personal email? Your Quicken files? The last Word document you edited? The last program you ran? For that matter, how many files are on your desktop right now? How many of them are related to each other?

This issue is compounded by several people accessing the same data; the hierarchical structure that may make sense for one person may be utterly incomprehensible for another, and even if they agree on a general structure, they will probably often disagree on where exactly to put individual items.

---

1. Shuttleworth is the former CEO of Canonical Ltd., creator of the Ubuntu family of Linux distribution. Ubuntu is an operating system that is based on the Linux kernel, with a strong focus on usability.
2. Read his essay at http://www.markshuttleworth.com/archives/223.
3. You can find the paper at http://people.cs.uct.ac.za/~gaz/publ.html.
4. Read it at http://www.eecs.harvard.edu/~margo/papers/hotos09/.

22.2 Space

Although we are able to understand reasonably obvious, intuitive hier-archies such as family structures and the logic governing where a store puts stuff, we're not really good at coming up with hierarchies for most other things. We typically don't arrange the stuff we own in a deeply hierarchical fashion. Sure, you may put all of your dinnerware into one cupboard and all of your kitchenware into another, but that's hardly a hierarchy. Instead, you're arranging things in space, putting related things next to each other. You don't remember where to find your plates by any kind of hierarchy. Instead, you remember where to find your plates because you know where you put them.

Similarly, your desk may be a huge mess, but you'll probably have a pretty good idea of where on your desk you put that letter you got last week. Not because you're using some kind of hierarchical organization scheme for your desk but simply because you know where you put it.

This is called *spatial reasoning*. Humans are good at it. If your product can make use of the human ability to think in terms of space and if you can let your users arrange their data in space, do it.

One example of this is Firefox's Group Your Tabs feature. It allows users to get a spatial view of all the tabs in a window and group them on a two-dimensional plane.[5]

---

5. Aza Raskin explains the thinking behind the feature at http://www.azarask.in/blog/post/designing-tab-candy/.

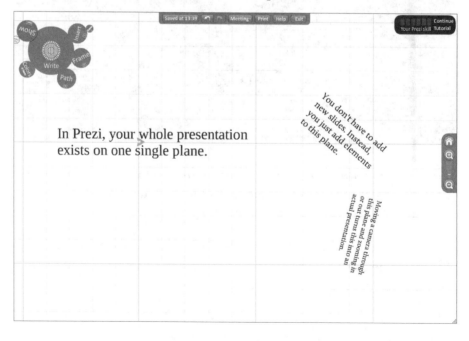

Another example is Prezi,[6] a presentation app that shows the whole presentation on one flat surface and breaks it down into individual screens by moving a camera across this plane.

---

6.   At http://prezi.com.

Keep in mind that in real life, stuff doesn't move on its own. In a spatial system, people expect to be able to find things where they left them. Make sure you never change things behind the user's back.

Spatial systems tend to break down when users have to manage large numbers of items. It's easy to create and keep track of a spatial arrangement of dozens or hundreds of items. It becomes harder when it's thousands of items, and it becomes almost impossible when the system has to manage hundreds of thousands of items.

22.3 Time

Millennia of living in a spatial world have taught humans how to organize and find things in such a world. Similarly, we have become pretty good at thinking about and organizing our world in temporal terms.

Although you may not remember exactly where inside a folder you've filed that report you wrote last week, you know for sure that you wrote it last week. You probably also remember the time of day it was, and you may even remember the specific day as well.

So, depending on your product, it may make sense to let users access their data in some kind of temporal view. Nintendo does a pretty good job of this; instead of a file system, Nintendo likes to use calendars to show user-created data. Using a Nintendo system, you never have to file a drawing or photograph you've made; instead, you just have to remember the month when you made it, and you'll probably be able to see a small version of the picture in the month view.

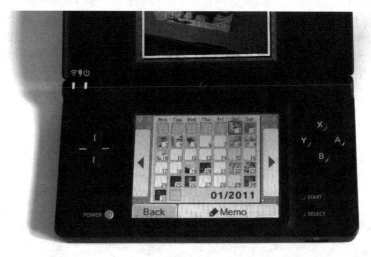

Another example of an application that uses a temporal view is Media Atelier's Mac app Alarms[7]—a to-do list that eschews the traditional hierarchical list view used by other task lists, opting instead for a temporal view in which to present to-do items.

If you can, allow people to access their data through a time-based view.

22.4 A Better Hierarchical System

In some cases, it is simply not possible to avoid hierarchical systems. If you feel that you need to go with a hierarchy, here are a few ideas that should help you make this system as usable as possible.

---

7. Find out more at http://www.mediaatelier.com/Alarms.

Restrict Depth

If you give people just a little bit of rope, they'll have a harder time using it to hang themselves. If you give people the ability to create only shallow hierarchies, they probably won't get lost in them. One example of such a system is the photo-sharing site Picasa, which allows its users to sort their pictures into albums but doesn't let them put one album into another album. An album contains a number of pictures, and that's it. It's unlikely that people will lose their albums, since they can't hide them inside other albums to begin with.

Show Hierarchies Spatially

When Apple added folders to its iOS operating system,[8] it did a very clever thing: as long as you don't put more than nine apps into a folder, you are always able to see all of the folder's apps inside the folder's icon. So even though this is technically a hierarchical arrangement of apps, users are unlikely to lose track of where things are, because the hierarchical arrangement *looks* like a spatial arrangement to the user.

Allow Items to Exist in More Than One Place

It's often not clear where individual items belong. Let's say you are using a document management system. It contains various directories, such as an Insurance directory for documents from your insurance and a Bills directory for your bills. Well, what happens if your insurance company sends you a bill? The same document needs to exist in two different places. Hierarchical file systems should always let people put the same file into more than one place.

Support Tagging and Other Metadata

Simply letting people sort items into a hierarchy is semantically weak. Hierarchies often express only one aspect of an item's nature. For example, the biological classification of animals uses the principle of common

---

8. iOS is an operating system most prominently used by iPhone, iPad, and iPod touch.

descent to sort animals into a hierarchy. That's useful if you're interested in how closely individual species are related to each other, but it's useless if you're compiling a list of all animals that are poisonous to humans, or a list of all aquatic animals. Allowing users to maintain metadata for the individual items in a hierarchy allows them to maintain data that is not expressed by the hierarchy itself.

Support Alternative Ways of Accessing Data

Even if items are primarily sorted into a hierarchy, you should allow users to access this data in nonhierarchical ways. For example, you should let people search through their data. Similarly, if you keep track of when individual items were changed, you can let people access their hierarchical data in a temporal view. Think about how people might want to search or browse through their data.

The BizTwit Case

Since every published Twitter message has a publication date, offering people a temporal view of their messages makes a lot of sense and makes it easy to go back to earlier conversations.

BizTwit lets people schedule messages that will be published automatically on a specified date. The temporal view could be expanded to include such messages, which would prevent any ambiguity about when messages will be published. Figure 22.1, on the next page shows a wireframe of how such a user interface might look.

In this view, people can filter what kinds of messages they want to see (sent messages, replies from other people, drafts, scheduled messages, or all messages). The dots in the individual days indicate the day's activity, from zero dots (no messages were sent or received) to three dots (lots of messages were sent or received). For days in the future, dots indicate scheduled messages. Finally, tapping a day shows the day's messages. This kind of view should be familiar to anyone who uses calendar apps.

This user interface gives people a quick overview over their Twitter account's activity, allows them to easily find past messages, and lets them quickly see what messages are scheduled to be tweeted when.

Takeaway Points

- Sometimes, hierarchies work well, but they need to be obvious and commonly accepted.

Figure 22.1: WIREFRAME OF BIZTWIT'S TEMPORAL VIEW

- Hierarchies work less well if people have to come up with them on their own, especially when several people share a hierarchy.

- Humans are pretty good at dealing with time and space. Try to use them, rather than hierarchies, to organize user data.

- If you must use hierarchies, try to keep the structure shallow, allow items to exist in more than one place, support metadata, and support alternative ways of accessing the data.

Further Reading

Information Architecture for the World Wide Web [MR06] by Peter Morville and Louis Rosenfeld provides some insight into hierarchical structures. Margo Seltzer and Nicholas Murphy's paper "Hierarchical File Systems are Dead" is also worth reading.[9]

William Jones, a research associate professor in the Information School at the University of Washington, has an interesting presentation about structuring personal information.[10]

---

9. You can find it at http://www.eecs.harvard.edu/~margo/papers/hotos09/.
10. You can watch it at http://www.youtube.com/watch?v=aufuHuNRqaE.

Chapter 23

Speed

When we do usability tests, one thing that often gets little attention is the product's speed and responsiveness. Usability tests will quickly show when users don't understand what a button label means. But they usually don't show that your product responds too slowly. People using your product in a usability test have a different motivation for doing so than your actual customers. The people in a usability test know that they are supposed to test your product; they won't suddenly abandon it and switch to a competitor because they grow frustrated when they have to wait.

Your real customers might. Tech investor Fred Wilson explains:[1]

> Speed is more than a feature. Speed is *the most important feature.* If your application is slow, people won't use it. I see this more with mainstream users than I do with power users. I think that power users sometimes have a bit of sympathetic eye to the challenges of building really fast web apps, and maybe they're willing to live with it, but when I look at my wife and kids, they're my mainstream view of the world. If something is slow, they're just gone. (...) When we see some of our portfolio company's applications getting bogged down, we also note that they don't grow as quickly. There is real empirical evidence that substantiates the fact that speed is more than a feature. It's a requirement.

---

1. Watch his presentation at http://thinkvitamin.com/web-apps/fred-wilsons-10-golden-principles-of-successful-web-apps/.

It's important to keep an eye on performance problems even if usability tests don't show obvious signs that speed or responsiveness might not be good enough.

23.1 Responsiveness

The first thing to look at is how responsive your product is. Research is pretty consistent on this topic.[2] If an action takes less than 0.1 second to finish, the user perceives it as instantaneous. If it takes less than 1 second to finish, the user no longer perceives it as instantaneous but will not lose track of what is going on. If an action takes longer than a second, the chance increases that the user gets distracted while waiting for it to finish.

Whenever possible, it's best to make sure actions take less than 0.1 second.

A somewhat related topic is continuous interactions on natural user interfaces, such as scrolling through a list by dragging the list with a finger. In those cases, performance is especially important. The user interface's response to the user's action must be immediate and fluid. The user interface must be able to keep up with the user's actions, and it must be able to do so at a high frame rate. Responsiveness can make the difference between the user getting the impression that she is interacting with actual physical objects and her consciously noticing that she is simply giving commands to a computer. In such user interfaces, indications of poor performance, such as input lag or choppy animations, can destroy the user's mental model of your product and can be extremely irritating. (I've written more on this particular topic in Chapter 13, *Natural User Interfaces*, on page 123.)

23.2 Progress Feedback

If an action takes longer than 0.1 second, you need to provide some kind of feedback. Determining the type of feedback required depends on two things: how long the action takes and what kind of action it is.

---

2. For more information, read Jakob Nielsen's essay on response time: http://www.useit. com/papers/responsetime.html.

If the action takes only one or two seconds, it's OK to change the cursor to an hourglass or add a small "I'm working" indicator that doesn't explicitly show how far the action has progressed.

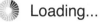 Loading...

The goal here is not to tell the user how long the action will take but to make it obvious that the computer has received the user's command and is working on it. The word *obvious* is quite important. If you watch people using web browsers, you will notice that they click a link repeatedly, thinking that the click didn't "take" on the first try. Perhaps you do this yourself. Why? Because the little "Loading" throbber or progress bar most browsers show is not obvious enough, and it's not where the user's focus is when she clicks a link.

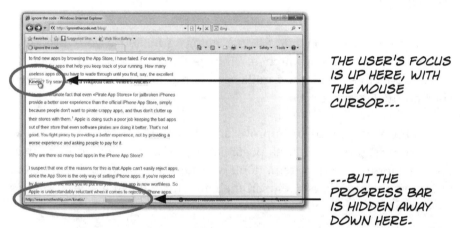

THE USER'S FOCUS IS UP HERE, WITH THE MOUSE CURSOR...

...BUT THE PROGRESS BAR IS HIDDEN AWAY DOWN HERE.

There is no clear feedback that the browser has received the user's click, so people often try to click again and again.

For actions that take longer than a few seconds, you need to provide some kind of progress feedback that indicates how long the action will take. This is typically done using a progress bar.

Loading...

In some cases, it may make sense to also tell the user what specific thing the computer is currently working on. This is especially important if it helps the user understand why he has to wait. For example, if the user is uploading a movie from a movie-editing tool, the task typically has two stages. First, the movie needs to be rendered and encoded.

Second, it needs to be uploaded. You could add some short explanatory text or even a little animation representing the active task near the progress bar, giving the user some indication of what is currently going on. Telling the user which stage the application is in provides an explanation for why the whole process is taking so long and can help make him comfortable with the idea of having to wait.

If a task takes a long time, it's likely that people will focus on something else. Eventually, they may forget that the task is running at all. You can use audio feedback to indicate that the task is done; that way, people will know even if they're paying attention to something else.

23.3 Perceived Speed

Speed is perception. People are not going to measure your product's response time with stopwatches. What *really* counts isn't how long an action takes in seconds and milliseconds but how your users perceive your product's speed.

One thing you can do to improve speed perception is to start showing partial results as soon as possible. If you are implementing a user interface for a search system, don't wait for the search to finish before you show the results to the user. Instead, start showing search results as soon as you start finding them.

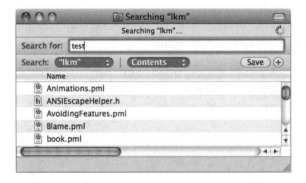

Another way of improving speed perception is to make sure that actions that take a long time don't block your product's user interface. If your users can do something else instead of being forced to wait for a process to finish, they are less likely to notice how long the process takes.

Here's a final idea. Adding simple ripple effects that move counter to the direction of a progress bar can make the progress bar appear to move faster.[3]

PROGRESS BAR MOVES TO THE RIGHT...

Trash

Emptying the Trash...

Items to delete: 4

RIPPLES ON PROGRESS BAR SHOULD MOVE TO THE LEFT

23.4 Slowing Down

Slow products are annoying, but the opposite can also be true. Sometimes, things can be too fast. A typical example of this is scrolling. If your application scrolls too quickly, users overshoot their target. It often makes sense to artificially slow down your product so people can keep up with it.

A similar problem once occurred to me when I was working on Appway, a business process management system. Its process editor includes a Save feature that allows users to manually save changes to a process. When people used the editor and wanted to save their changes, they often repeatedly clicked the Save button rather than just clicking once and sometimes complained that it did not work properly.

It turned out that the application was simply too fast for them. Saving the workflow took only a fraction of a second. The absence of a progress indicator meant users had no obvious feedback indicating that the document had actually been saved, but saving a document felt so important to them that they expected to see something reasonably substantial happen when they clicked the button. The solution was to throw up a "fake" progress indicator that took about half a second to finish.

---

3. As shown here: http://www.newscientist.com/blogs/nstv/2010/12/best-videos-of-2010-progress-bar-illusion.html.

This reassured users that something substantial had happened. User experience consultant Harry Brignull refers to a similar story[4] about coin-counting machines. Supposedly, the machines counted coins so quickly that customers did not trust that they could have counted them correctly. To fix this user experience problem, the manufacturer changed the machines to display the results more slowly and added speakers to produce coin-counting sounds while the machines waited for the counter to get to the final amount. As a result, people felt that the machine put the proper effort into counting their money and trusted the result.

Takeaway Points

- Responsiveness and speed are extremely important properties of your products. Usability tests don't always reveal these kinds of problems.

- To be perceived as instant, actions should take less than 0.1s.

- Actions taking more than a second should show some kind of indicator that the application is working. This should appear where the user's focus is.

- Perceived speed is more important than actual speed. Sometimes, tricks can help you make your product *feel* faster.

- It's possible for things to happen *too* fast. In some cases, artificially limiting the speed of some features of your product can improve the user experience.

---

4. View the article at http://www.90percentofeverything.com/2010/12/16/adding-delays-to-increase-perceived-value-does-it-work/.

Further Reading

Jakob Nielsen's essay on response time is an invaluable source of information on this topic.[5]

Bruce Tognazzini talks about latency in his list "First Principles of Interaction Design."[6]

---

5. Read it at http://www.useit.com/papers/responsetime.html.
6. At http://www.asktog.com/basics/firstPrinciples.html.

Chapter 24

Avoiding Features

Product design is a never-ending race. To avoid being overtaken by competitors, you need to keep running and running—or, in our case, designing and designing. But this race has no clear finish line; your product is never really "done." At most, it simply becomes a bit less unfinished with each new release. This is the best we can hope for.

Like a species of shark that needs to keep moving in order to supply its gills with oxygenated water, if your product remains stagnant for too long, it dies. This is a problem, because it means you must constantly add new things. As a result, most products are forever acquiring new features, without much thought going into it.

As you add new features, your product can quickly grow from its original state—an elegant solution to a well-defined problem—into a byzantine mess of unrelated functions. It may be that, on the whole, the product solves a number of problems, but chances are that it solves most of them poorly. The fact that a product could (in theory) solve many problems is meaningless if its users have trouble figuring out how to find the features that solve *their particular problem.*

Although those users with existing knowledge of your product may be able to keep up with all of the features, you are essentially closing the door for new users who do not have the benefit of starting out with a simple product and learning how to use all of the additional features as they appear.

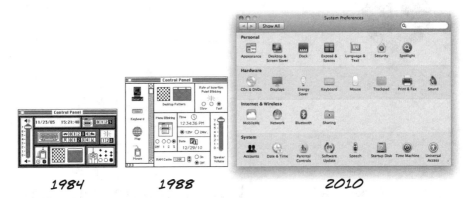

1984   *1988*   *2010*

What's worse, your existing users, who grow alongside your product, will turn into advanced users, which means they will continue to push you to add more advanced features. If you do this, your customer base will skew even more toward advanced users.[1] It's a vicious cycle.

How do you manage product growth and avoid adding countless new features?

24.1 Remember the User's Goals

Think about what your users want to achieve with your product. Does the new feature help them produce better results? Does it allow them to reach new goals? Does it make the product easier to use? As Kathy Sierra puts it,[2] "People are not into your tool, they are into what the tool enables."

24.2 The Five Whys

When receiving user feedback, your first task is to find out what exactly the user is trying to achieve. Often, the solution to the user's problem can be found without adding new functionality to your product.

One process you can use to find the root cause of a problem is "The Five Whys." According to legend, this approach was originally developed by Sakichi Toyoda, the founder of Toyota Industries. It works pretty well when trying to find out what caused somebody to send in a particular feature request: you simply keep asking "why?" (or something along

---

1. Chris Clark mentions this problem at http://releasecandidateone.com/236:crotchety_old_power_users.
2. You can read more of her writing at http://headrush.typepad.com.

those lines that sounds a little less unfriendly) until you figure out what prompted your users to think they needed an additional feature. You don't have to ask exactly five times. Sometimes, fewer times does the trick, and sometimes, more asking is required to get to the bottom of the issue.

Let's look at an example of how this works:

User: *Hey, it would be awesome if you could add a feature where BizTwit regularly saves a copy of the message I'm currently writing.*

Designer: *That sounds interesting. If it is OK with you, I'd like to ask you a few questions to make sure I understand how you would use this new feature. This way, I can do the best possible job of making the feature as useful to you as possible, if I decide to add it to the product.*

Can I ask you what you would use this feature for?

User: *Well, I often need to go back to an earlier version of a message I'm writing.*

Designer: *Yes, I see how this could be useful. Is there a specific purpose for which you want to use earlier versions of your documents?*

User: *I sometimes make changes to messages that I am unhappy with. If I had earlier versions, I could just copy parts of one into my message.*

Designer: *There is already an Undo feature in the product that should allow you to reverse unwanted changes. Does that not work for you?*

User: *It usually works, I guess, but every time I save my draft of the message I'm writing, for some reason I can't undo past that point. Also, your product sometimes crashes when I try to paste formatted text into a message, so I've made it a habit to save as often as possible, every few minutes, which means that the Undo command often doesn't work properly.*

In this example, the user's initial request was for a versioning feature. But it turns out that the actual root cause of her request was one bug in BizTwit that prevented the Undo command from undoing saved changes and another bug that caused it to crash regularly. Instead of adding new features to the product, the user's problem can be solved by fixing these two bugs.

Always try to see the bigger picture. What do people *really* want? What actual problem are they trying to solve with the feature they've asked you to add to your product?

24.3 Instead of Adding a New Feature, Make an Existing Feature More Usable

If a lot of feature requests are coming in that can be solved using your product's existing feature set, chances are you should invest time into fixing your existing features, rather than creating new ones. Similarly, if your product has a neat feature that nobody seems to know about or use, it's generally a good idea to investigate how you can improve that feature.

Essentially, rather than adding a completely new feature, the goal is to make an existing feature available to more of your users. By taking this approach, you're actually simplifying your product—not making it more complex. At the same time, you're essentially adding functionality for all of the people who didn't realize the feature even existed or who didn't know how to use it.

It's also possible that a new feature might replace an existing feature. When considering a new feature, you should ask yourself whether it makes an already existing feature obsolete. An argument in favor of implementing the new feature is if you can remove an existing feature because the new feature provides the same or similar functionality but in a much better, easier-to-use way.

24.4 Solve Several Problems with One Change

Instead of adding new features individually, it often makes sense to consider similar (or even seemingly unrelated) features as part of one problem to solve.

For example, consider these feature requests for a word processor:

User 1: *I often write letters, so it would be really useful if I could insert my letterhead automatically into my documents.*

User 2: *I would like a way to change the default font.*

User 3: *Is there some way I can change the footer style on several documents at the same time?*

Ostensibly, these requests don't have much in common. However, they could all be satisfied by implementing a templating system. Giving people the option to create their text document from a set of templates solves a number of different user requests.

24.5 Consider the Cost

Every new feature has both a value and a cost. To properly evaluate the impact a new feature will have, it's important to consider both aspects.

A feature's value is usually quite obvious—namely, what it allows your users to do.

But the cost of adding a new feature to your product might not be readily apparent: the additional complexity might take a toll on people who aren't interested in using the feature. Adding a new feature to your product prevents you from working on other things, and having it in your product might slow down future progress because you have to maintain yet another feature. A feature that relies on systems you can't control, or that is error-prone for other reasons, might lead to rising costs in user support.

Consider the cost of a feature, rather than just its benefits.

24.6 Make It Invisible

If you can add a useful feature in a way that does not add to the user's "cognitive load," do it. Invisible features are the best, because they make your product better without making it more complex. Can you improve text rendering so documents created with your product look better than documents created with your competitor's product? If you add HTTPS support to your web application, can you just switch your users to HTTPS and make them more secure without forcing them to enable the new feature manually?

These features make your product better, but people don't have to consciously deal with them.

24.7 Provide an API and a Plug-in Architecture

You don't have to implement every feature on your own. Often, it makes sense to let others chip in and help. Twitter, for example, started out with an extremely simple service. But its API[3] allowed other developers to step in and create a whole ecosystem of great products that revolve around Twitter. Photoshop is another great example. Although

---

3. An application programming interface (API) allows developers to create applications that interact with your product.

Adobe has added an incredible number of features to Photoshop, it couldn't possibly implement every feature that its customers might want. Instead, Adobe allows third-party developers to create plug-ins for Photoshop, thus broadening the market for the product without investing any of their own money or making Photoshop even more complex than it already is.

By adding an API and a plug-in architecture, you can avoid implementing features that will help only part of your audience, leaving that to other developers. You could even use your own plug-in architecture to implement new features yourself.

24.8   Listen to Your Users

It's important to keep in mind that you are not your users. At most, you are *one* of your users; one user typically constitutes a minority of all users. You may think that a new feature sounds extremely useful, but chances are that many of your users disagree. This disconnect is sometimes called the *internal-audience problem*: the people who design and implement solutions do so for people who are like them, rather than for people who are like their actual customers.

You know too much about how your product works and too little about how people use it. Your users, on the other hand, know a lot about how they use your product but very little about how it works.

It's often tempting to add what amounts to useless complexity. You understand how your product works, so it doesn't seem complex *to you.*

It is always smart to run new feature ideas by your users. Note that people are often reluctant to provide negative feedback, so it's important to show them simple draft sketches, rather than actual implementations. This gives the impression that you're not yet heavily invested in the idea so they are less reluctant to burst your bubble. It also helps to explicitly ask for negative feedback, saying, for example, "Tell me three things you don't like about this new feature."

You might be surprised by your users' reactions—I know I've been surprised whenever someone has told me that a proposed new feature sounded really cool but that they saw no reason to ever use it. ▶

24.9 But Don't Listen to Your Users Too Much

Writing about the people who still tell him that the Mac version of Microsoft Word 5.1 was the perfect version of the product,[4] Microsoft's Rick Schaut points out that if you ask these same people what they really want in a word processor, they almost always require at least one unusual, additional feature. It's not just "Word 5.1," it's "Word 5.1 plus one feature." But everybody has a different "plus one" feature, and if you add all of these additional features, Rick notes, you eventually arrive at the feature set of a modern Word version.

When your users envision your product, they envision a product that is tailor-made for them, a product where the features the product offers are exactly the features they use. This often includes one or two specific, quirky features that almost nobody else uses.

If you add most of the "I just need one unusual feature" requests, you end up with a product where most features are unusual and very few features are used by many people. This works well for Microsoft, but it's not necessarily a good idea for your product.

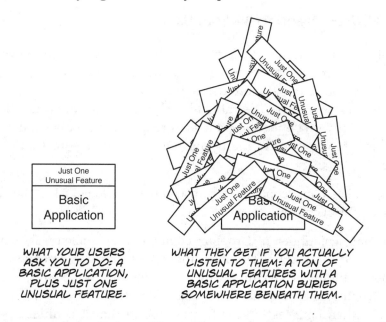

WHAT YOUR USERS ASK YOU TO DO: A BASIC APPLICATION, PLUS JUST ONE UNUSUAL FEATURE.

WHAT THEY GET IF YOU ACTUALLY LISTEN TO THEM: A TON OF UNUSUAL FEATURES WITH A BASIC APPLICATION BURIED SOMEWHERE BENEATH THEM.

Recent research by Debora Viana Thompson, Rebecca W. Hamilton, and Roland T. Rust has shown that, when asked, most users say that

---

4. You can read Rick Schaut's entire essay here: http://blogs.msdn.com/rick_schaut/archive/2004/06/18/159325.aspx.

they prefer products with more features. People think that they might want to use these features in the future, even if they see no immediate need for them.[5] However, when the same people get around to using the product they said they wanted, they wind up being frustrated by all the features. They thought they would prefer a product with more, but they end up being happier with fewer, even if a simplified product doesn't provide all the features they think they might want to use in the future. People who pick up your product because it offers the most features quickly turn into a liability when they end up being unhappy with their purchase.

Similarly, in *The Paradox of Choice* [Sch05], Barry Schwartz notes that as the number of choices people have goes up, the satisfaction they derive from their choice goes *down*. Giving people more things to do may make them less happy.

If you want satisfied, happy customers who will recommend your product to their friends, be careful when adding new features.

24.10   Not All Users Need to Be Your Users

Finally, it's important to keep in mind that you don't have to own 100 percent of your market. It's true that adding more features to your product allows you to target more users, but doing so comes at a cost. Your product becomes more desirable to the people who would not be able to use it if it didn't offer a specific feature. However, it also makes your product less desirable to the people who have no use for that specific feature.

It's OK to let some people go to your competitors to get what they need; you can't be everything to everybody.

Isaac Hall, cofounder of Dropbox competitor Syncplicity, writes that he ran into the CEO of Dropbox and asked him why Dropbox didn't support multifolder synchronization. The answer,[6] Hall says, explains why Dropbox is so popular. Dropbox added multifolder support early on but, when beta testing the feature, found that it confused people.

---

5. You can read more about their research here: http://hbr.org/2006/02/defeating-feature-fatigue/ar/1.

6. Read his full answer at http://www.quora.com/Dropbox/Why-is-Dropbox-more-popular-than-other-programs-with-similar-functionality.

Dropbox couldn't get the user interface right. Because it was too hard to use, Dropbox removed the feature.

Not having that particular feature may have cost Dropbox a few customers, but this less-is-more philosophy made Dropbox incredibly easy to use and, consequently, the most popular application of its kind.

Being feature-rich comes at a cost. Users are more enthusiastic about a product that does one thing incredibly well than a product that does everything kind of OK.

In their book *Rework* [FH10], the people from 37signals explain that "we're willing to lose some customers if it means that others love our products intensely. That's our line in the sand."

Takeaway Points

- Adding more features can make your product more desirable to people who need those features but less desirable to the people who don't. Usually, for any given feature, the second group is the larger one.

- Use "The Five Whys" to evaluate user feedback and find the root of the problem.

- Instead of adding a new feature, improve an existing one.

- Try to add features that solve several problems at once and perhaps allow you to remove existing features from your product.

- Consider the cost of a new feature as well as its benefits.

- Focus on features that make your product better without increasing user interface complexity.

- Provide an API and a plug-in architecture. Implement niche features as plug-ins, or leave them to third-party developers.

- Do proper user research before adding new features to find out whether people really need the feature and what they need it for.

- If you implement every "I just need this one feature" request, you end up with a product where most features are unpopular.

- Accept that not every person needs to be your customer.

Further Reading

Kathy Sierra's blog has many, many of articles on this topic.[7] *The Paradox of Choice* [Sch05] by Barry Schwartz is also worth reading, as is the research by Debora Viana Thompson, Rebecca W. Hamilton, and Roland T. Rust.[8]

On his blog, Mint.com lead designer Jason Putorti recommends some tests for deciding which features to implement.[9]

Brent Simmons, developer of the popular Mac RSS application Net-NewsWire, writes about how seemingly simple features can have a lot of hidden complexity.[10]

---

7. Read it at http://headrush.typepad.com.
8. You can read about it at http://hbr.org/2006/02/defeating-feature-fatigue/ar/1.
9. Read it at http://jasonputorti.com/post/229492382/how-to-avoid-feature-creep/.
10. At http://inessential.com/2009/07/30/anatomy_of_a_feature.

Chapter 25

Removing Features

The previous chapter was about avoiding feature creep—how to make sure you don't overload your product, and your users, with too many features. But you might find yourself in situations where it's not about refraining from adding unnecessary features anymore. What you really need to do is get rid of some of your existing features.

You might have reached this point for a number of reasons. Maybe your technology has become outdated. A decade ago it might have been absolutely reasonable to add FTP syncing to your application, but today there are better ways, and the FTP feature has become a liability. Perhaps you added a feature because the backend supported it and it was free for you to add, but feedback shows that few people use it now. Or maybe you inherited a product from somebody who wasn't quite as selective as you are about adding features.

No matter how you got there, you are now in the unfortunate and unpopular position of having to take away features from your users. Having to tell your users that you are removing a feature is much harder than telling them that you are not going to implement something. Even your product's most pointless feature will be *someone's* favorite. The fact is, removing any feature will make some of your customers really unhappy.

But keeping unnecessary features in your product sends the message that you don't really care. Soon, these features start piling up, and eventually, your product changes from a small, elegant solution that people love into an unwieldy mess of outdated features that most people don't care to understand.

This chapter contains some ideas that might help you remove features from your product.

25.1 Do the Research

Before deciding to remove a feature, make sure you have all the data. Do you know how many of your customers use that particular feature?

The best approach is to get usage data from your customers. Add a "Send anonymous usage statistics" checkbox to your settings, and ask your users whether they would like to opt in.

☑ Help improve BizTwit by automatically sending
  anonymous usage statistics.

If you can't get hard data, you can ask your users how they use your product. Polling your users can lead to interesting results. You should make sure to give people the option of also sending in a written reply to your poll, detailing exactly how they use your product.

That's what Mac and iOS developer Manton Reece did for his Mac app Wii Transfer.[1] As a result of the survey he ran on his users, he decided to remove a feature from his app. He wrote:[2]

> I eventually did remove a feature, and the survey to customers served as a nice sanity check that the feature wasn't heavily used. The interesting part, to me, is that the feature I removed was the entire 1.0 product for Wii Transfer. Literally everything that 1.0 did is now gone.

> It's been two weeks so far without any complaints. I like to think that it removes a distraction from the app—one less place in the app that could lead the customer down the wrong path. And hopefully it'll eliminate a tiny part of my support load, as no one can ask me questions or have problems with that feature again!

Eventually, you should have a pretty good idea of the popularity of your features. Should the results show that a feature is particularly unpopular and therefore a good candidate for removal, you should ask yourself the following:

- If only a few of my users use this feature, is it because the feature was intentionally designed that way? Is it very important but only rarely used because of its nature?

---

1. See his survey results at http://www.manton.org/2009/07/wii_transfer_survey.html.
2. Read what he had to say at http://www.manton.org/2010/02/removing.html.

- Do few people use the feature because the user interface is incomprehensible, hidden, or poorly named? Would people use it more often if they knew how?

- Do people largely ignore this feature because it is simply unnecessary?

Low usage data doesn't necessarily mean you should or even can cut a feature. For example, most users of a backup application very rarely use the restore function. Obviously, that doesn't mean it's OK to cut the restore function from your backup app.

Low usage is one indicator that something might be wrong. Use the data to help you come to a conclusion, but rely on your knowledge and experience to decide which features to remove, which to replace with better solutions, and which to keep.

There's more about collecting data in Chapter 34, *Collecting Usage Data*, on page 291.

25.2 Inform Your Users

Before you yank a feature, it's always best to tell your users what you intend to do and ask for their input on your decision. It's entirely possible that you missed something when deciding which features to cut. Identify the features you intend to cut, and explain why you intend to cut them.

Don't let people vote on which features to cut (a vote doesn't tell you anything about *why* people voted the way they did, and if you have to override the results, you're inviting a user revolt), but do take their opinions and feedback into account. These people are the ones who actually use your product, so they might have useful insights into how your product is being used in the real world—insights that you might have missed.

25.3 Provide Alternatives

Only a few of your customers might use a particular feature; however, it's possible that they really rely on it. So, it's always a good idea to try to provide some kind of alternative. For example, you could contact somebody who creates a product that could replace the feature you're removing and try to negotiate a discount for your existing users.

When the people at Bohemian Coding[3] wanted to remove the bitmap features from their application DrawIt, they contacted Flying Meat's Gus Mueller.[4] They were able to work out a deal, and every DrawIt customer got a free copy of Flying Meat's image editor Acorn. Bohemian Coding's Pieter Omvlee told me:

> The feedback I got was mixed. Some people were happy with the improvements I made to the vector part in the same update and said they never used the bitmap part anyway. Some complained because they only used the bitmap part, but I could point them to Acorn. Lastly, I received some complaints from people who really liked the combination of both vector and bitmap in one app. Fortunately, only very few people felt that way. In general, it all went well, and I think that's for a big part thanks to Gus Mueller's generous offer.

If you can't find a similar solution, another option would be to spin the feature off into its own independent, small utility. However, this sets the expectation that you will support this utility at least at a basic level. If you aren't ready for that responsibility, don't pick this option.

If none of these options works for you, you can also consider keeping the old version of your product available for a time so that everybody who relies on its unique features has the opportunity to download it again and, if necessary, create a local backup copy for later use.

25.4 It's Your Product

The most important point is to remember that *you* are responsible for your product. Your customers can switch to another product if yours doesn't suit them anymore. You can't. You customers don't know how popular a feature is. You do. Your customers don't know how much work it is to support a feature and to keep it running. You do.

You are stuck with your product, so you should make sure it remains something you want to work on and can be proud of.

---

3. Find them at http://www.bohemiancoding.com.
4. Flying Meat is at http://flyingmeat.com.

Takeaway Points

- Sometimes, you have to remove features from an existing product. This is never an easy decision.

- Get usage data to find out how people use your product.

- If you're considering removing a feature, get feedback from your users before going ahead with your decision.

- Try to provide alternatives.

Further Reading

Mac developer Brent Simmons has written repeatedly about removing features.[5]

On his blog, product manager Jeff Lash tells you not to be afraid of removing features.[6]

---

5. Here's a good essay on the topic: http://inessential.com/2008/07/22/more_about_deleting_features.

6. Read his article at http://www.goodproductmanager.com/2008/02/17/do-not-be-afraid-to-remove-features/.

Chapter 26

Learning from Video Games

We want to make our products fun. But how? A lot of different things can be fun. For example, some people think that being scared is fun. They like riding roller coasters and visiting haunted houses. Obviously, in most cases, we can't make our product more fun by making it scarier. Instead, the kind of fun we most typically experience when we use applications and websites is the one associated with what psychology professor Mihály Csíkszentmihályi calls *flow*.

26.1 What's Fun?

Fortunately, there is a lot of great research on the psychology of this kind of fun, and the results are rather consistent. In his book *Flow: The Psychology of Optimal Experience* [Csi02], Mihály Csíkszentmihályi explains that people experience fun when they have a goal, a way of measuring progress toward that goal, constant feedback on their success, and skills that match the challenge, neither exceeding it nor falling short. He notes that "by far the overwhelming proportion of optimal experiences are reported to occur within sequences of activities that are goal-directed and bounded by rules—activities that require the investment of psychic energy, and that could not be done without the appropriate skills."

Similarly, in his book *A Theory of Fun for Game Design* [Kos04], Raph Koster comes to the conclusion that people who play video games have fun when they are able to master tasks; the game presents what appear to be difficult problems that make sense to the player in the context of the game's world. The player's ability to solve these problems is what makes the game fun. Koster writes:

Fun is all about our brains feeling good—the release of endorphins into our system. (...) One of the subtlest releases of chemicals is at that moment of triumph when we learn something or master a task. This almost always causes us to break out into a smile. After all, it is important to the survival of the species that we learn—therefore our bodies reward us for it with pleasure. There are many ways we find fun in games, but this is the most important.

So, let's quickly recap these points. People experience fun when the following three criteria are met:

- They have a meaningful challenge or task.

- They have a way of measuring whether they are getting closer to mastering that challenge.

- They have the ability to master that challenge.

To be an actual challenge, the user's task can't feel too easy, because that's boring. On the other hand, the task can't be too hard; otherwise, it will be stressful. People experience fun when their skill level matches the challenge.

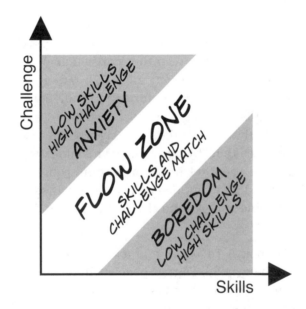

The mechanism that makes a video game fun is very similar to the one that makes your application or website fun.

26.2 Why Your Product Is Not Like a Game

What we've discussed so far applies both to games and to your product. However, there are two important differences between them: where tasks come from and who sets the tasks' difficulties.

Games Need to Provide Tasks; Your Product Doesn't

When playing a game, the game itself provides the tasks. With your product, the user provides the tasks.

I sometimes hear user interface designers say something like:

> Games make the player do unnecessary tasks, such as collecting coins. But people have fun playing games. So, it's probably OK for my application to make the user do unnecessary tasks; they'll still have fun using my product.

This rationalization seems to offer some justification for overly complicated design. Overly complicated design provides more things for the user to do. Games also provide things for the player to do: evil Bowser has kidnapped the princess, and the player needs to get her back by jumping on turtles.

Your product, however, is different from a game. You don't have to provide any tasks. The *user* will provide the tasks—for example, creating a movie or a presentation or finding a specific piece of information. The application or website is the tool used for accomplishing these tasks.

Games Need to Control the Difficulty; Your Product Doesn't

In a game, the designer controls the difficulty of the task. With your product, the user controls the difficulty of the task.

This might sound like an inconsequential difference, but it affects how you should design your product. Here's something I've heard designers say about difficulty:

> Games can be difficult to play, but people still have fun playing them. So, it's OK to make my application difficult to use. That'll just make it more fun for my users.

An application or website that is hard to use does not present a *meaningful* challenge if the difficulty is unrelated to the actual task. It merely makes the user feel stupid and gives him the impression that he is not completely in control.

You don't need to make a task harder for your users. If a user doesn't feel sufficiently challenged by her task, *she* will make it harder. She will add more complex transitions and titles to her movie. She will create a beautiful letterhead for her letter. She will learn how to use layer effects when editing photographs.

There's an additional issue with the idea that we should emulate games by making our products more difficult to use. As it turns out, most modern games aren't actually difficult; they are specifically and carefully designed to merely *give the impression* of being hard.

At the beginning of Nintendo's seminal game Super Metroid, the heroine of the game is attacked by a huge monster. The fight seems impossible, and it takes all of the player's skill to dodge the monster's attacks while still fighting back. Just when her energy is about to run out and she thinks she's done for, the monster gives up and flees. Wow, that was hard! A lesser player wouldn't have made it!

Actually, the monster always gives up seconds before the player dies. Anyone would have made it. It just *feels* like it was a nearly insurmountable challenge.

In an article called "Hot Failure: Tuning Gameplay With Simple Player Metrics,"[1] game developer Chris Pruett describes the system he uses to balance the difficulty of his Android game Replica Island.[2] To test his game, he released to players a version that reported where the players died. From this data, he created a heat map, shown in Figure 26.1, on the facing page, that showed where in each level people died the most. Brighter colors indicate areas where people died more often.

Using the heat map, he eliminated areas that were too difficult or caused deaths that were unfair to the player (such as pits that were invisible during a jump).

Additionally, his game employs a dynamic difficulty-adjustment system that allows him to decrease the difficulty for players who die more often. He explains:

> This system secretly increases the player's life and flight power after a certain number of consecutive deaths.

---

1. Read it at http://www.gamasutra.com/view/feature/6155/hot_failure_tuning_gameplay_with_ .php.
2. Find out more at http://replicaisland.net.

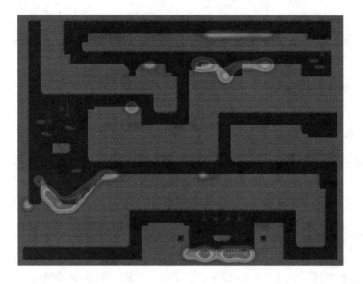

Figure 26.1: HEAT MAP SHOWING WHERE CHARACTERS DIED IN REPLICA ISLAND

Many modern games use systems like these. When I talked to Bruce Oberg, co-owner of Sucker Punch, a game studio that developed titles like inFamous and the Sly Cooper series, he told me the following:[3]

> We want people to make progress at a steady pace; we don't want them to die all the time. If we have a recording of where everyone died and we see that everyone's dying in one spot, maybe we need to change that spot. (...)

> Basically, we want everyone to be able to have a good time playing the game, whether you're high-skilled or low-skilled. We want everyone to be able to make progress and have fun.

Modern games are not fun because they are hard. They are fun because a lot of testing goes into making them appear to be challenging, while still allowing players to overcome any problem thrown at them. Constantly failing is not fun, but mastering challenges that *seem* hard is.

You can apply this to your product. People really love apps like Garage Band for the iPad, because it takes something that is hard (creating

3. You can read the whole interview at http://wisegamers.ch/artikel/417/gamescom_interview_bruce_oberg_infamous_2/. Scroll down for the original English transcript of the interview.

music that sounds good) and makes it possible for people to actually achieve great results. It's the same concept found in games: take a challenge that seems hard and allow people to master it.

But that's not all we can learn from games.

26.3 What We Can Learn from Games

Game designers have decades of experience in making things that are fun. If we keep in mind how games are different from our own products, user interface designers can learn a lot from how games are designed.

Progress

In his paper "Heuristics for Designing Enjoyable User Interfaces: Lessons from Computer Games,"[4] Thomas W. Malone notes:

> For both toys and tools, however, users need some kind of performance feedback to know how well they are achieving their goals. In games, this performance feedback is provided by things like the missing bricks in Breakout and the position of the incorrect arrows on the number line in Darts. There may be similar ways to incorporate performance feedback for the external task into tools. For example, the Writer's Workbench developed at Bell Laboratories measures various stylistic features of manuscripts such as word length, sentence length, percentage of sentences using passive voice, and so forth. These rudimentary kinds of performance feedback for the external goal of producing a readable manuscript may enhance the challenge of using the tool.

In other words, measuring progress and providing feedback about that progress makes an activity more fun.

Video games like Capcom's Ghosts 'n Goblins provide an overview map. After every world the player masters, the game's knight progresses a bit further. This shows the player's task, and it also gives constant feedback on her progress. EpicWin[5] is an iPhone tasklist app that uses the same metaphor to show the user's progress at ticking items off the tasklist.

---

4. Find it at http://portal.acm.org/citation.cfm?id=801756.
5. Get the app at http://www.rexbox.co.uk/epicwin.

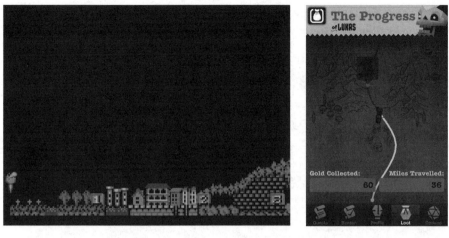

PROGRESS IN GHOSTS 'N GOBLINS   PROGRESS IN EPICWIN

Similarly, the online presentation program Prezi[6] shows a small progress bar that depicts how much of the tutorial the user has already gone through. Until she finishes the tutorial, this small badge is always visible, reminding her of her progress regardless of what she's currently doing.

I'm usually not the kind of person who goes through these tutorials, but this simple progress bar induced me to finish Prezi's tutorial.

6.   At http://prezi.com.

But progress doesn't have to be shown quite so literally. When creating a movie trailer in iMovie, progress is shown as a list of scenes the user has to set up.

Again, this shows the task and tells the user how far he's progressed.

Skill Growth

Another aspect of games design that can apply to product design in general is skill growth, or learning. Games get harder as the player's skill improves. Users of your product will create greater challenges for themselves on their own—if they can. To keep your users in the "flow zone" where the challenge and the user's skill match, your product needs to be able to grow alongside the user's skill.

A good example of this is the image-editing application Pixelmator.[7] At first its user interface seems deceptively simple. But as the user's skill grows, she can discover and learn new aspects of the application that are initially hidden.

PIXELMATOR SEEMS DECEPTIVELY SIMPLE AT FIRST...

...BUT AS THE USER'S SKILLS GROW, SO DOES THE APPLICATION.

---

7. Find out more at http://www.pixelmator.com.

To make it possible for people to increase their skills, your product needs depth. It should be easy for new users to learn, but it also needs to provide advanced features for advanced users to discover. Thomas W. Malone suggests making this progression an explicit part of your product:

> For example, a multilayered text editor could be designed so that beginning users need only a few simple commands and more advanced users can use more complicated and more powerful features of the system.

> The point here is that a multilayered system could not only help resolve the trade-off between simplicity and power, it could also enhance the challenge of using the system. Users could derive self-esteem and pleasure from successively mastering more and more advanced layers of the system, and this kind of pleasure might be more frequent if the layers are made an explicit part of the system.

Discovery and Rewards

Modern games often combine conveying progress with discovery. They do this using something called *achievements*. Microsoft's Xbox first introduced achievements, and other consoles have followed suit since then. Some systems call them trophies, challenges, or badges, or they use other names. By now, regular applications and websites have started using them.

Achievements are awards given out to users either for discovering a new aspect of a product or for doing something positive. They are used both to encourage experimentation, as well as to reward good behavior.

Audible's mobile app uses badges as well as usage statistics that show the user's progress to encourage people to listen to audiobooks more often. Figure 26.2, on the next page shows this. Audible also uses this data to assign different levels to users, from "newbie" to "master," further encouraging them to use the app more often.

Location-based social networking site Foursquare uses secret badges to encourage exploration: users are rewarded for figuring out unusual situations for using Foursquare.

Figure 26.2: PROGRESS FEEDBACK IN AUDIBLE

Question-and-answer site Stack Overflow[8] uses badges to encourage and reward good behavior. In addition to this, Stack Overflow awards points to users. It even has something called *user flair*, a piece of HTML their users can include in other sites to showcase their points and their badges.

Competition

Publicly showcasing points introduces another element commonly found in games: competition. Systems like Nike+[9] or RunKeeper[10] use scores and competition to get users to use their systems more regularly.

Twitter is another system that uses competition to engage users. Online community architecture expert Amy Jo Kim notes[11] that Twitter followers are less like a typical game score and more like a collection game.

Collecting Things

Trying to get followers in Twitter is very much like collecting baseball cards or playing Pokémon and collecting monsters.

8. At http://stackoverflow.com.
9. At http://nikeplus.com.
10. At http://runkeeper.com.
11. Watch her presentation on the topic at http://www.youtube.com/watch?v=ihUt-163gZI.

HIRO received TOTODILE!

GETTING A NEW POKÉMON...

...IS A BIT LIKE GETTING A NEW FOLLOWER ON TWITTER.

Many games and applications involve collecting things. iPhone owners tend to collect apps, for example, in part because the beautiful icons look valuable. It's fun to collect them, even if you don't use most of the apps on your phone.

Consistent Rules

Finally, good games have an easily understandable, static, consistent set of rules. If the rules change during the game, players feel cheated. The same applies to your product. For example, a tool should always have the same effect, regardless of where and to what it is being applied. When discussing how rules in video games work in *Rules of Play: Game Design Fundamentals* [SZ03], Katie Salen and Eric Zimmerman write:

> Rules are complete and lack any ambiguity. For example, if you were going to play a board game and it wasn't clear what to do when you landed on a particular space, that ambiguity would have to be cleared up in order to play. (...)

> Rules are repeatable from game to game and are portable between sets of different players.

If the rules governing your product are ambiguous or not repeatable, people will be unable to form correct mental models of how your product works.

These kinds of elements commonly found in games can make your product more fun to use and at the same time seduce your users into exploring your product, learning more, and behaving in a positive way.

26.4 Fun vs. Usability

Being usable is a bit like being edible.[12] A lot of things are edible, but being edible alone doesn't mean that something is also *delicious*. Similarly, a lot of things are usable, but that alone doesn't mean that we *want* to use them.

But while being edible is not sufficient for being delicious, it *is* required. Similarly, being usable is not sufficient for being fun, but it *is* required.

So although not every usable product is necessarily fun, every fun product has to be usable—otherwise it will just be frustrating.

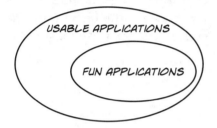

Actually, this may not be entirely true. There is a kind of product that can be unusable yet still fun: art.

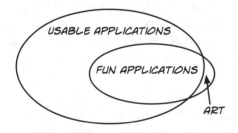

If challenging your user is your only goal, then you're basically creating art. This book is not about art; it is about applications and websites that humans use to reach specific goals.

Victor Papanek was particularly harsh in his book *Design for the Real World* [Pap05], when he wrote that "the cancerous growth of the creative individual expressing himself egocentrically at the expense of the spectator and/or consumer has spread from the arts, overrun most of

---

12. I didn't come up with the usable/edible comparison. I think I first saw it in Aarron Walter's essay "Emotional Interface Design: The Gateway to Passionate Users" at http://thinkvitamin.com/design/emotional-interface-design-the-gateway-to-passionate-users/.

the crafts, and finally reached into design." He lamented that many designers no longer have the good of the consumer in mind.

Making your product fun is a great goal, but fun can and should never come at the expense of usability.

Takeaway Points

- Merely being usable doesn't make your product fun. However, if your product isn't usable, it's probably not fun either.

- People experience fun if they have a meaningful challenge, a way of measuring their progress toward mastering that challenge, and the skills to master the challenge.

- Don't provide the challenge. Your users will do that for you.

- You don't need to set the difficulty. Your users will pick a challenge that is suitably difficult for them.

- Providing feedback on people's progress, and allowing them to grow along with the challenges they master, makes their experience more fun.

- Try to find a way to reward exploration and positive behavior.

Further Reading

Both *Flow: The Psychology of Optimal Experience* [Csi02] by Mihály Csíkszentmihályi and *A Theory of Fun for Game Design* [Kos04] by Raph Koster provide useful insight into what makes things fun. *Rules of Play: Game Design Fundamentals* [SZ03] by Katie Salen and Eric Zimmerman is also worth reading, as is Thomas W. Malone's paper "Heuristics for Designing Enjoyable User Interfaces,"[13]

Replica Island developer Chris Pruett writes a great blog about game design that sometimes touches on usability issues.[14]

On YouTube, there's an interesting presentation called "Putting the Fun in Functional: Applying Game Mechanics to Functional Software" by Shufflebrain CEO Amy Jo Kim.[15]

---

13. You can find it at http://portal.acm.org/citation.cfm?id=801756.
14. At http://replicaisland.blogspot.com.
15. Watch it at http://www.youtube.com/watch?v=ihUt-163gZI.

Part III

Implementation

Finally, we can start actually writing code!

We've done user research, looked at the problems people have, and figured out solutions for them. We've come up with designs, tested these designs, iterated, and made them as useful and usable as we possibly can.

At this point, you know what you want your product to look like. It's time to start actually creating it.

But this is not the end of your design process. In fact, it's only just starting. This is your opportunity to see your ideas in action, to find out whether they actually translate, and to change the direction of your product as early as possible should you find out that things aren't working.

Once your product is out in the wild, you'll start working on the next version. But how do you know what to improve and what to keep? Techniques like A/B testing and collecting usage data will help you make these decisions.

Chapter 27

Guerilla Usability Testing

Research	Design	Implementation

What's the Technique?

Usability testing typically involves inviting people to come to you. This creates a number of issues with scheduling, setting up simple test labs, and finding people who are willing to help you out as testers. You can circumvent these problems by doing one simple thing: going to people instead of having them come to you.

Why Is This a Good Idea?

You can do the best job possible planning and designing your product, but until you test it with real people, you don't know how well it works.[1] By going out and asking people to do simple tasks with our product, you can quickly identify areas where your design needs additional work and fix these areas while the code is still easy to change. If you don't invest time in finding out where your product's problems are now, you'll find out about them after you've launched it.

---

1. Expert opinions are no replacement for tests, as outlined in http://uxmyths.com/post/3086989914/myth-30-if-you-are-expert-you-dont-need-to-test-your-des.

> ### Why "Guerilla"?
>
> Ostensibly, it's called *guerilla usability testing* because, analogous to guerilla warfare, it circumvents many of the tools and techniques of traditional usability testing in favor of a simpler, less people-intensive approach that relies heavily on mobility and on the element of surprise. However, I think, it's mainly called guerilla usability testing because we programmers and designers like to make our jobs sound much more badass than they really are. Hi there, Code Ninjas and Rock-Star Designers!

Are There Any Prerequisites?

Yes. You need to have running code, and at least part of your user interface needs to be working. You also need to be able to run your product on a portable device, such as a notebook, cell phone, or iPad.

Guerilla Style

In a typical usability test, you invite people to come to you. You sit them down in front of a specially prepared workspace and ask them to do specific tasks while you record their actions. You then use the information gleaned from this interaction to improve your user interface.

This kind of testing involves quite a bit of preparation. You need to set up a workspace and devise a way of recording your testers; you need to find testers, schedule them, and maybe also pay them for their participation.

As usability testing became more widespread in the software community, people developed a set of techniques that circumvent all the process issues. This is commonly known as *guerilla usability testing*.

The main difference to a regular usability test is that we go to testers, instead of having them come to us.

27.1 How Often to Test

Guerilla testing is simple, requires almost no preparation, and can be done pretty much at any time. As a result, it's often a good idea to do guerilla testing when you actually have a question you need answered.

Say you've come up with a new way of letting people send messages in your Twitter app. You've implemented it, and it works. But will people get it? Don't guess. Instead, test.

27.2 Preparing for the Test

You should have your code running on a portable device. If your product relies on a service or is a service, prepare a guest login so people don't have to supply their email addresses or other personal data. If your code relies on an Internet connection, make sure this works where you're going. Check that your portable device's battery is full (keep a spare if possible and necessary).

You should also think about how to explain your product and come up with some simple tasks you want people to perform. Then, make sure your product is bug-free for these specific tasks; run through each task to see whether it works. Your aim is to find issues with the user interface, not bugs in your code.

If you want to, you can install something like Silverback or Jing[2] on the computer to record the user's actions.

27.3 How Do You Find Testers?

Simply visit a nearby café, look for people who don't appear to be buried in the newspaper or a laptop, and ask them whether they are interested in participating in a short usability test.

If you're working in an office building, it's often also possible to find people near the watercooler or people who are on a cigarette break. Unless you specifically want to find out how well a new feature works for existing users, you should try to avoid people who are overly familiar with your product, though.

27.4 How Many Testers

Since you don't have to schedule testers in a guerilla-style usability test, you can test with as many people as you need to until you feel you have a solid answer to your question. Three to five people is usually

---

2.   Find these products at http://silverbackapp.com and http://www.techsmith.com.

a good idea, but even a single tester often yields useful insights into potential issues with your design.

27.5 Running the Test

This is pretty simple. Find somebody willing to lend you five minutes. Explain what exactly you are doing, what the application does, and what the task is that you want the person to perform. If you intend to record the session, get the user's permission.

> We're working on a new Twitter app. You know what Twitter is? OK, great. We're working on this app, and in order to make sure that we got the design right, we want to see whether people can figure out how to use it, so we're testing our design. We're not testing *you*. Don't worry if you don't immediately get something, because that's exactly the kind of feedback we're looking for. It means we got something wrong with our design. If it's OK with you, we'll record this test so that we can go through it later. We won't publish the recording or anything like that. OK? Great. For the first test, we want to test our "new message" user interface. We're already logged in, and we just want to see whether people can figure out how to post Twitter messages. Feel free to talk during the test and explain what's going through your mind while you're using the app.

Then, sit back, observe, and take notes.

It's very likely that the tester will run into issues rather quickly. If you feel that he gets frustrated, intervene and either give a hint or stop the test. Otherwise, just keep your mouth shut.

I will talk more about how to run usability tests in later chapters, but for now, this is really all you need to know.

27.6 The Results

Once you've done this with a few people, you'll end up with a list of problems. Some of them will likely have occurred with more than just one person, and those are the ones you want to focus on first. Think about why people didn't get your design. Think about how to fix it. Implement a fix. Test again, until people get it.

Takeaway Points

- Usability testing can be simple yet still yield useful, actionable results.

- Run informal, guerilla-style usability tests whenever you need to test a change to the user interface.

- Prepare for the test by installing your product on a portable device, making sure it runs, and coming up with some simple tests.

- Go to a nearby café or find bored people in your office building. Ask them whether they're willing to spend five minutes helping you out.

- If you find a tester, explain how the test works, explain the premise of your product, and give him or her a simple task.

- Don't interrupt, unless you feel the tester is getting frustrated or is stuck. Take notes.

- After a few tests, you'll have a pretty good idea of where your user interface still has issues. Fix them, and then test again.

Chapter 28

Usability Testing

Research	Design	Implementation

What's the Technique?

In the chapter about paper prototypes (Chapter 11, *Paper Prototype Testing*, on page 97), you got a first taste of usability testing. Now, we want to do the same kinds of tests with real running code. In many ways, testing code is actually easier than testing paper prototypes, because you don't need to simulate a computer. Testing running applications also allows you much more freedom in how to perform a usability test. This chapter reviews some ideas covered previously, while also introducing a number of new concepts that are not applicable to paper prototypes.

This chapter focuses on explaining usability testing and on preparing for such a test. The next two chapters show how to run usability tests.

Some of the concepts introduced in this chapter work well for larger teams; others work well for smaller teams or even for people running the whole show on their own. There should be something for everybody in this chapter, even if not everything directly applies to your situation.

Why Is This a Good Idea?

If you want to know if your design *works*, you need to see whether people get it. You can do this using simple guerilla-style usability tests, shown in the previous chapter. Doing more extensive usability tests allows you to get better results.

Are There Any Prerequisites?

Yes. You need to have running code, and at least part of your user interface needs to be in working order.

You should also have read Chapter 11, *Paper Prototype Testing*, on page 97, since that chapter introduces concepts that are used in this and the following chapters and are not explained in detail again.

28.1 Usability Tests Don't Have to Be Expensive

The basic goal of a usability test is to observe users while they use your product or a prototype of your product and to thus identify areas of your user interface that might be difficult for people to navigate.

At the expensive end of the spectrum, this can mean hiring a usability expert, using a lab with two-way mirrors, planning the tests for weeks, running several tests with different testers, evaluating and discussing the results, and producing a report (possibly including videos) of all the problems and possible solutions.

At the very low end of the spectrum, you can simply take your laptop to a café and ask people to do some simple tasks with your product.

This chapter is about the middle ground: getting great results but still keeping your investment as low as possible.

Usability expert Jakob Nielsen notes[1] that even poor usability testing yields *some* useful results.

> Better usability methodology does lead to better results, at least on average. But the very best performance was recorded for a team that only scored 56% on compliance with best-practice usability methodology. And even teams with a 20–30% methodology (i.e., people who ran lousy studies) still found 1/4 of the product's serious usability problems.

---

1. Read more at http://www.useit.com/alertbox/discount-usability.html.

> Finding two serious usability problems in your design is well worth doing, particularly if you can do so after testing only three users—basically, an afternoon's work. (...)
>
> Bad user testing beats no user testing.

So, even doing poor tests is still a lot better than doing no tests at all. But with a few simple guidelines, we can do pretty good usability tests on a pretty small budget.

Many designers and developers don't do usability tests, because they think they don't have the time. Schedules are often tight, and spending even a day on something other than adding features to the product can mean that the project is now one day behind schedule.

The problem isn't that companies don't do good enough usability tests; it's that they don't test at all. This chapter isn't about running the best usability tests in the world—it's about running simple, cheap usability tests that still yield actionable results.

Here we'll take a look at different approaches to running usability tests. Some of them take more time than others, but you can get great results by investing even a few hours each week.

28.2 How Often to Test

Doing usability tests is like jogging: the more you do it, the easier it gets, and the better you become at it. Experts often recommend spending a few days each month, but setting aside a few days for usability testing can be hard to do—plus, if you do it only once a month, you won't get used to it. Between it being hard to reserve the time and you not getting used to it, you'll eventually stop doing tests altogether. So, I'm recommending a schedule that is a lot simpler: set aside half a day each week.

Soon you'll discover that the feedback cycle becomes addictive. Each week, you'll find new problems, and after you've come up with potential solutions, you'll be eager to see whether they work. Instead of waiting a month for the next test, it's much more exciting to see early on how our new design does—whether it solves the problem and whether it introduces new issues.

28.3 How Many Testers

Jakob Nielsen famously wrote that only five users are needed to find almost all the usability problems that a larger group would have found.[2] But even testing with such a small group takes a lot of work. Remember, our goal is to spend only half a day each week. Finding five testers, scheduling them so they can all come in on the same day, making sure somebody takes care of them if they come too early or too late, preparing all the paperwork five times—you can't do that in half a day.

Instead, you can get useful results by doing only one test with only one person each week.

Before covering the reasons for testing a single user, let's look at the arguments against it. Nielsen points out two of the disadvantages in his essay.

For one, you won't have anybody to compare that one person's results to. If you test with five people, it's easier to identify the pressing problems because more than one person will stumble upon them. Usually, you can make a reasonable guess as to the importance of a problem even when testing with only one person—but not always. However, that's not a huge problem; since you're going to test your design each week, you can just ignore problems if you're not sure they're urgent. The urgent problems will pop up again pretty soon.

Another problem is that your test preparation yields only one test result, which is especially problematic when running more extensive tests that require more preparation. A pretty big investment can result in a pretty meager outcome. If the plan is to run extensive usability tests that require a lot of preparation, then you need to test with more people. However, the kinds of tests introduced in this chapter do not require a lot of preparation.

So, there are disadvantages. Fortunately, testing with only one person also comes with clear advantages:

- It's easier to find testers since you have to find only one person at a time.

- It removes the overhead of trying to match the schedules of several people. It's usually easy to find a date that works for two people: the designer and the tester. Trying to get an additional person to

---

2. Read more about it here: http://www.useit.com/alertbox/20000319.html.

show up on the same day significantly increases the complexity. There's a reason why most people that we make appointments with have waiting rooms in their offices: scheduling people is hard, and it usually doesn't work out properly.

Even if you manage to find a date that works for everybody, you will run into problems during the test. With just one user, you can let the test session run a bit longer than expected; if somebody else is waiting, you'll have to stop the test when the allocated time is up.

- If you have only one user, it's easy to run the whole thing by your-self. If you have more than one user, you might need somebody who can help take care of the people who are waiting and who can welcome people who arrive while you're in a test.

Of course, given sufficient time, budget, and helpers, testing with three to five users offers more insight than testing with only one. But don't let a lack of time and budget prevent you from doing usability tests.

(Note that this restriction does not apply to guerilla-style usability tests introduced in the previous chapter. If you go to your testers instead of having them come to you, the issues with doing multiple tests essentially disappear. In those cases, I recommend doing more than one test at a time.)

28.4 Who Should Test Your Product?

Unless you are designing a product that targets a very specific group of people, who you invite for usability tests typically doesn't matter much. And even if you do target a particular group, it still makes sense to test with people from outside of that group as well. There are two reasons for this.

One is that people are surprisingly consistent in how they behave. If you have big problems in your design, you'll probably find them regardless of who you recruit as a tester.

The other is that even if you target specific groups of people, the members of this group may not be entirely homogeneous. Certain people will be more experienced with the topic than others. By intentionally picking testers from a specific group of people, you could miss design issues that affect less experienced members of the target group. For example, say you're testing a product used in a hospital. If you test only with people who already work at that hospital, you will get testers who are familiar with the hospital's processes and all the related medical jargon. However, new hires at that hospital may not be familiar with these things and may encounter usability issues that nobody in your test group did. So although it makes sense to include people from your target audience, you should never limit your testers to people from that group.

The same applies to existing users or people who have already participated in usability tests for a specific product. If you are designing an update to a product, it often makes sense to do a subset of your tests with people who have some familiarity with your product. These people may have learned specific behaviors that cause them to navigate your user interface differently from novice users. Focus on testing with people who don't bring any preconceptions to the test but do include some tests with existing users.

When it comes to testing, one thing that can matter a lot is cultural background. Symbols and colors mean different things to people from different parts of the world. For example, Japanese video games often indicate victory by displaying a huge red ring, which kind of looks like a stop sign. Although this indicates winning to Japanese audiences, it typically conveys the opposite message for Western audiences.

If you're expecting a lot of people with different cultural backgrounds to use your product, it makes sense to reflect this diversity with your testers.

And finally, although this book doesn't cover accessibility,[3] I will mention here that it often makes sense to do usability tests with people with poor eyesight, with older people, and generally with people who have disabilities that might affect how they can interact with your product. Doing this can help uncover accessibility issues that would have gone unnoticed.

The main point remains: don't spend too much time trying to recruit testers from a specific demographic. Most of the time, people will find the same kinds of usability issues, regardless of their background.

---

3. If you're looking for information on accessibility, check out Mark Pilgrim's "Dive Into Accessibility" at http://diveintoaccessibility.org, and Joe Clark's website at http://joeclark.org.

28.5 How to Find Testers

There are many different avenues you can use to find testers. Here are some ideas to get you started:[4]

- *Friends and relatives.* The easiest way to start recruiting testers is to ask friends and relatives. It's OK to reuse testers, but don't overdo it by using the same people over and over. I would advise against using workmates for testing, since they tend to have at least some level of insight into your product that normal users won't have.

- *Professional recruiting agencies.* There are professional recruiting agencies that will help you find testers, but definitely compare costs before committing to one of them. If you use agencies, you're a bit more likely to get people who regularly participate in such tests, which is not always what you're looking for.

- *Through your website.* You can also look for testers through your website; the downside there is that you're likely to get existing users of your product.

- *Through a local newspaper.* Simply putting an ad in a local newspaper often works out well. If you live near a university, they probably have a pinboard where you can advertise for testers.

Keep in mind that depending on how the testers were recruited, it might be necessary to compensate them.

28.6 Different Types of Tests

If you're doing a paper prototype, you're quite restricted in how you can run usability tests. The nature of a paper prototype pretty much dictates how you test it. Usability tests with actual running code are more forgiving, and there are different schools of thought on how they should be run. I'll roughly group them into three different types of tests: moderated tasks tests, unmoderated tasks tests, and free-form tests.

Since the type of test determines how you prepare for it, I'll introduce the different types of tests now and explain how to run each test later.

---

4. Christine Perfetti offers some additional ideas in this great video introduction to usability testing: http://uxideas.com/shows/usability_tests_nutshell/.

Moderated Tasks Tests

In a moderated tasks test, a facilitator moderates the tests and introduces the testers to different activities or tasks. The moderator then observes the testers while they work on the tasks. The facilitator stays with the testers during the test and interacts with them.

Unmoderated Tasks Tests

In an unmoderated tasks test, the facilitator introduces the user to the usability test and explains how everything works. The facilitator then gives the user a number of tasks on a sheet of paper and leaves the room. There is no or very little interaction between the tester and the facilitator in this type of test, which rules out any influence the facilitator might exert on the tester.

Free-Form Tests

In a free-form test, the testers are given no tasks. Instead, the facilitator encourages the testers to explore the product on their own and do the tasks that interest them. This works best if you've recruited people who already have an interest in your product (say, you've recruited testers via your website).

In reality, you will often combine aspects of different types of tests. For example, tests often start with the facilitator encouraging the tester to explore the product and then switch to task-based tests.

28.7 Preparing for the Test

Depending on the type of test you're running, there are different things you need to do to prepare. In most cases, you will need a computer. Uninstall all the extraneous stuff that might interrupt the test, such as virus protection software. Install the product in a way that will allow you to easily reset the system to its default state (you don't want to confuse testers with data other users have entered into the system). Install screen-recording software and a microphone. If you decide to record the user, you also need a webcam.

It's important to be as faithful to the product as possible. For example, you wouldn't test an iPad application running in a simulator on a computer if you could avoid it. Instead, you would get an iPad for the tests and run the application on the device itself. Otherwise, you would miss important problems—such as buttons that are too small to be touched with a finger but can be clicked using a mouse.

If you're going to test software that doesn't run on a computer, you might need a camera that allows you to record the session.

If you're running a moderated test, where the facilitator stays with the user, recording the session is not strictly necessary. It can sometimes be useful, though.

Preparing Tasks

For a task test (either unmoderated or moderated), you prepare by creating tasks for your testers. Think back to the very beginning of this book, where I talked about activities, and start with those. Focus on the most basic, most important activities of the product.

Programmers use code coverage as a measure of how much of their code is covered by a test suite. When testing user interfaces, you can't measure how much of the user interface is covered by a test quite so easily. But keep "user interface coverage" in mind as a goal. You want to design your tasks so that they touch on many different areas of your user interface.

Just like with designing tasks for paper prototypes (in Chapter 11, *Paper Prototype Testing*, on page 97—in fact, if you want to, you can probably reuse tasks from your paper prototype usability test), you don't want your tasks to be too prescriptive, so you should come up with a scenario that one of your users might actually experience. Describe the situation and the goal; do not describe any of the actual steps, and do not use words that are visible on-screen.

Prepare at least five tasks. For a moderated test, print each task on an individual piece of paper. Otherwise, print them all on one piece.

28.8 Running the Test

When running the actual test, you basically have two choices: either meet the tester in person or do a remote test. In most situations, doing remote usability tests is a lot simpler and cheaper, and it removes some of the issues that in-person tests have.

I recommend starting by doing a few in-person tests first to get a feel for how usability tests work and to get used to interacting with testers. This is a lot easier if you can sit right there next to them.

In the next chapter, I explain how to do in-person usability testing. The chapter after that will explain how remote testing works.

Takeaway Points

- If you want to know whether a user interface works, you need to test it with actual people.

- Usability tests don't have to be expensive or take a lot of time.

- You should do tests regularly; the more testing you do, the better you get at it, and shorter iterations make it easier to test user interface ideas to see whether they work.

- It's better to do smaller tests more often, rather than testing less often with more people. It's fairly simple to do one usability test with one (different!) person each week.

- You should test with novice users, as well as with people who already know how to use your product, because the two groups of people are likely to find different kinds of issues.

- When selecting testers, look for diverse cultural backgrounds. Don't forget to test accessibility issues as well.

- There are different kinds of usability tests, including moderated or unmoderated, and they can be task-based or free-form. Often, you will combine aspects of different types, first asking people to explore the product on their own and then switching to predefined tasks.

- If you're doing a task-based test, you need to prepare tasks before-hand. Tasks should not be too prescriptive, instead outlining a scenario and letting the user come up with a solution.

Chapter 29

Testing in Person

Research	Design	Implementation

What's the Technique?

Basically, you invite people, observe them while they use your product, and use information from these tests to make your product better.

Why Is This a Good Idea?

Doing usability tests of any kind gives you great insight into where your user interface has problems.

In addition to that, even if you want to focus on doing remote usability tests, you should start by doing some in-person tests to get a feel for how to run usability tests in general.

Are There Any Prerequisites?

Yes. You should read the previous chapter (Chapter 28, *Usability Testing*, on page 241) before reading this one.

29.1 Running the Test

At this point, let's assume you have found a tester and have prepared everything you need for the test. So, let's jump ahead to the actual test. The first thing you'll do is to introduce the tester to the test. Similar to the paper prototype test (back in Chapter 11, *Paper Prototype Testing*, on page 97), you give a short introduction to usability testing. Here's an example of what you might say:

> Hi, I'm Lukas. I work for BizTwit Inc. as a software designer. Today, we are testing a new version of our Twitter client BizTwit to see whether it works the way we intended. I want to make it very clear that we are testing the product, not you. This new product has never been used outside of our team here, so we are hoping to find problems by observing how people interact with it. So, don't worry if you get stuck or if something doesn't work as you expect it to—this is exactly the kind of feedback we are looking for! Feel free to say whatever is on your mind while interacting with the product. This will help us understand what you're thinking while you're using the product, which will make it easier for us to figure out how to improve the product. With your permission, I will record this session. This will help us see what we can do to fix problems with our design. We will never publish this recording in any way.

Depending on what type of test you're running, you also need to explain how the test itself is going to work.

What happens next depends on the type of test.

Moderated Tasks Tests

You start by explaining how moderated tasks tests work. This includes pointing out that while the tester is welcome to ask questions, you may not always be able to respond.

Then you turn to the computer (or device). Before you initiate the test, the computer should be in a neutral state. You start your product (if it's a website, by entering the URL into the browser's address bar; if it's an application, by launching the application) and hand over control to the tester.

The first thing you want to know is whether the tester can figure out what the product is, so you start the test by saying something along the lines of this:

> Take a look at this website. Feel free to scroll around. What kind of service do you think this website offers?

If the tester can't figure out what the website is all about, you've found your first usability problem.

Next, you want to know whether the tester can figure out how to use the product. To do this, you have prepared a number of tasks, each one on its own slip of paper. Say something like this:

> To test this website, I'm going to give you a task. I'll read it to you first, and then I'll give it to you in written form.

Then, hand the tester the piece of paper, shut up, and observe. It's OK to take notes, but try to avoid influencing the tester as much as possible. Don't make any noises. Definitely don't laugh. Sit back a little.

If the tester finishes a task, say something to acknowledge that fact, and move on to the next task. If, on the other hand, the tester looks unhappy or seems to be stuck, feel free to stop the current task. If you have to stop a task, you must avoid discouraging the tester; you can do that by ensuring he knows that the result of the test was helpful, even if he didn't finish the task. Say something like this:

> Yes, I had a hunch there might be a problem with this inter-face. I can see what we have to change now. I think we've learned all we can from this task—let's move on to the next one.

This is pretty much the only time you should interrupt the tester. If you have something that you'd like to talk to the tester about, you can make a note and ask after the task is done. If the tester has a question, just reply in a noncommittal way:

> How would you deal with this question at home, if you were alone?

After the last task, ask any remaining questions, ask the tester to give feedback on how the test was run, and thank your tester for his time. Make sure to end the test on a positive note.

Unmoderated Tasks Tests

Moderated tasks tests pose a bit of a problem. That problem is us. As facilitators, we have to stay with the tester during the test, so we are very likely to influence her in subtle ways, even if we do our best to avoid doing so (for more on this, see Chapter 31, *How Not to Test: Common Mistakes*, on page 271).

Facilitators can also make people anxious; we probably wouldn't like it if somebody was constantly looking over our shoulder and making notes about everything we are doing, either. Finally, testers often subconsciously try to please the facilitator, so if we're sitting right next to them, they will be more likely to keep trying until something works.

The simplest solution to this problem is to take ourselves out of the equation.

In an unmoderated tasks test, you introduce the tester to the test, hand him a list of tasks on a sheet of paper, start recording, and leave him alone.

The one obvious problem with this approach is that you can't easily intervene when the tester gets stuck. At the beginning of the test you need to explain what to do if this happens. Depending on your equipment, there are different ways of dealing with this. If you're doing the test in a usability lab furnished with a two-way mirror, the question is moot; you'll be observing the test, and you'll be able to communicate with the tester.

If you're doing the test in a place where communication is impossible, you could say something like this:

> If you get stuck on one of the tasks, don't worry. This is exactly the kind of thing we're looking for. Feel free to keep trying for a bit, but as soon as you get bored or think you can't figure out how to continue or that there's a problem

with the product, which is entirely possible because it's not finished yet, just move on to the next task. If for any reason this is not possible, I'm in the next room, so you can always come over if there is any kind of problem.

Besides minimizing the influence of moderators, unmoderated tests are less stressful for testers, because there is nobody sitting next to them, constantly looking over their shoulder.

Free-Form Tests

In a free-form test, there are no tasks. The goal is to see what people do if they don't already know what they are *supposed* to do. Just introduce the tester to the test, let him have at your product, and see what happens. I *do* recommend observing the test, either in person or from another room, in order to intervene when the tester gets bored or stuck. If that happens, suggest some tasks, and move to a task-based test.

Should You Encourage Talking?

It's a good idea to tell people that they are free to talk during the test if they want to, but you should take care not to force the issue. Some people just don't like to talk, and constantly encouraging them to speak their mind will make them uncomfortable or distract them (especially if they have to speak in a non-native language, as is sometimes the case when testing with people from different cultural backgrounds). Avoid screening testers for people who like to talk; you don't want to test your product only with extraverts.

Although it is often useful to hear what's on people's minds, it's not required information. In most cases, the problems your testers find are quite obvious even without knowing what's going through their heads.

In my experience, people tend to offer *opinions* when they are encouraged to speak. Your main job is to pay attention to what people are *doing*, not what they are saying. If people are getting sidetracked and start offering their opinions rather than doing a task, just gently remind them of what you need them to do. Say something like this: "What are you looking for right now?" to get them back on track.

Should I Record Tests?

If you're doing a moderated test, you don't have to record the test, since you can see what the tester is doing and take notes during the test. But even if you don't *have* to, should you record?

I usually don't go back to watch recordings if I have them. But making recordings is easy and cheap to do, and from time to time, they can be extremely useful. If you can easily do it, record tests. But if that's not possible, don't worry about it.

For Macs, I recommend Silverback, a screen-recording application that is specifically geared toward usability tests.[1] It's also possible to do simple screen recordings using QuickTime Player by selecting File→New Screen Recording.

For Windows PCs, TechSmith offers a number of different solutions.[2]

For Linux, use something like xvidcap.[3]

What Should You Do with the Results?

You need to list the problems you've found. Prioritize them. Fix the most important ones. Test again. Don't worry if it's impossible to fix all problems; if a problem is important and you haven't fixed it, it will eventually reappear in a future test.

If more than one person is observing the test, do a Post-it post-mortem. Have everybody write their ten most important issues on Post-it notes. Stick them on a wall, placing duplicate issues next to each other. Pretty quickly, it'll be clear which problems get more "votes" and should be fixed sooner.

Don't write reports unless it's really necessary, because they often create more work than simply fixing the problems would. Usually, no one reads these reports anyway. Instead, identify the most pressing issues, and make sure these get fixed.

Takeaway Points

- Do one test with one (different!) user each week. This makes it easy to schedule testers, and you can iterate quickly.

- Use one of the test types explained in this chapter, or combine them. It's often a good idea to let users play around with your

---

1. Find out more at http://silverbackapp.com.
2. You can find TechSmith's products at http://techsmith.com, where they also offer Mac apps.
3. You can find xvidcap at http://xvidcap.sourceforge.net.

product on their own, see how they do with it, and then move to a task-based test.

- Always end tests on a positive note.

- Use common sense when evaluating test results. Find the most pressing issues, fix them, and test again.

- If you are unsure about how widespread a problem is, simply postpone its resolution; since you will do another test soon, the problem will come up again at some point if it is important.

Further Reading

If you're ready to learn more, I recommend that you start with Steve Krug's *Rocket Surgery Made Easy* [Kru09].

Chapter 30

Remote Testing

Research	Design	Implementation

What's the Technique?

Doing traditional, in-person usability tests requires you to either go to a tester or have a tester visit you. Scheduling and meeting people usually involves quite a bit of work—so much work, in fact, that it gets put off way too often.

Fortunately, you don't have to physically meet with people to do usability tests. Instead, you can do remote tests. This chapter explains how to do that.

Why Is This a Good Idea?

Testing remotely is often easier than testing in person, since it gets around some of the harder parts of usability testing, such as finding willing testers who live nearby and scheduling them to show up for a test. Being free of these problems means you can test more often, which helps you identify and fix more usability problems.

Are There Any Prerequisites?

Yes. You should read the previous two chapters before reading this one.

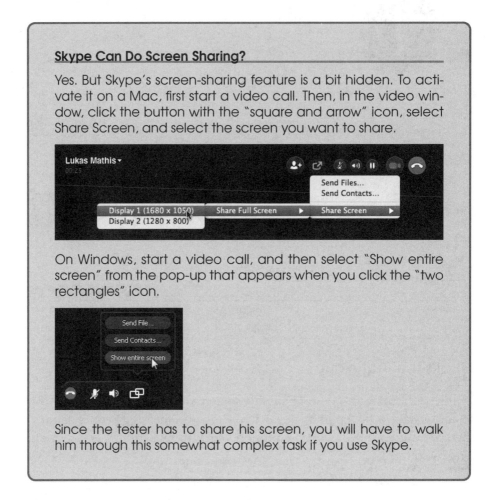

Skype Can Do Screen Sharing?

Yes. But Skype's screen-sharing feature is a bit hidden. To activate it on a Mac, first start a video call. Then, in the video window, click the button with the "square and arrow" icon, select Share Screen, and select the screen you want to share.

On Windows, start a video call, and then select "Show entire screen" from the pop-up that appears when you click the "two rectangles" icon.

Since the tester has to share his screen, you will have to walk him through this somewhat complex task if you use Skype.

30.1 Moderated Remote Testing

Let's say you want to run a usability test, but you can't find any testers who live nearby. Or you want to test with a more diverse group of testers, so it may make sense to test with people who live in different places. Or you want to recruit testers on your website, so they might be from all over the place. Or maybe you just want to simplify testing even more and avoid that whole meeting-in-person thing.

You can do this using screen-sharing apps such as Skype, iChat, or Copilot.[1] Instead of meeting your testers physically, you meet them online.

---

1. At https://www.copilot.com.

Recruiting

When you do a traditional usability test, first you have to recruit testers, and then you have to schedule a date for the test. So, recruiting often happens days or weeks before the test. With remote testing, you don't have to schedule a physical meeting, so you don't need to recruit as far in advance of the test.

Remote testing offers another way of recruiting that isn't possible with a traditional usability test: "live recruiting." Just put a note on your website that you're looking for people to help you test a new application or website, with a link to a recruiting page.

To increase the number of respondents, you can offer participants some kind of reward—a small Amazon gift certificate, for example.

People who click the link should get a form where they can enter their contact info (perhaps their email address, Skype name, or phone number, depending on how you run the test) and any other information you need in order to screen people for the test. In their book *Remote Research* [BT10], Nate Bolt and Tony Tulathimutte recommend using this form to weed out potentially poor testers who have visited your site specifically to participate in a test. (This problem occurs only if you offer rewards to participants.) They suggest asking a question like "Why did you come to the site today?" They write:

> This question not only helps determine whether a user's motives for coming to the site match the goals of the study, but also helps to root out fakers. (...) Most authentic visitors will have a good specific reason for being there, and by asking open-ended questions, you can usually get a strong intuitive feel for authentic visitors. We almost always begin our screeners with the simple question "Why did you come to

[Web site name] today?" If the answer is suspiciously vague ("for info," "just looking around," "to see the offerings"), you should be careful to screen the user further if you choose to contact him/her. If the answer is straightforward and specific and fits the study goal nicely ("I came here to compare prices between the iDongle and the iDongle Pro"), you can probably be more confident.

They recommend Ethnio, their live web recruiting tool, for setting up a live recruiting form.[2] When somebody responds to your form, you can immediately call them back and (if the potential tester agrees) start the test.

Introductions

When doing remote testing, you're not physically in the same place as the tester, so building rapport and getting a feel for the tester's mood can be difficult.

Start the session with a phone call or a video chat to introduce yourself and explain the procedure. The introduction should be similar to a regular usability test: explain exactly what you're doing and what you want the tester to do (this is explained in the previous chapters). Make sure that the tester understands that you will be able to see her screen for the duration of the test. If this is unclear to the tester or if the tester seems uncomfortable with what you're asking, stop the test and find somebody else to test with.

If the tester agrees to screen sharing, walk her through the process of sharing her screen. (The details on how to do this depend on the screen-sharing system you're using.) Make sure you know *exactly* what the tester has to do to access your application or website.[3]

Running the Test

In many ways, running a remote test is easier than running an in-person test, since you're a lot less likely to influence the tester. Simply pay attention to what the tester is doing, and keep your mouth shut unless the tester explicitly asks a question. As with any other usability

---

2. Check it out at http://www.ethnio.com.
3. If you're testing a product that doesn't appear on the tester's screen, say, an iPhone app, simply have her turn her webcam to the product so you can see what the tester is doing.

test, avoid guiding the tester, but do stop the test if the tester seems uncomfortable or agitated.

Because you're not in the same room, it can be harder to sense when the user is getting frustrated. Pay constant attention to the tester's tone of voice to make sure you catch any frustration before the test goes south.

At the end of the test, you can pretty much do the same debriefing you do in a traditional usability test. Ask any questions you might have had during the test, ask the tester to give feedback on how the test was run, thank your tester for his time, and finally give him his reward (if you've offered one).

Disadvantages

There are a number of downsides to moderated remote testing, compared to in-person testing.

Because you aren't sitting next to the tester, you miss out on a number of physical cues. Is the tester getting agitated or frustrated? It's hard to tell when doing remote testing, so you need to pay particular attention to this and be prepared to stop the task if the tester shows signs of fatigue or annoyance. Pay attention to the tester's tone and choice of words.

Additionally, you can't see what the tester is looking at. If you get confused by what the tester is doing or are not sure whether the tester is still engaged in the task, simply ask, "What are you looking at right now?" or tell the tester that it would be helpful if he indicated what he is looking at by pointing at it with his mouse.

When testers aren't in the same room, you need to go through some extra steps to get your consent forms signed. You can send the consent form by email in advance of the testing session. Then when you call the tester, before starting the test, you review the main points that she is consenting to and ask her to give a verbal agreement. Whether these steps are enough to cover everything you need, in terms of getting proper consent, depends on the laws in your particular location, though.

When doing remote testing, you typically can't control the tester's environment. The downside to this is that it might take a while to get your product running; the upside is that it means you can observe the tester in his own surroundings, so his behavior most likely is more natural than in a controlled environment. Additionally, this lets you see how your product performs on a typical computer, rather than the high-end model you're likely to be using. But it also means that he might get distracted during the test—for example, stopping to take a phone call or check incoming email. If possible, ask the tester to turn off the phone, shut down any chat programs, and disable periodic email checking.

Since you can't set up the environment exactly the way you want it to be, you need to walk the tester through some things before doing the test. Find out what system he is running and what applications and versions he has installed. (If you are recruiting using your website, you can do that with a small questionnaire.) Make sure you know how to walk him through getting everything up and running. Also, make sure that the tester's Internet connection is fast enough to allow for remote testing.

As an alternative to having the tester share her screen with you, you can use your own system for testing and share your screen with her. In some cases, this can be necessary, because it's not always possible to get your product to run on the tester's computer. But avoid this option, if you can. Sharing your screen with the tester decreases the quality of the graphics on her end and produces a small delay between input and response, which can be very irritating to many people and may skew the test results.

Advantages

I've already mentioned that one potential advantage of remote testing is that you get to test your product in the tester's natural surroundings. This is not the only advantage that remote testing offers.

Another huge advantage of remote testing is that it allows you to easily recruit testers if you have a website that is reasonably well visited.

Also, you pretty much eliminate the chance of unduly influencing the tester. Since remote testers can't see your facial expressions or body posture, they won't be influenced by your behavior.

And, of course, remote testing makes it easier to schedule testers—you don't have to physically meet them and can even eliminate scheduling altogether.

Pulling It All Together

To give you a feel for how a typical remote test would work, here's a hypothetical, somewhat abbreviated version of a session.

For this test, let's assume that the tester provided his Skype name on your online form, and you're now contacting him via Skype. Be sure to wear a headset so you have your hands free to take notes.

Facilitator: *Hey, this is Lukas Mathis, from BizTwit.biz. How are you? Listen, about twenty minutes ago, you filled in a form on our website, indicating that you'd like to help us make BizTwit even better.*

Tester: *Right, yeah. Didn't think I'd hear from you!*

Facilitator: *So, do you have fifteen minutes for this?*

Tester: *Yeah, sure.*

If the tester replies in the negative, stop the test.

Next, we want to know if this is the kind of participant we're looking for.

Facilitator: *So, have you ever used our Twitter app, BizTwit?*

Tester: *No, not so far.*

Facilitator: *And you visited our website because you might be interested in such an app?*

Tester: *Right. I was looking for a Twitter app for businesses and found you on Google.*

Facilitator: *Great, you're exactly the kind of person we're looking for. So, here's what this is about. We're currently testing a new design for our app, and we want to know whether people can figure it out, you know, find out what parts of the design we have to make better. This is about testing the new design and seeing whether it works, not testing you. How this works is, you'll have to share your screen with me. Is this OK with you? During the duration of the test, I'll be able to see your screen.*

Tester: *Sure, not a problem.*

Facilitator: *OK. From now on, I'll record this call. We'll use this recording to look for problems with our design. It won't be made public—it's purely for us to improve our product.*

Tester: *OK.*

If there's any hesitation with the last two questions or if the tester doesn't seem to be quite sure, stop the test. If everything is OK, start recording now.

Facilitator: *OK, great. Before you get to that, I sent you a consent form by email. Did you receive that?*

Tester: *Yeah, got it a few minutes ago.*

Facilitator: *Did you have time to go through it?*

Tester: *Yeah, I skimmed it.*

Facilitator: *OK, let's quickly go through the important points so you know what you're getting into here.*

Explain exactly what he's consenting to, and get verbal agreement (and whatever else you need, according to the legal requirements where you live).

Facilitator: *Now that this is done, let's start the actual test. First, you need to share your screen with me. From now on, I can see everything you do until this test is over. So if there's anything personal on your screen—emails, for example—now is the time to close them.*

Explain how to share the screen.

Facilitator: *Great, now I can see what you're doing. First, we're going to get the most recent version of BizTwit running on your system. Go to biztwit.biz...*

Explain how to get your product running. Since people probably don't want to enter their own login information, you should set up an example account in advance, if something like this is required by your application.

Facilitator: *Now that BizTwit is running, tell me what you think. Does this look like something you might want to use? Do you think that just by looking at the app, you have a pretty good idea of what it does and how to use its features?*

Do a short product introduction and ask for first impressions and then move on to task-based tests.

Facilitator: *OK, let's start with the first task. I'm going to explain the task to you. While you're doing the task, please feel free to think out loud and tell me what's going through your mind. If you have questions, feel free to ask, but I probably won't be able to give you detailed answers.*

It's just part of the test. If something doesn't work or is boring you or upsetting you, you can stop the test at any time. OK?

Tester: *OK.*

Give the first task. For information on how to design tasks, see the previous chapters, as well as Chapter 11, *Paper Prototype Testing*, on page 97.

Once the tasks are done, first explain how to stop screen sharing. Then ask any questions you might have.

Finally, move on to the debriefing. The goal here is to end the test on a positive note. Being observed while making mistakes can be a bad, stressful experience. Telling the tester that his effort really helped you can offset that bad experience and make the tester's investment feel worthwhile.

Facilitator: *Now I can't see your screen anymore. OK, that was great; that helped clear up a lot of questions we had. Using the stuff we discovered today, we'll be able to improve BizTwit's user interface a lot. Thank you so much for helping us out! Now, do you have any questions or feedback for me?*

Tester: *I was kind of confused at first about how to share my screen, but I guess it worked out in the end.*

Facilitator: *Yeah, I'll try to find a better way of explaining that in the future. Now, we've promised you an Amazon gift certificate, and I'll send that to your email address, if that's OK?*

Tester: *Sure.*

Facilitator: *Great. If you have any additional questions or comments, just send me an email. I'll put my email address into Skype's chat window. Thanks again for helping us, and have a great day!*

Don't forget to send out the reward, if you've promised one.

Do not write any reports. Do not create movies showing the results. Instead, after doing the test, make a list of the issues you found that you feel are most important to you, and fix them for the next test. If you are unsure about an issue, let it go for now, and see whether other testers encounter the same issue in future tests. If an issue is important, it will eventually show up again.

To Remote, or Not to Remote?

Considering everything involved, when it comes to getting useful data out of the test, how does moderated remote testing compare to regular usability testing?

On the whole, whether remote testing yields better or worse results than regular old in-person usability testing is a topic that is hotly debated in the usability community. Remote testing may not be quite as effective as in-person usability testing, but it's definitely a lot better than not testing at all. And since it is easier to set up, it allows you to do more tests and run tests more regularly.

30.2 Unmoderated Remote Testing

An even easier way of doing remote testing is to completely avoid inter-acting with the tester. Simply ask testers to record their screens while they are using your product or while they follow a number of predefined tasks.

As always, there are advantages and disadvantages to this approach. With unmoderated, task-based remote testing, you can't intervene if the user gets stuck or frustrated. On the other hand, you get a pretty good idea of what people do when using your product on their own, and this situation is closer to how most of your real users will behave.

Another upside to unmoderated testing is that you don't have to do any scheduling at all. You can explain the procedure to the tester and let her run the test when she has the time. In fact, you can even use online remote testing services, which allow you to forego recruiting alto-gether.[4]

Takeaway Points

- If you've never done any usability tests, start by doing a few tra-ditional, in-person usability tests. You can ask your friends to act as testers until you're comfortable running tests.

- Once you have a pretty good feel for how to run usability tests, move on to remote testing.

---

4. Online services such as http://usertesting.com or http://fivesecondtest.com. Both of these services work only for testing websites, though, and not for desktop apps or mobile apps.

- Try to do at least one remote test every week.

- Recruit testers using your website, as well as other venues such as mailing lists, discussion groups, or even newspapers. Using a website for recruitment is extremely convenient and essentially free, but if you *only* recruit this way, you may skew your results toward people who already have experience with your products because they're more likely to visit your website.

- Screen out potential testers who are only in it for the reward.

- When calling a potential tester, make sure to alert her to the fact that you'll be able to see her screen, and get consent for the test.

- When running a remote test, you typically won't be able to see facial expressions or where people are looking. Make sure to watch out for signs that the tester is getting frustrated or upset, and stop the test if this happens.

- At the end of the test, thank the tester for his time, explain that you can't see his screen anymore, and send the reward (if you've promised one). End the test on a positive note.

Further Reading

Remote Research [BT10] by Nate Bolt and Tony Tulathimutte contains a ton of useful information on remote testing. If you're considering remote testing, you owe it to yourself to pick up this book.[5]

On A List Apart, Nate Bolt also has an article on remote usability testing.[6]

---

5. You can find it at http://www.rosenfeldmedia.com/books/remote-research/.
6. Read it at http://www.alistapart.com/articles/quick-and-dirty-remote-user-testing/.

Chapter 31

How Not to Test: Common Mistakes

Usability tests are surprisingly resilient to mistakes. No matter how poorly you do them, chances are that you will get *some* useful information out of them. You might not uncover the most important problems, and maybe you'll get only a small subset of all problems, but you'll get *something* that will help you improve your product.

Still, if you take the time to test properly, you will get better results.

I've already mentioned some of these points in earlier chapters, but I think it's useful to do a quick recap here.

31.1 Don't Use Words That Appear in the User Interface

It's important not to use your application's terminology when you create tasks and when you talk to your tester. You want to know whether people are capable of using your application. You don't want to know whether they are able to find a specific word in your user interface.

Let's say you're testing a word processor, and you want to see whether people can use its spell-checker. Figure 31.1, on the next page, shows how this feature might be accessed in one of your application's menus.

Now, if you were to phrase the task along the lines of "Check your document's spelling," your tester could simply look through your application's menus and find the one with the matching words. It's best to avoid describing the task at all; instead, describe the goal: *"Make sure that there are no typos in your text."*

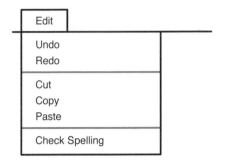

Figure 31.1: COMMON WORDS IN A WORD PROCESSING MENU

Tasks phrased like this are more aligned with what your users' goals might actually be, so the tester's behavior is more along the lines of how a real user might behave.

31.2 Don't Influence the Tester

Wilhelm von Osten was a German math teacher who lived around the early 1900s. As a hobby, he trained horses. You can probably see where this story is going: he tried to teach his horse how to do math. To everybody's astonishment, the horse (aptly named Clever Hans) quickly learned to do a number of reasonably complex math calculations: additions, subtractions, multiplications, divisions, and date calculations. The horse was capable of understanding math questions asked in plain German, and it could also read math questions if they were written on a piece of paper.

Obviously, the horse couldn't write down the results. Instead, it tapped the correct number with its hoof.

Psychologist Oskar Pfungst became suspicious and decided to investigate Clever Hans. Quite quickly, he was able to establish what was happening: Clever Hans didn't actually do any calculations. The animal didn't read, and it didn't understand German. Instead, it responded to involuntary cues in the body language of its trainer, von Osten, who, in turn, was the one who solved the math problems. The horse simply watched him and tapped its hoof until von Osten would indicate that it had reached the correct number.

Interestingly, von Osten was completely unaware that he was providing these cues to the horse.

This piqued Pfungst's interest, and he continued his experiments on the topic. He was eventually able to show that the same kind of interaction occurs between humans and, furthermore, that it is impossible to suppress these involuntary cues, even if we are completely aware of their existence.

What does this mean for us?

It means it is easily possible for a facilitator to involuntarily lead the tester through the whole test, thereby utterly invalidating the test. This is why formal usability tests are always done behind two-way mirrors; this eliminates any possibility of outside influence on the tester.

There are a few things you can do to improve the situation. First, even though you can't consciously avoid giving involuntary cues, you *can* cut down on your voluntary cues. So, don't interact with the tester unless absolutely necessary.

Second, you have to remove yourself from the tester's field of vision, sitting a bit behind the tester so he is less aware of your presence.

Third, if possible, run a test that doesn't require sitting with the tester. Remote testing is perfect for this (see Chapter 30, *Remote Testing*, on page 259).

Finally, don't worry about it too much; just be attentive. You are not doing a statistically valid double-blind study here; you are merely trying to find problems in your user interface. If the tester hesitates or looks to you for guidance, you already know that there might be a problem with the user interface, even if your reaction allows her to figure out what to do next.

31.3 Avoid Stressful Situations

All medical students are taught this principal precept of medical ethics: "Primum non nocere," or, "First, do no harm." The same should apply to usability professionals. When we run usability tests, we put people in a situation where we want them to make mistakes. But making mistakes can be a stressful situation; nobody likes to make mistakes. You can do a number of things to make testers feel OK with the situation they find themselves in.

First, you need to make sure you explicitly and clearly point out that you are not testing them, but the user interface.

Second, if a tester gets stuck and it becomes obvious that he's on the wrong track or becoming agitated, intervene. Say something to make it clear that the tester is not to blame, something along the lines of, "This is exactly why you're running these tests. This design still has some serious issues here. I think you'll have to go back to the drawing board on this one." Then, move on to the next task.

Third, do not repeatedly tell testers to speak out loud. It's OK to make this point at the beginning of the test by saying something like, "Feel free to speak out loud during the test; this helps me better understand where problems in your user interface are." It's also OK to ask something like "What's on your mind right now?" when it's not clear what the tester is doing during the test. But keep in mind that some people just aren't comfortable with what amounts to talking to themselves.

Fourth, if it appears that a tester is starting to get stressed out by the experience, stop the test. Besides being at risk of putting the tester through a horrible experience, you won't get any value out of forcing a tester who is upset and unable to concentrate to finish the test. His behavior typically won't be representative of your real users, who have the ability to take a break or work on something else if your product is annoying them.

Finally, always end tests on a positive note. Thank people for their time. Tell them that their participation in the test was valuable to you and will help you improve your product.

Takeaway Points

- When designing tasks or talking to users during usability tests, avoid using words that appear in the user interface.

- Avoid influencing the tester during tests.

- Watch out for situations where the tester looks to you for guidance, since these indicate usability problems.

- Avoid putting the tester through stressful situations.

- Don't constantly ask the tester to speak out loud.

- Stop the test if the tester seems to get upset or annoyed.

Chapter 32

User Error Is Design Error

When people fail at using our products, we may be tempted to attribute that failure to user incompetence. It's a "user error," we may say. This response has its own acronym: "PEBKAC," which stands for "Problem Exists Between Keyboard And Chair."

When you do your first usability test, it's natural to experience some amount of denial—surely your product can't be *that* bad. You probably just happened to pick a few truly inept people to test it, right?

This tendency to blame users is often supported by users themselves, who also tend to blame themselves for problems with your product. When they are unable to figure out how to use it and you show them how, they will often respond with something like "Oh wow, I have no idea how I did not see this! It seems so obvious now!" They tend to blame themselves for not seeing something, rather than blaming your product for not making it obvious enough.

Blaming the user for your product's errors does not fix the error. If tens of thousands of people use your product, every problem you see in a usability test will be experienced by hundreds or even thousands of users. Rather than assigning blame, fix the problem. In his book *The Design of Everyday Things* [Nor88],[1] Don Norman puts it like this:

> Don't think of the user as making errors; think of the actions
> as approximations of what is desired.

People don't make errors. Your product makes errors when it doesn't interpret the user's actions correctly.

---

1. If you haven't read *The Design of Everyday Things* [Nor88] yet, drop this book right now and go pick up Don's book instead.

32.1 Don't Blame Your Users in Your Error Messages

We've all encountered an error message like this:

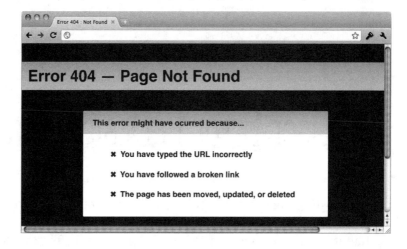

The first thing people will read is, "You have typed the address incorrectly." This error message blames the user for trying to access a URL that doesn't lead to a page. But the user very likely didn't do anything wrong. When people encounter "page can't be found" errors, it's more likely that they simply clicked a broken link, probably a broken link on the very website where the address leads to.

Instead of blaming the user, we should start by apologizing for the problem. This is good usability, because it helps people calm down and deal with the issue. In *The Man Who Lied to His Laptop* [NY10], author Clifford Nass writes about an experiment with a computer that provides "emotional support" while the user plays a game. He concludes that "actively acknowledging and addressing people's emotional states alleviated the high negativity and high excitement associated with frustration. In other words, people feel better when you show that you have heard them, understand their feelings, and sympathize."

Another problem with the error page shown earlier is that it uses a lot of jargon to explain what the problem is. Most people don't know and don't care what 404 means or what a "URL" is.

And finally, the error page isn't helpful. It offers reasons for the problem but doesn't offer any solutions. The site could determine where the user intended to go, based on the information available to the site. For example, links to blog posts often contain the year, month, and day that a blog post was written. Even if the last part of the URL got cut off

People Don't Like to Be Insulted

At folklore.org, Andy Hertzfeld recounts a funny experience that occurred while doing usability testing for Apple's Lisa computer.* He explains that the two default buttons in dialog boxes were originally called Cancel and Do It. In usability testing, however, they found out that a few users regularly clicked Cancel when they should have clicked Do It instead. When they talked to a user who seemed particularly confused by the dialog box, he replied "I'm not a dolt; why is the software calling me a dolt?"

People simply didn't notice the space between "Do" and "It" and read it as "Dolt." As a result, the Lisa team changed "Do It" to "OK."

---

*.   Read the full story, and many other interesting stories about the development of the Mac, at http://www.folklore.org/StoryView.py?project=Macintosh\&story=Do_It.txt\&sortOrder=Sort%20by%20Date\&detail=medium\&search=Do%20it.

---

or was entered incorrectly, the remaining information can be used to determine likely candidates for the specific page the user was trying to open. How about something this:

Rather than putting the blame on the user, this screen acknowledges that the site itself is more likely at fault and apologizes for the problem. It explains what went wrong in reasonably understandable language, but it also offers possible solutions to the problem. If nothing helps, it offers a direct way for people to contact you.

32.2 No Error, No Blame

It's good practice not to blame users for the errors they make. It's even better practice to include error messages that help users figure out how to fix the problem. But it's best not to let the problem occur at all. If something goes wrong, it's usually not the user's fault; it's your fault. If your product worked differently, then the problem might never have occurred.

You can prevent a number of common errors from occurring simply by changing the user interface. Let's look at two sources of such errors.

Mode Errors

Problems we perceive as "user error" can often be attributed to products not clearly indicating their current state or what specific action they expect from the user. I've written about this in Chapter 20, *Modes*, on page 169, but since modes are such a common source of errors that we often perceive as "user errors," let's quickly recap.

A typical example of a mode error is a cell phone that goes off during a movie; most cell phones don't have obvious "silent" modes. A cell phone's current state is not clear just by looking at it. It's too easy to forget whether it is currently in "silent" mode.

30 MINUTES INTO THE MOVIE, ONE OF THESE TWO CELL PHONES WILL MAKE A LOT OF NOISE. CAN YOU TELL WHICH ONE?

An obvious hardware button on the device that toggles between the two modes, like the one found on iPhones or webOS devices, would help prevent this problem.

A similar issue can occur in modal applications when the application doesn't clearly indicate what mode it is in or when it switches the mode unexpectedly. For example, picture-editing applications often have a modal tool selection that indicates the currently selected tool by changing the cursor. It's easy for users to miss this hint and, say, paint a line by clicking an image when they thought the clone tool (rather than the paint tool) was currently active.

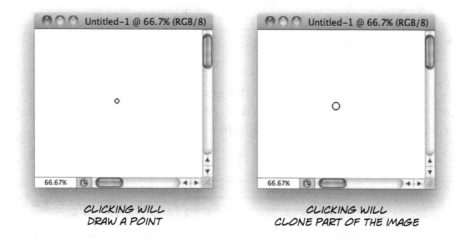

Using different cursor images for different tools would help prevent this problem. Here's how the same two tools look in Acorn:[2]

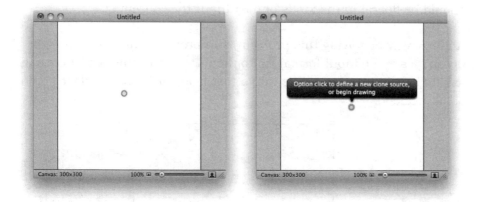

Acorn reminds users of the tool they're using. The chance of being confused about the active tool is much smaller.

2. Learn more about Acorn at http://www.flyingmeat.com/acorn.

Input Errors

Another common example of "user errors" occurs when products don't clearly explain what they expect users to do, for example in overzealous and nonobvious form data validation schemes:

Birth Date:

Credit Card Number:

It's not clear what format the product expects for the date and credit-card number. As a result, users will try to enter all kinds of different formats. This often doesn't work properly.

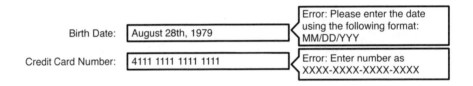

Birth Date: | August 28th, 1979 — Error: Please enter the date using the following format: MM/DD/YYY

Credit Card Number: | 4111 1111 1111 1111 — Error: Enter number as XXXX-XXXX-XXXX-XXXX

Apps and websites either should explicitly state what they expect the user to do (for example, by entering example data into the fields) or should be liberal in the kinds of user input they accept.

Another way of solving this problem is to provide a user interface that doesn't leave the input format up to the user. For example, rather than asking people to enter a date into a text field, the user interface could show a calendar.

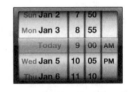

ICAL ONLY LETS YOU CHANGE ONE NUMBER AT A TIME, MAKING SURE THE FORMAT IS ALWAYS CORRECT.

WINDOWS USES A CALENDAR THAT LETS YOU PICK A DATE BY CLICKING ON ITS DAY AND ONLY USES TEXT ENTRY FOR THE TIME OF DAY.

THE IPHONE USES A DATE ENTRY INTERFACE THAT AVOIDS TEXT ENTRY BY THE USER ALTOGETHER.

Takeaway Points

- Take responsibility. "User errors" are really user interface design failures; they are *designer errors*. Simply assuming that the user is responsible for a problem doesn't make the problem go away.

- Don't blame the user in your user interface. It makes your customers feel bad, and the problem was probably your fault to begin with.

- Present useful error messages. If something goes wrong, explain what went wrong, but more importantly, explain how the user can fix the problem.

- Prevent the problem. It's always best to avoid errors altogether. If users encounter errors, think about how you can change the product so that the error doesn't occur again.

- Prevent mode errors by avoiding modes or by clearly indicating your product's current mode.

- Prevent input errors by clearly showing what you expect users to do or by preventing invalid input from ever occurring.

Chapter 33

A/B Testing

Research	Design	Implementation

What's the Technique?

So far, I've mainly talked about usability tests that involve observing how individual users behave. This is great for finding problems with your designs, but it's not good if you need to compare two (or more) different designs and find the best one.

Let's say you're working on the text of your sign-up page, and you're not sure which version works best for convincing people to sign up. Or you're trying to decide between two different positions for the login form on your home page, and you're not sure which one will work better for your users. The most common way to answer such questions is with A/B testing. With an A/B test, you can find out which one of two (or more) designs works best.

Even though it's called A/B testing, you don't need to compare only two different designs; it can be used to test several different versions of a design. For this reason, it's sometimes also called A/B/n testing.

Why Is This a Good Idea?

A/B testing lets you improve your design using hard data. There's no guessing involved. If you need to make your design perform better, A/B testing is the tool that will help you do that.

Are There Any Prerequisites?

Yes. You need to have a working version of your product, and it should be used by a fair number of people.

Multivariate Testing

Multivariate testing (sometimes called *multivariable testing*) is a version of A/B testing. With a regular A/B test, you test different fully implemented designs.

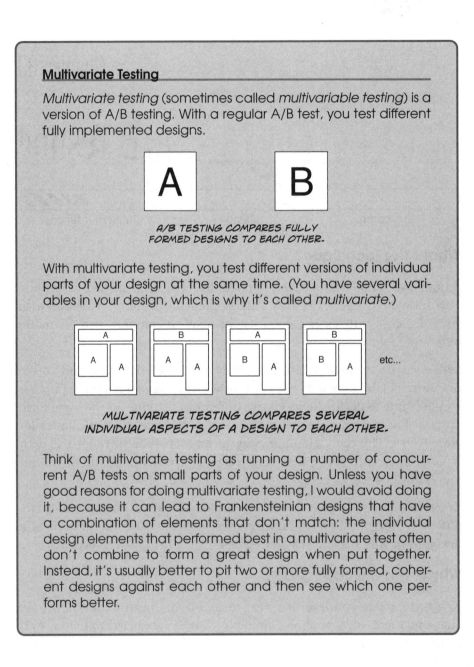

A/B TESTING COMPARES FULLY
FORMED DESIGNS TO EACH OTHER.

With multivariate testing, you test different versions of individual parts of your design at the same time. (You have several variables in your design, which is why it's called *multivariate*.)

MULTIVARIATE TESTING COMPARES SEVERAL
INDIVIDUAL ASPECTS OF A DESIGN TO EACH OTHER.

Think of multivariate testing as running a number of concurrent A/B tests on small parts of your design. Unless you have good reasons for doing multivariate testing, I would avoid doing it, because it can lead to Frankensteinian designs that have a combination of elements that don't match: the individual design elements that performed best in a multivariate test often don't combine to form a great design when put together. Instead, it's usually better to pit two or more fully formed, coherent designs against each other and then see which one performs better.

33.1 When to Do A/B Testing

A/B testing is useful for comparing two or more designs and finding out which one works better. Generally speaking, there are two situations when this is useful:

- You've redesigned or rewritten something, and you want to know whether the new design or the new copy works better than the previous version.

- There are several possible solutions to a problem, and you want to find out which one works best.

You can use A/B testing to compare everything from vastly different layouts to small changes in color or wording.

If, like Google or Amazon, you have millions of people using your site every day, even minuscule differences in usability can result in tens of thousands of people either running into a problem or not. You probably don't have *that* many people using your product, so small differences in usability may not matter much. There's no need to check every little change with an A/B test. But when making larger changes, or for areas of your product that are particularly important (say, the sign-up screen of your web service), A/B testing is tremendously useful.

33.2 What's Success?

The basic idea behind A/B testing is to implement two different designs and see which one works better. But there's an inherent problem with this. What exactly does "works better" mean? At what point has the user successfully used your product? Sometimes, the answer is obvious. For example, in designing a checkout system, the system "works" when the user is able to finish the checkout process. Often, however, there is no immediately obvious answer to what constitutes "success."

One way to define "success" is to go back to the very beginning of the design process and think about your users' goals. If you know why they use the product, then you can define success: the product works better if a higher percentage of your users are able to reach their goals.

Sometimes, all it takes is to measure the percentage of people who click a link on a website or the percentage of your website visitors who sign up for your service. Other times, answering this question is more involved. How many people who start a task actually finish it? The definition of success depends on your product.

33.3 Preparing for the Test

At this point, you have two (or more) designs you want to test, and you have a definition of success. Now, you have to implement both designs and find a way of distributing them to your users.

If your product is a desktop application, either you need to create two (or more) different builds and distribute the appropriate build to your individual users or you need to add both designs to the same application and decide which design to show when the user launches the application.

If your product is a website, you need to implement a way of accessing the different versions of your website, either by giving the two designs different URLs or by deciding which design to show when the user accesses the single URL. A number of online tools are available for running A/B tests on websites. You can use Google Analytics[1] for A/B testing, but Google also offers Website Optimizer[2] to test changes to websites. Vertster[3] is another tool that helps you create multivariate tests for websites.

33.4 Running the Test

When running A/B tests, you want to make sure that individual users don't switch between the two different designs. (Seeing one version of the design and then, after clicking a link or restarting the application, suddenly seeing the other version would be really confusing.) To do that, you should partition your users into different groups that consistently see the same design.

While the test is running, you'll need a way of collecting the results. This is simple when you're dealing with a website (since you can "see" what each user is doing), but it can be harder when dealing with a desktop application.

You also need to inform users that you're receiving usage data and explain exactly what you're going to send back and why. Here's how Google does this on Chrome's download page:

---

1. To find out more on how to use Google Analytics to run A/B tests on your website, read the essay by George Palmer at http://www.rowtheboat.com/archives/39.
2. At http://www.google.com/websiteoptimizer.
3. At http://www.vertster.com.

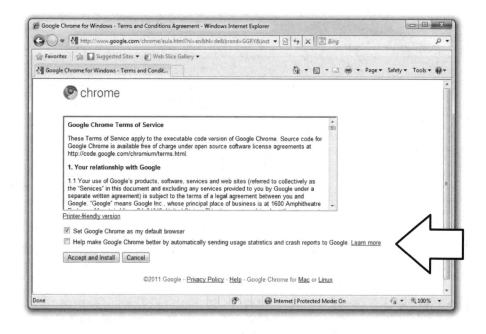

33.5 Interpreting the Results

Most A/B tools interpret the results for you; quite often, you can see early trends indicating which design performs best. But be careful: humans are pattern seekers, and it's easy to see patterns where there are none. One thing to keep in mind here is statistical significance. You need to have some idea of how big the probability is that the results you're seeing have occurred because of random chance.

The company User Effect[4] has a simple calculator[5] that reveals whether the results of an A/B test with two designs are statistically significant. If they're not, the calculator also tells you how many more visitors you need to get a significant result.

If you have more than two designs in your A/B test, you can compare individual designs to see whether the difference is significant.

33.6 Keep in Mind

If you use A/B testing to compare the performance of small, incremental changes to your design, keep in mind that A/B testing will only

---

4. Find them at http://www.usereffect.com.
5. You can find the calculator at http://www.usereffect.com/split-test-calculator.

Partitioning Users

Partitioning users into two groups is pretty simple when testing a desktop application. Give each user one of the builds at random when he downloads your app; typically each user downloads the app only once, so you don't have to worry about individual users switching from one design to the other. Similarly, if both designs are in the same build, pick a design at random when the user first launches the application, and store the design you've picked as a user setting.

Dealing with a website is a bit more complex. One way of picking a design for each visitor is to use a modulo of the hash of the visitor's IP address to determine which design to show* and then set a cookie indicating which design to show on the user's computer. For repeat visitors, first check whether they have a cookie, and if they don't, fall back to the IP address to determine which design to show. This system is not entirely fool-proof (users might not allow cookies and change their IP address), but it should cover almost all cases.

---

*. Since IP addresses are not random, simply taking the modulo of the IP address itself would skew the number of people in the different partitions; applying a hash function to the IP address removes that bias.

---

bring you to a local maximum of usability. Making many incremental changes will get you to a good design but may not get you to the best design possible.

Imagine all possible designs for your product. Some of them are more usable; others less. If you could plot them on a graph, you might get something like this:

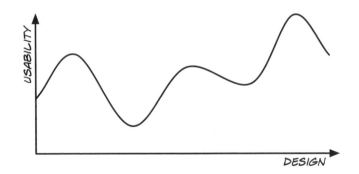

If you change your design, the usability changes.

If the quality of your design is currently somewhere in the middle of this graph, then you won't be able to get to the best design possible by making only small, iterative changes and A/B-testing them. Think of it like this: if you go mountain climbing and decide to always climb *up*, you'll eventually reach the peak of the mountain, but you'll never reach the nearby mountain peak, which might be even higher. You have to climb down first to reach that higher peak.

Similarly, you sometimes have to make a fresh start with a design that performs worse if you want to eventually arrive at a design that works much better.

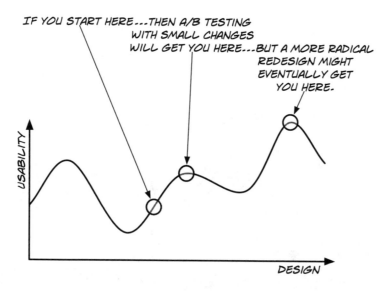

To avoid this problem, you might need to let go of this type of iterative design and take a chance on an entirely different design. A/B testing is a great tool in every designer's tool belt. Just be aware of its limitations.

Takeaway Points

- A/B testing allows you to compare different designs and find out which one works best.

- The definition of what "works" depends on your users' goals.

- Getting usage data is simple for websites but harder for desktop or mobile applications. Remember to get your users' consent and tell them exactly what you're doing.

- Make sure to check whether results are statistically significant before basing decisions on this kind of data.

- When you compare your highly optimized old design to your new design, realize that even if the new design performs worse in a direct comparison, it might eventually perform better if you give it the same kind of attention you gave to the previous design.

Chapter 34

Collecting Usage Data

Research	Design	Implementation

What's the Technique?

Now that you've designed and released your product, it's done, so your job is done as well, right? Well, application and website design is never really done. When people start to use your product, it's time to figure out how well your design works and what people do with your product. This chapter presents some ideas that help you do exactly that.

Why Is This a Good Idea?

When your product is out in the wild, people use it in ways you never expected. You need to know what people actually do in order to know how to improve your product.

Are There Any Prerequisites?

Yes. You need to have a working, released version of your product.

34.1 Measure Speed

Performance matters. If your product involves a lot of waiting, people will not like the experience. You can and should test your product's performance while it is still in development, using test data. But you just know that your users are going to do crazy things with your product—things you never even thought about.

If you're writing a DVD cataloging application that allows people to keep track of the movies they own, you might assume that most people would own no more than 200 DVDs, so you might make sure that your product performs well for collections around that size. In reality, a sizeable portion of your customers are movie collectors (this being their reason for buying your product in the first place). So instead of keeping track of hundreds of DVDs, they might want to keep track of *tens of thousands* of DVDs.

Or let's consider a website that allows freelancers to track the time they spend on their various projects and clients. The service might perform beautifully during testing, so you figure you could just take the performance you saw during testing and linearly scale up from that to the number of users you expect to have after launch. However, this assumes that each of your users will hit your sites in (what appear to you as) random intervals. Consider what happens once you release your product and people start using it. Every morning, many of the users living in the same time zone start working at roughly the same time. They all fire up their computers, open your website, and start working on a project. In other words, all of them are hitting your service at the same time, causing a spike in traffic. Instead of access being spread out over the whole day, you get peaks and valleys of traffic. How does your service perform during the peaks? Will your users' first experience every day be a bad one, because your servers are not able to cope with the sudden peak in demand?

Once you've finished your product and people start using it, make sure to keep track of how well it performs in real-world situations.

For more on how fast your product has to be, go back to Chapter 23, *Speed*, on page 193.

34.2 Exit Points

One of the questions you want to answer when looking at how people use your product is "when do people *stop* using it?" The point at which people exit your product can tell you a lot about the kinds of problems they are experiencing. Are they exiting the product once they've finished a task? In that case, you're probably in the clear. Are they exiting the product in the middle of a task? For example, are they abandoning a full shopping cart in your online store? If so, you probably have a problem somewhere. Maybe people are getting bored with your product. Maybe they don't understand how to finish a task. Maybe they're not sure what will happen when they continue. But something is probably going wrong.

Exit points in the middle of tasks are indicators of usability issues. Keep track of them in order to find out where potential issues with your product lie.

34.3 Measure Failure

It's often obvious when your product has failed its users, so this is one area where it can be simple to get useful data on areas that require improvements.

If your users encounter a 404 page or a similar error when using your website, you know that something went wrong. Keep track of such errors and of the referring sites, and fix the issues if possible.

If your users search for something and get zero search results or don't click any of the search results they receive, it might make sense to look at the search string they entered and try to figure out why they didn't find what they were looking for. Is there anything you can do to fix this issue?

Whenever people undo something, it might be because your product didn't do what they expected it to do. Keep track of what people do before they undo their changes.

Although crashes are not, strictly speaking, usability issues, they are clearly very detrimental to the user experience. Make sure to give your users a simple way of reporting crashes to you and fix the issue whenever possible (and sometimes even when impossible).

Similar to how game designers measure where exactly people die in games (see Chapter 26, *Learning from Video Games*, on page 217), you can measure where your product fails and fix these problems.

34.4 User Behavior

After you have deployed your product, you can start running analytics on it. Which links do people click, and which ones do they never use? Which features are popular, and which ones are not? Services like ClickTale and Crazy Egg[1] allow you to get information on how your users behave. Use this information to evaluate design and feature ideas or even to help decide which features you can remove. (See Chapter 25, *Removing Features*, on page 211 for a bit more on that.)

This doesn't just apply to websites. You can also give users of a desktop application the option of regularly sending you usage data.

Once somebody consents to sending you data, you need to determine what kind of data is useful. Microsoft's Jensen Harris writes[2] that "we collect anything we think might be interesting and useful as long as it doesn't compromise a user's privacy."

Microsoft collects keyboard shortcuts people use, how much time people spend on different tasks, even what and how much people create (such as how many mail folders they have), and much more. The better you know what your users actually do, the better informed your design decisions are.

When your product has been out in the wild for a while, you can also start doing usability tests with experienced users or visit some of your users and observe how they *actually* use your product (as opposed to how you envisioned your product would be used in the real world—the two are often vastly different).

Takeaway Points

- Once your product is being used by real people, it's time to start measuring how well it performs.

- Speed is one important aspect of performance, because it's often hard to figure out how well your product performs until it's in your users' hands.

- Keep track of exit points, since they indicate potential issues with your product.

- Measure failures such as broken links, empty search results, or crashes.

---

1. Find these services at http://www.clicktale.com and http://www.crazyegg.com.
2. You can read the whole essay at http://blogs.msdn.com/b/jensenh/archive/2006/04/05/568947.aspx.

- Measure user behavior to get a better grasp of where to improve your product, which features to add, and which ones to remove.

- Now that people are getting their hands on your product, it's not time to stop designing. It's time to look into what people *actually* do with your product and how you can use that information to make it even better.

Further Reading

Jensen Harris, director of Program Management for the Microsoft Windows User Experience Team, writes a fascinating blog.[3] He often writes about how Microsoft uses data when making design decisions.

---

3. At http://blogs.msdn.com/b/jensenh.

Chapter 35

Dealing with User Feedback

Once your product is out there, the hard part starts. Real people will use your product in ways you've never imagined. They will encounter issues you never thought of, and they'll complain to you about them. I've already mentioned some aspects of how to deal with user feedback in Chapter 24, *Avoiding Features*, on page 201, where I explained how to use "The Five Whys" to evaluate feedback. In other parts of the book, I've talked about when to listen to your users and when to take their feedback with a grain of salt.

This chapter covers some additional aspects of user feedback.

35.1 Unexpected Uses

One important thing to keep an eye out for is unexpected ways people use your software. In the 1970s and 1980s, IBM vastly underestimated the market for personal computers, not realizing that people would find uses for these devices that IBM itself could not think of.

When Tim Berners-Lee proposed the World Wide Web at CERN in 1989, his stated goal for the technology was "to link and access information of various kinds as a web of nodes in which the user can browse at will." Today, we write *whole applications* that run on his platform.

For a more recent example, when the podcasting company Odeo came up with the idea of building a simple system for posting the kinds of status messages that people would otherwise put into their Skype status, they had no clue that their users would "abuse" Twitter as a microblogging site.

The point is that people do not always use your product the way you want them to or the way you thought they would use it when you built it. And that's not a bad thing; it means you've stumbled upon a market you didn't know would be interested in your product or perhaps didn't even know existed.

There are three ways of dealing with this:

- Ignore it. This mostly applies if the additional market is smaller than your "main" market. If these people are happy with what your product does, great. You're getting a few more users for free.

- Adapt your product to it. If this new market is much bigger than your original target market, it may make sense to change the direction of your product and specifically target this new market.

- Split your product. If both your original market and this new market seem interesting, create specific editions of your product that are uniquely targeted at each individual market.

Each of these choices can be valid, but it's important that you think about your options before going with one.

35.2 Bad Feedback

People are often vicious when writing feedback. One of the reasons for this is that people sometimes don't expect anybody to read their messages. So, they use your feedback form as a way of venting their frustration.

Don't take it personally. After all, the fact that these people took the time to yell at you means they at least care enough about your product to take the time to yell at you. It could be worse: they could not care at all.

When I talked about his design process with interaction designer Chris Clark,[1] he told me the following:[2]

> I'm kind of weird; I love negative feedback. Unsolicited complaint means somebody cared enough to write it down, and then when you fix their pet peeve, they transform into a fan. Plus you got to fix a real problem for a real person, which is

---

1. Find him at http://releasecandidateone.com.
2. Read the whole interview at http://ignco.de/320.

pretty rewarding. The oft-bemoaned fact that iOS developers can't reply directly to App Store commenters is all the more reason to fix the root of the problem.

Customer comments do ease the planning of future software releases a little. They're the squeaky wheels. It'd be foolish to ignore your own ideas and priorities in favor of being 100 percent feedback-driven...you'd find yourself in the Henry Ford "my customers wanted a faster horse" situation pretty quickly, but it's helpful nonetheless. Popular feature requests jump up the queue, others languish.

Some negative feedback just isn't helpful, but that's life. The world has its share of caustic assholes with nothing better to do than give one-star reviews on iTunes, but if mean words really bother you, you have no business making things and selling them to the public. Don't be a musician, either. Or a writer. Or a chef.

Rather than taking bad feedback as an insult, take it as an opportunity to turn a passionate user of your product into a passionate *fan* of your product.

Take a deep breath. Don't be defensive. Think about what the user actually said. Does he have a valid reason for being angry? Is there anything you can do to help this person? Is there something you can do to make sure that nobody else encounters the problem this person encountered?

We are designing products because we want to help people achieve their goals. This is exactly why you've read this book: you want to make people's lives better. Bad user feedback doesn't mean you've failed. It merely means that you still have work to do.

Takeaway Points

- People may not use your product the way you intended. This can often be a great opportunity to take your product into new directions.

- Don't let bad feedback get you down. Instead, use it to turn an angry customer into a fan.

Chapter 36

You're Not Done

This is the last chapter of the book but not of your development process. At the very beginning of this book, I said that a typical development process looks a bit like this:

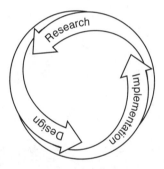

It's not a coincidence that the last chapters of the implementation part of the book are about collecting data and dealing with user feedback. These things are *research*. In other words, you're back where you started. Now that you've reached the end of the implementation part of your development process, it's time to start anew, to rethink everything. Are people using your product the way you expected them to use it? Who is your *real* audience? Did your product solve the problems you wanted to solve?

This chapter may be

The End

of the book, but your work has really only just begun.

Appendix A

Acknowledgments

A ton of people helped me create this book. I'll do my best to list them all, but if I've missed you, please accept my sincerest apologies and a box of Swiss chocolate to make up for my mistake.

Speaking of mistakes, all the mistakes in the book are, of course, my own, and none of the fine people listed here should be blamed for any of them.

First and foremost, I want to thank my editor *Jill Steinberg*, who turned my incoherent babbling into proper English.

I want to thank my tech editors, who scoured the book for mistakes and offered tons of amazingly great feedback and ideas. In no particular order, they are as follows:

Keith Lang, interaction designer at skitch.com. You can find his blog at http://UlandUs.com.

Jon Bell. He's an experience designer for Windows Phone. Read his personal blog at http://www.lot23.com and his design blog at http://www.designdare.com.

Max Steenbergen. As a resident graphic and UI designer, he designs the UI and graphics for software used on the bridge of luxury yachts. His blog is at http://facevalue.virb.com, and you can find him on Twitter at @maxsteenbergen.

Charlotte Simmonds, who is an author of poetry and short stories. You can find out more about her book *The World's Fastest Flower* [Sim09].[1]

---

1. At http://www.victoria.ac.nz/vup/2008titleinformation/worldsfastestflower.aspx.

Duncan Wilcox writes software for Macs, iPhones, and iPads. You can read his blog at http://duncanwilcox.com.

Chris Clark, or Clarko, is an interaction designer and *enfant terrible.* His website can be found at http://releasecandidateone.com.

Sharmila Egger, who will finish her studies in psychology at University Zürich in 2012. As well as editing the book, she also helped me with research.

David Naef, creative director and member of the management at a Swiss identity firm. You can read his writings at http://www.wisegamers.ch.

Sibylle Aregger is an expert developer who writes risk management tools for banks. Unfortunately, she does not have a blog I can link to.

Michael Trummer is a senior Appway engagement manager at Numcom Software AG. You can find him at http://ch.linkedin.com/in/trummer, and you can read his thoughts on the development of business applications at http://twitter.com/DrummeratWork.

I also want to thank *Chris Pruett* (find him at http://replicaisland.blogspot. com) for allowing me to use his Replica Island death heat map in Chapter 26, *Learning from Video Games*, on page 217, as well as *Clayton Miller* (at http://rclayton.net), for allowing me to use his "delayed passive confirmation" mock-up in Chapter 19, *Instead of Interrupting, Offer Undo*, on page 165.

Amadé Fries from http://zuendung.ch took the two car pictures in Chapter 23, *Speed*, on page 193 and kindly allowed me to use them in this book.

I want to thank Lynx co-designer *RJ Mical* for answering my questions about the development of the Lynx video game console (see Chapter 1, *User Research*, on page 5). You can find him at http://www.mical.org. *Pieter Omvlee* from Bohemian Coding helped me out with Chapter 25, *Removing Features*, on page 211 when he talked to me about his experience with removing features from DrawIt. Bohemian Coding is at http://www.bohemiancoding.com.

I want to thank *Amanda Kiefer* for helping me with the psychology research for this book.

Many more people helped me with this book by allowing me to use quotes from their books or blogs, and I want to thank all of them as well.

A lot of people have allowed me to use their Twitter pictures, names, and tweets in this book's pictures. Their Twitter handles are, in alphabetical order: 7WP, aidanhornsby, AlphabUX, CoryCalifornia, designdare, fetjuel, gauravmishr, ienjoy, jonbell, larryv, lorentey, louije, maxsteenbergen, neave, oliverw, shawnblanc, thibautsailly, timeboxed, and workjon. Thank you!

And finally, I want to thank *Damaris Kiefer*. She shot some of the pictures in this book and also appears in a few.

Appendix B

Bibliography

[BB10]   Cennydd Bowles and James Box. *Undercover User Experi-
           ence Design*. New Riders Press, 1 edition, 2010.

[BT10]   Nate Bolt and Tony Tulathimutte. *Remote Research*. Rosen-
           feld Media, 2010.

[Bux07]   Bill Buxton. *Sketching User Experiences: Getting the Design
           Right and the Right Design*. Morgan Kaufmann, 2007.

[CL99]   Larry Constantine and Lucy A.D. Lockwood. *Software for
           Use: A Practical Guide to the Models and Methods of Usage-
           Centered Design*. Addison-Wesley Professional, 1999.

[Cla10]   Josh Clark. *Tapworthy: Designing Great iPhone Apps*.
           O'Reilly Media, 2010.

[Coo95]   Alan Cooper. *About Face: The Essentials of User Interface
           Design*. John Wiley & Sons, New York, 1995.

[Coo99]   Alan Cooper. *The Inmates Are Running the Asylum*. Sams,
           1999.

[Cor99]   Stanley Coren. *Sensation and Perception*. John Wiley &
           Sons, 1999.

[Csi02]   Mihaly Csikszentmihalyi. *Flow*. Rider, 2002.

[FH10]   Jason Fried and David Heinemeier Hansson. *Rework*.
           Crown Business, 2010.

[FHL09]   Jason Fried, David Heinemeier Hansson, and Matthew Lin-
           derman. *Getting Real*. 37signals, 2009.

[Fru98]   Adrian Frutiger. *Signs and Symbols: Their Design and Mean-ing.* Watson-Guptill, 1998.

[Gil07]   Daniel Gilbert. *Stumbling on Happiness.* Vintage, 2007.

[Hoe06]   Robert Hoekman. *Designing the Obvious: A Common Sense Approach to Web Application Design.* New Riders Press, 2006.

[HT00]   Andrew Hunt and David Thomas. *The Pragmatic Program-mer: From Journeyman to Master.* Addison-Wesley, Reading, MA, 2000.

[Kin00]   Stephen King. *On Writing.* Scribner, New York, 2000.

[Kos04]   Raph Koster. *A Theory of Fun for Game Design.* Paraglyph Press, 2004.

[Kru09]   Steve Krug. *Rocket Surgery Made Easy: The Do-It-Yourself Guide to Finding and Fixing Usability Problems.* New Riders Press, 2009.

[McC94]   Scott McCloud. *Understanding Comics.* Harper Paperbacks, 1994.

[MR06]   Peter Morville and Louis Rosenfeld. *Information Architecture for the World Wide Web.* O'Reilly Media, 3rd edition, 2006.

[Nor88]   Donald A. Norman. *The Design of Everyday Things.* Double-day/Currency, New York, 1988.

[NY10]   Clifford Nass and Corina Yen. *The Man Who Lied to His Lap-top: What Machines Teach Us About Human Relationships.* Current Hardcover, London, 2010.

[PA06]   John Pruitt and Tamara Adlin. *The Persona Lifecycle.* Mor-gan Kaufmann, 2006.

[Pal99]   Stephen E. Palmer. *Vision Science: Photons to Phenomenol-ogy.* The MIT Press, 1999.

[Pap05]   Victor Papanek. *Design for the Real World.* Academy Chicago Publishers, 2nd edition, 2005.

[Ras00]   Jef Raskin. *The Humane Interface: New Directions for Designing Interactive Systems.* Addison-Wesley Professional, Reading, MA, 2000.

[Ros86]   Caroline Rose. *Inside Macintosh.* Addison Wesley, 1986.

[Saf08]   Dan Saffer. *Designing Gestural Interfaces.* O'Reilly Media, 2008.

[Sch05]   Barry Schwartz. *The Paradox of Choice: Why More Is Less.* Harper Perennial, 2005.

[Sim09]   Charlotte Simmonds. *The World's Fastest Flower.* Victoria University Press, 2009.

[SJ94]   Michael Steehouder and Carel Jansen. *Quality of Technical Documentation.* Editions Rodopi, 1994.

[Sni03]   Carolyn Snider. *Paper Prototyping: The Fast and Easy Way to Define and Refine User Interfaces.* Morgan Kaufmann, 2003.

[Spe09]   Donna Spencer. *Card Sorting: Designing Usable Categories.* Rosenfeld Media, 2009.

[Spe10]   Donna Spencer. *A Practical Guide to Information Architecture.* Five Simple Steps, 2010.

[Spo11]   Joel Spolsky. *User Interface Design for Programmers.* Apress, 2011.

[SZ03]   Katie Salen and Eric Zimmerman. *Rules of Play: Game Design Fundamentals.* The MIT Press, 2003.

[War04]   Colin Ware. *Information Visualization: Perception for Design.* Morgan Kaufmann, 2 edition, 2004.

Index

More from PragProg.com

HTML5 and CSS3

HTML5 and CSS3 are the future of web development, but you don't have to wait to start using them. Even though the specification is still in development, many modern browsers and mobile devices already support HTML5 and CSS3. This book gets you up to speed on the new HTML5 elements and CSS3 features you can use right now, and backwards compatible solutions ensure that you don't leave users of older browsers behind.

HTML5 and CSS3: Develop with Tomorrow's Standards Today
Brian P. Hogan
(280 pages) ISBN: 9781934356685. $33.00
http://pragprog.com/titles/bhh5

The RSpec Book

RSpec, Ruby's leading Behaviour Driven Development tool, helps you do TDD right by embracing the design and documentation aspects of TDD. It encourages readable, maintainable suites of code examples that not only test your code, they document it as well. *The RSpec Book* will teach you how to use RSpec, Cucumber, and other Ruby tools to develop truly agile software that gets you to market quickly and maintains its value as evolving market trends drive new requirements.

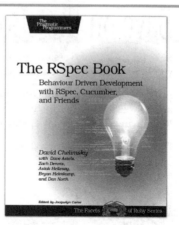

The RSpec Book: Behaviour Driven Development with RSpec, Cucumber, and Friends
David Chelimsky, Dave Astels, Zach Dennis, Aslak Hellesøy, Bryan Helmkamp, Dan North
(450 pages) ISBN: 978-1-9343563-7-1. $42.95
http://pragprog.com/titles/achbd

The Pragmatic Bookshelf

The Pragmatic Bookshelf features books written by developers for developers. The titles continue the well-known Pragmatic Programmer style and continue to garner awards and rave reviews. As development gets more and more difficult, the Pragmatic Programmers will be there with more titles and products to help you stay on top of your game.

Visit Us Online

Homepage for Designed for Use
http://pragprog.com/titles/lmuse
Source code from this book, errata, and other resources. Come give us feedback, too!

Register for Updates
http://pragprog.com/updates
Be notified when updates and new books become available.

Join the Community
http://pragprog.com/community
Read our weblogs, join our online discussions, participate in our mailing list, interact with our wiki, and benefit from the experience of other Pragmatic Programmers.

New and Noteworthy
http://pragprog.com/news
Check out the latest pragmatic developments, new titles and other offerings.

Save on the eBook

Save on the eBook versions of this title. Owning the paper version of this book entitles you to purchase the electronic versions at a terrific discount.

PDFs are great for carrying around on your laptop—they are hyperlinked, have color, and are fully searchable. Most titles are also available for the iPhone and iPod touch, Amazon Kindle, and other popular e-book readers.

Buy now at pragprog.com/coupon.

Contact Us

Online Orders:	www.pragprog.com/catalog
Customer Service:	support@pragprog.com
Non-English Versions:	translations@pragprog.com
Pragmatic Teaching:	academic@pragprog.com
Author Proposals:	proposals@pragprog.com
Contact us:	1-800-699-PROG (+1 919 847 3884)